GEOFF HILL is the features editor of the *News Letter*, one of the world's oldest newspapers. He has either won or been short-listed for a UK travel writer of the year award nine times. He is also a former Irish travel writer of the year and a former Mexican Government European travel writer of the year, although he's still trying to work out exactly what that means. In 2005 he was given a Golden Pen award by the Croatian Tourist Board for the best worldwide feature or broadcast on Zagreb. He has written about travel for the *Daily Telegraph*, the *Sunday Telegraph*, the *Independent*, the *Independent on Sunday* and the *Irish Times*. He has also won one UK and three Northern Ireland feature writer of the year awards, and two UK news-paper design awards. His first travel book, *Way to Go: Two of the World's Great Motorcycle Journeys*, was published in 2005, was *Mail on Sunday* book of the week, and was shortlisted for UK travel book of the year.

Geoff lives in Belfast with his wife Cate, a cat called Kitten, a hammock and the ghost of a flatulent Great Dane. His hobbies are volleyball, flying, motorbikes, skiing, and thinking too much.

PRAISE FOR GEOFF HILL'S TRAVEL WRITING

'Geoff Hill has an outstanding writing talent with a wicked sense of fun. For all the hilarious observations and polished one-liners, there is also thoughtful, informative travelogue. Brilliant writing, genuinely and originally funny, and a supremely entertaining read.'
MARTYN LEWIS, broadcaster

'Geoff Hill has travel writing genius in his very soul ... The funniest travel writer in our business.'
JULIE SHMUELI and DAVID ROSENBERG,
Travelex UK Travel Writing Awards

'Good travel writers are in short supply, great travel writers are prizes ... Geoff is one of the most talented travel writers ever to cross my path.'
MELISSA SHALES, Chairperson, British Guild of Travel Writers

The Road to
Gobblers Knob
From Chile to Alaska
on a Motorbike

GEOFF HILL

BLACKSTAFF
PRESS
———
BELFAST

First published in 2007 by
Blackstaff Press
4c Heron Wharf, Sydenham Business Park
Belfast, BT3 9LE
with the assistance of
The Arts Council of Northern Ireland

© Text, Geoff Hill, 2007
For picture acknowledgements, see above.

All rights reserved

Geoff Hill has asserted his right under the Copyright, Designs and Patents Act 1988 to be identified as the author of this work.

Typeset by CJWT Solutions, St Helens

Printed in England by Cromwell Press

A CIP catalogue record for this book is available from the British Library

ISBN 978-0-85640-804-5

www.blackstaffpress.com

For Catherine, always

I confess to a sigh of regret, not at a lost opportunity, but at something inevitably lost, something which, to me, seems precious – the idealism, the directness, the simplicity of youth. I lived with a secret image of perfection in my heart. My hope, my belief in myself and in life, was boundless, vague and vast as a cloud horizon before sunrise. The prosaic and worldly things – money, position, self-interest – out of which men build their little sand-castles of vanity and power, meant nothing. They slipped by, ignored. Everything you did should be the best possible. You should live gloriously, generously, dangerously. Safety last!

CECIL LEWIS, *Sagittarius Rising*

The first step in the birth of any great nation is the development of its roads, their decay the first sign of disintegration.

ROBERT EDISON FULTON JNR, *One Man Caravan*

Geoff making one of his record 122 appearances for the Northern Ireland volleyball team.

I

At the age of forty-eight and a half precisely, I decided to retire at the height of my fame.

Only to find that I hadn't reached it.

Faced with such a shock, I did the only thing possible, and had a mid-life crisis.

In any case, it was about time, and all the signs were there. I was in the middle of my life, for a start. Unless I got knocked down by a bus, of course. Then, buses being what they are, immediately knocked down by another one.

I had also started sighing deeply when I drove past my old university, or picked up a photograph of myself as an international volleyball player, a disturbingly distant quarter of a century ago. Not to mention flicking through sports car magazines in Sainsbury's and attempting to do thirty press-ups in the bathroom after a few beers on a Saturday night.

'Are you all right, dear? You look a little flushed,' my wife Cate would say as I reappeared in the living room and sank onto the sofa.

'Bear in the bathroom, love. I had to wrestle the machine gun off him before I could throw him down the stairs.'

'Of course. Now what's really the matter?'

'Oh, I don't know. I'm just overcome by a feeling these days that I've made a complete failure of my life.'

'As in international sportsman and winner of so many writing awards we've had to get the mantelpiece reinforced twice? That sort of failure?'

'I know, I know. I just have this nagging feeling that I could have done better.'

'Listen, count your blessings, and stop struggling so much. We've had the happiest of years, and you're just having a mid-life crisis.'

'See? I thought so.'

Now, men deal with a mid-life crisis in different ways. Some die, like Jackson, one of my best mates from university, perishing on the eve of his fiftieth birthday, his heart giving up the struggle in much the same way as the complex hydro-pneumatic suspension systems of the ancient Citroëns he had loved in life.

I could have done the same, but I've always had an unnatural fear of death, if only because it stops you finding out what happens next.

I could have bought a red sports car, but it would have clashed with my nose.

So I did what Cate said, and counted my blessings. And she was right. We had just had the happiest year imaginable. After five years together, we'd got married in September, followed by a glorious honeymoon in Slovenia, where I'd rowed her across Lake Bled to the wooded island there, carried her up the ninety-nine steps to the little white church, as Slovenian grooms traditionally do with their brides, then rung the bell three times and wished for a happy and successful life together. After Slovenia, there'd been Venice, then home on the Orient-Express, one of the great experiences of an adult life, particularly as I'd blagged my way into not paying for it by selling our honeymoon rights to *Wedding Journal* magazine for a fiver. Which I could ill afford.

In work, Cate's PhD and research project was going well, and I'd been named Northern Ireland feature writer of the year and finished second in the UK travel writer of the year award in the Over 6′ 6″ section.

'Oh well,' I said, 'at least I'm a bloody good travel writer.'

Two days after Christmas, I went back to work as the features and travel editor of the paper I worked for and sat down at my desk. It was ten in the morning, and mid-life crisis or not, I was the happiest man in the world.

Little did I know that by two minutes past, I would be the unhappiest.

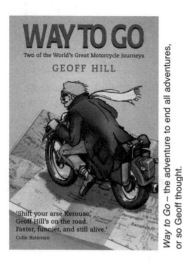

2

'What do you mean, you want to take me off travel?' I asked the editor in disbelief.

'It's not that I want to take you off travel. It's just that we're launching a new metro edition to increase our circulation in Belfast, and I want you to spearhead it with a page every day, which means you won't have time for travel.'

'You can't be serious,' I said, vaguely aware that I sounded like John McEnroe.

'I am. Perfectly. All I hear from the readers is how much they love your stuff, so I want you in the paper every day. Therefore no travel.'

'But it only costs you twenty-five days a year. That's two days a month. I do the same again in my own time and it doesn't cost you a penny. I single-handedly produce half our travel coverage and we've got the most award-winning travel section of any regional paper in the UK – and several of the nationals. Plus travel and tourism is the biggest industry in the world, and our surveys show that readers love it. What exactly is the problem?'

'It's not a problem. I just want to use your skills more effectively. Now, you'd better get a move on. We're launching the new edition in two weeks.'

And that was that. Twelve years' work down the tubes. I walked out of his office, sat down at my desk so stunned I could hardly speak, and phoned Cate.

'You can't be serious,' she said.

'It's funny you should say that,' I said.

A month before, I had been up a river in Guyana, talking to a woman who rescued orphaned river otters. The day after the conversation with the editor, I found myself trudging to a fish and chip shop in the pouring rain to ask the owner how he got his cod so crispy.

The fact that our city circulation increased by a remarkable 30 per cent did nothing to stop me plunging into utter gloom. For me, a world without travel had become as empty as a world without love.

For a month, I virtually stopped sleeping. I lay awake at four in the morning, convinced that my entire life had been a disaster, my future would be even more so, and I would end up as one of those old men who haunt public libraries, their eyes as empty as the lace holes of their shoes.

I was haunted by the words of Letitia Gwynne, an old friend who had said to me once: 'We all thought you would go all the way.' Haunted by the sight on TV of successful people I knew. When John Irvine, ITN's Far East correspondent, came on, it was all I could do not to burst into tears and hide behind the sofa.

In daylight, of course, you realise that people who are concerned with success are never happy, for no matter how successful they get, there are still people more successful than they. And probably just as unhappy.

In daylight, too, you know there is no point in regretting the past or worrying about the future, since worrying never does anything except make you worried. But logic does not live in the dark, and there is nothing quite so dreadful as lying in bed in the middle of the night, your nerves taut and icy sweat on your brow, listening to the clock tick away the hours yet not bearing to look at it.

Because if it says only three or four, a small part of you will be glad that you still have half a dozen hours left in which you are at least safe and warm, and no harm will come to you. And yet another part of you fears that for those hours, you will be lying as you are now, your mind racing with a thousand anxieties, until the clock strikes the rising hour and with a superhuman effort you get up like a dead man, dress and make your way to work with dread in your heart and a knot in the pit of your stomach.

If you are lucky, that knot of fear will pass as the day goes on, to be replaced by a numb, grey feeling, as if you are going through the motions but can find no joy in anything.

And if you are really lucky, evening will bring a sense of calm, as it did for me when Cate picked me up from work and we drove home together to cook, talk, eat, have a glass of wine and watch an old movie. On evenings like that, I felt for a few precious hours that life was possible. Until I went to bed, took a sleeping tablet and fell into a dreamless sleep, then woke a few hours later as the whole process started over again, a daily struggle between hope and despair.

Every morning, I woke in dread that something terrible was about to happen, and yet if you had asked me what, I would have been hard pushed to say: something happening to Cate, the end of the world, reality TV being made compulsory. What I did know was that I had lost happiness. I looked for it everywhere; down the back of the sofa, or in the clearing sky after rain, but found it only in evenings with Cate, or the moment I woke beside her, before the nameless horror of the day began again.

You see, for me, travel was like love. When I went away for a few days, every six weeks or so, it gave me that feeling you get when you fall in love: when you wake every morning with a song in your heart, fling back the shutters and go walking through the rain-washed streets with a spring in your step. For the people around you, it is just an ordinary day, but for you, the miracle of travel, like the miracle of love, has made the ordinary extraordinary: that little girl with the ice cream, her face tilted to her mother, that old man on the park bench, the clouds mirrored in his cataracted eyes.

Deprived of that, I stopped seeing the world through the eyes of a child, and therefore stopped being a writer, and became instead a tired and disillusioned hack, trudging around Belfast in the pouring rain every day trying to turn base metal into gold. Had I been young, free and single, I would have told the boss to stuff his job and gone off to forge in the crucible of destiny the glittering sword of my future. But mortgages make cowards of us all.

Ironically, two months later, I won an award for the best piece in the known universe from the Croatian Tourist Board, and my first travel book, *Way to Go*, came out, was reprinted twice and nominated for UK travel book of the year. I was, it seemed, a prophet in his own land.

Only two things kept me from crawling into a hole in the ground, curling up and going to sleep until the world became young again.

Cate. The song of her heart, the hymn of her soul. The way she smelt of hay and salad cream when the sun shone, and autumn woods even when it didn't.

'Salad cream? How can that be?' she laughed.

Cate.

And the Pan-American Highway, funny enough.

You see, *Way to Go*, the book that had just been published, was about two great motorcycle trips: Delhi to Belfast on a Royal Enfield and Route 66 on a Harley, and the year before my little world fell apart, I had been wondering about another one.

Then, one night, I had wandered into the bedroom and picked up the several books on the floor beside the bed.

One was *Biggles Flies West*, which I had already read, one was *A Cultural History of the Penis*, which I had no desire to read, since everyone knows that a penis has no conscience, never mind a culture, and the third was *The Adventure Motorbiking Handbook* by Chris Scott.

I picked it up, and it fell open at the section on the Pan-American Highway, dreamed up at the Fifth International Conference of American States in 1923 as a project to link North and South America with the world's longest road. Although each of the countries along the route had agreed to contribute money to it, the US had shouldered most of the burden, seeing the road as a pathway to international communication, cooperation and commerce. Construction had begun around 1930 and was nearly finished by the start of the Second World War. As a measure of the difference it made, in 1928 three Brazilians set off by road to Washington DC. It took them nine years. In 1941, four Argentinians completed the same journey in seven months.

In the years since then, the initial route had spawned so many side roads that if you asked four people where the Pan-American went, you got five different answers.

Some versions had it starting at the southern tip of Argentina, veering off on a whim to Brazil and grinding to a halt in a São Paulo cul-de-sac, scratching its head and looking at a street map. One opinion, that of *Independent* travel editor Simon Calder, had it dashing off with gay abandon as far east as Winnipeg, although why any self-respecting road would want to dash off to Winnipeg was quite beyond me, since the city's only charms are wide streets and the coldest, windiest corner in Canada, at the junction of Portage and Main.

The most accepted version, it seemed, had the Pan-American Highway starting in Puerto Montt in southern Chile, and ending in Fairbanks, Alaska, with the option of going on past the Arctic Circle to Deadhorse, just a few seal lengths from the icy shores of Prudhoe Bay.

At 16,500 miles, it was the world's longest road: a road on which travellers faced being baked in deserts, frozen in mountains, kidnapped and murdered by Colombian drug barons, buried under Peruvian avalanches, drowned by the Guatemalan rainy season, fleeced by eight-year-old Ecuadorean border touts, wasted by Montezuma's revenge, driven mad by blackflies in the Yukon, eaten by Alaskan grizzlies and, worst of all, limited to a glass of Chardonnay a day in California.

The Pan-American Highway. It sounded brilliant. The next day, I went out to buy every book I could find on it. And found that there weren't any.

Then it's about time I wrote one, I thought.

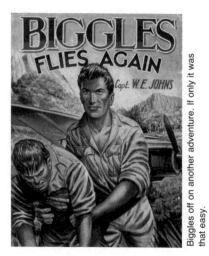

Biggles off on another adventure. If only it was that easy.

3

Biggles books invariably start like this, and I should know, since I've read most of them.

Major James Bigglesworth, better known to his many friends, and indeed his enemies, as Biggles, looked up from the flying magazine he was reading, stifled a yawn and looked around him. In various chairs around the room, his colleagues, the Right Honourable Algernon Lacey, better known as Algy, Lord Bertie Lissie, and their protégé, Ginger Hebblethwaite, were in positions of similarly languid repose.

'I don't know about you chaps, but unless we see some action soon, I'm going to perish of boredom,' he said. 'Hang on, I hear footsteps.'

No sooner had he spoken than there was a gentle tap at the door, which opened to reveal the distinguished figure of Air Commodore Raymond.

'Ah, Biggles,' he said. 'I'll get straight to the point. You don't happen to remember old Bunny Fetheringston-ffortescue by any chance, do you?'

'Of course I do,' said Biggles, putting down his magazine. 'He was with Wilks during the war, then headed out to Burma to help

get their air force started, if I recall.'

'Old Bunny? He was at Eton with me. Spiffing chap all round. Rugger and cricket blue, what?' piped up Bertie, taking out his monocle and polishing it vigorously.

'Yes, that's him all right. Or was,' said the Air Commodore.

Raising an eyebrow, Biggles reached for a cigarette, tapped it out on the back of his hand, and lit it.

'Was, you say?'

'That's what I fear. He set out from Rangoon on a flight to Singapore three weeks ago, and hasn't been heard of since. And what's worse, two other aircraft from the same outfit have gone west on the same route since then.'

'My sainted aunt!' ejaculated Biggles, absent-mindedly stubbing out his cigarette on the back of Algy's hand. 'Looks like we'd better be getting out there. We were just saying it was about time we had another adventure.'

'Yes, I was rather hoping you'd say that,' said Air Commodore Raymond, a wan smile playing across his lips.

Three weeks later to the day, a Shorts Imperial flying boat came to rest gently against a jetty in Rangoon harbour and Biggles stepped lightly out to survey an evening sky which was turning fantastic shades of orange, purple and pink.

'Mmm. Better take it easy on the acid this evening,' he thought to himself as he watched Flight-Sergeant Smyth tie the aircraft up for the night.

Well, it doesn't quite work like that in real life. The day after I thought of the Pan-American idea, I wrote out a basic list of things to do if it was to happen. When I got to number 78, I sat looking at the screen thinking that motorbikes were supposed to be all about freedom from sitting looking at a screen all day, but organising an adventure on one involved exactly that.

Still, one thing at a time, as my grandmother was so fond of saying on her deathbed. Money was the first thing. I picked up the phone and called Brian Davis of Nambarrie, the tea

company which had sponsored the Nambarrie Run, as the
Delhi to Belfast expedition to bring back the first tea leaves of
the season had been christened.

'Here, you don't fancy lunch tomorrow, do you? I've got a
mad idea for you for Nambarrie Run II,' I said.

The next day, I spent the first two courses spelling out the
plan, and he spent the third thinking about it. By the time his
cup of tea arrived, he'd made a decision.

'Yes. We'll do it. I don't know quite how we'll find a tea
connection in South America, but we'll think of something,' he
said. 'Will Paddy Minne, the world-famous Franco-Belgian
motorcycle mechanic, be going with you again?'

'Doubt it. He got married last year, and his wife's pregnant.
Looks like I'm on my own for this one, although it's going to be
tough,' I said.

I went back to the office, hauled out a calculator and worked
out that at 180 miles a day, the trip would take about three
months. I toyed briefly with the idea of just leaving my
computer switched on and a cup of tea sitting on the desk to
give the impression that I'd just nipped around the corner for a
sandwich. But then I realised that I'd have some explaining to
do when I came back without the sandwich, so there was
nothing else for it but to ask the editor. In those days, I'd been
getting on with him very well.

'You'll get a really good piece out of it every single day. And
Nambarrie are sponsoring it, so it won't cost the paper a penny.
And the readers loved the previous ones, from Delhi to Belfast
on an Enfield and Route 66 on a Harley,' I said in what was
supposed to be a strong, authoritative voice, but probably came
out sounding like a gerbil on helium.

'Indeed, I enjoyed them myself. All right. Let's go for it,' he
said, surprising both of us.

Splendid. Now all I needed was someone to fly me out there,
and a motorbike to get me from Quellón to Deadhorse.

I emailed British Airways in March, and finally heard from
them in July, to say they probably wouldn't. Thinking that they

could surely have done better than that, after keeping me waiting so long, I phoned my old mate Mary Stuart-Miller, a PR guruess I'd met two years before on a trip to Slovenia. We'd got on so well that we had immediately, for reasons which will be obvious to any right-thinking person, founded a lesbian dormouse-hunting collective. It never worked out in the end, possibly because neither of us were lesbians and because the dormouse-hunting season in Slovenia is only a week long, but we had remained the best of friends, and she was always the first person I turned to with apparently insoluble marketing difficulties.

'Not a problem,' she said. 'I'll call Debbie Marshall of Zoom.'

Five minutes later, Debbie called to say she'd be glad to fly me and a motorbike out as far as Toronto, and back from Vancouver to London.

'Debbie, you are a wonderful, warm, caring human being, and that colour suits you. And tell Mary she's a genius the next time you're talking to her,' I said.

Now all I had to do was get someone to lend me a motorbike for three months.

I wrote to BMW, since they'd recently done a similar deal with Ewan McGregor and Charley Boorman. As you may know, after saving the known universe armed with only a light sabre, a dodgy haircut and a Glasgow accent, Ewan had set off with Charley around the world on two BMWs, with only a huge budget, back-up crew, film unit, fleet of 4×4s, string of local fixers and satellite phones between them and disaster.

When they returned, they came out with the book, the TV series, the DVD, the soundtrack, the T-shirt and the PlayStation game, and at this point were still travelling around the world promoting BMWs at such vast expense to the company that, when I phoned BMW to see if they fancied lending me a bike, they laughed for several minutes, then said they'd spent their entire publicity budget on Ewan and Charley right up to about the time the sun becomes a red dwarf and swallows up this corner of the universe in a blaze of unfinished business, while the lone voice of the last person left on the planet cries out a final rhetorical question: 'Here, what was it all about, anyway?'

I stroked BMW off the list and wrote to KTM, who said they weren't interested, and Honda, Harley and Yamaha, who said nothing at all.

Finally, God bless her sprockets, Andrea Friggi at Triumph said they'd be happy to come up with a Tiger if I could guarantee coverage of the trip in a national newspaper.

I wrote to every national travel editor I'd ever written for, and they wrote back saying they didn't even plan a week in advance, never mind a year. Sighing deeply, I picked up the phone and called Mary again, and within her standard five minutes, I had an email from her chum Maggie O'Sullivan at the *Sunday Telegraph* giving me a commission.

Splendid. I mailed Triumph to tell them the good news, adding as an aside that they'd better teach me to fix the bike they were lending me, since the nearest Triumph dealer to Chile was in Brazil, then signed up at Queen's University for evening classes in Spanish.

I asked Tony in IT at work to see if we could find some way of emailing stories and pictures home using a laptop and a mobile phone, and he sent Sarah at T-Mobile an email headed Nambarrie Run II, with a list of the countries we'd be going through.

'I'll check that out,' she mailed right back, 'but can you tell me where Nambarrie is?'

When I'd stopped laughing, I made another attempt to find some books on the Pan-American, but found only some by people who had travelled part of it. Half of them seemed to be self-published diaries by German bikers which went something like: 'Rose at dawn. Adjusted clutch. Rode all day. Spent evening adjusting overhead underhang where it connects to bonglesprocket to stop it interfering with diagonal steam trap. Had goat and beer for supper, again. Told barman German joke which goes: "There were these three Germans.

That's it." Barman failed to laugh. Went to bed wondering why no one appreciates efficiency of German humour.'

At the other end of the scale was the purple prose of Toby Green, who had followed the journeys of Darwin on a horse. 'The sky was still cast as a pale shadow of death, and lumbered uncertainly against the dark shadows which stood aloofly with the declining darkness,' he wrote on page 55 of *Saddled with Darwin*. Wondering vaguely how a pale shadow can lumber, I made it as far as 'His work was a swollen vein bursting with faint tragedy' on page 118 before throwing it in the bin and going out to buy every guide book on every country in North and South America.

When I got home, laden with bags, I sat down and wrote to the tourist boards or embassies of Chile, Peru, Ecuador, Colombia, Panama, Costa Rica, Nicaragua, Honduras, El Salvador, Guatemala, Mexico, California, Washington State, Oregon, Vancouver, British Columbia, the Yukon and Alaska to ask them for weird and wonderful stories en route.

Actually, that's not strictly true. Since everyone I had asked whether it was safe to ride a motorbike through Colombia just laughed hysterically and put the phone down, what I actually asked the Colombian embassy was how likely I was to be alive by the time I got to the Panama border. Not to mention how to get over the slight problem of the Darien Gap, the 83-mile break in the road in the jungle between Colombia and Panama, and the fact that the Crucero Express, the ferry which was the only way of getting round that gap, had stopped running ten years before and never been replaced.

I never heard back from them. What I did hear were horror stories of kidnappings and murders, or stories like the one about the biker who stopped at traffic lights in Bogotá.

'Nice bike,' said the well-dressed pedestrian standing on the pavement.

'Thank you. Harley-Davidson, made in USA,' said the proud motorcyclist.

'Now get off it,' said the pedestrian, producing a gun from

an inside pocket of his elegant suit, climbing on the bike and riding off.

Ron Ayres, a rough, tough adventure motorcyclist who had been all over South America, had this to say: 'Stay out of Colombia. The cops can't protect you.'

But then, as Biggles would say, if these things were easy, everybody would be doing them, and everything had been moving along nicely until the boss took me off travel.

Although he said he would stick to his word to let me do the trip, for a while after that, I lost the will to live, never mind go anywhere. I would lie awake at nights, thinking about it, then slip into strange half-dreams. Once I woke in a panic because I dreamed that I needed to photocopy my hair, but by the time I found a colour copier, it had turned grey.

I told this to Cate when she woke. She laughed, and I laughed nervously with her.

Once in the street, an old woman stopped me, squeezed my hand, and said: 'I want to thank you. Every day you make thousands of people happier. My husband wakes me at night to read out the things you write, but I don't mind, they make me laugh so much.'

I make everyone smile except myself, I thought, going home to another sleepless night. At four in the morning, I looked at Cate's sleeping face.

The thought of leaving her for three months, of waking alone in a Colombian hut without even a photocopier to copy my hair, seemed intolerable.

Exhausted and disheartened, I was on the verge of calling the whole thing off.

But sometimes when you think you are drowning, someone throws you a fish.

Clifford and Geoff's crash course in Triumph maintenance at McCallen's in Lurgan.

4

The voice on the phone was definitely Scottish, and definitely enthusiastic.

'Listen, I hope you don't mind me ringing you at work, but I've just read *Way to Go*, and I thought: "Bloody hell, this is my life story." My dad used to race motorbikes just like yours, I rode an Enfield in India, and I was in Los Angeles exactly the same time as you when you finished university. We have to meet.'

He turned out to be Clifford Paterson, a former Isle of Man TT winner turned successful businessman who had given it all up to run one of the hundred Camphill communities world-wide which give people with mental, emotional and behavioural disabilities useful and rewarding work.

I drove down through the Mountains of Mourne to see him the next day.

As I walked towards the front door, it was flung open and an animated elf leaped out and grabbed my hand. That was my first sight of Clifford, one of the weirdest and most wonderful people I was ever to meet. We went walking through the workshops, where everyone was making exquisite guitars and lyres, past the organic farm, orchard and gardens which made them self-sufficient, past the pottery, bakery and weaving room, past the Zen garden where Clifford raked the gravel every day, and past his Royal Enfield, shining in the sun.

'You see, after my dad gave up racing, he worked hard all his life building up the family business, garages and hotels, and all that time he was looking forward to retiring,' he said as we walked. 'Then he had a stroke, and eventually died before he could enjoy any of the fruits of his labours. I was running the business, and I thought: "This is no life, working every hour of the day and looking forward to a future that might never happen." So I handed over to my brother, and went off and travelled in India, Japan and the States, then came here,' he said.

We discovered other remarkable parallels: we had been born within weeks of each other, were both Geminis, and had both suffered from severe doom and gloom when we were thirty-eight.

We shook hands, and he hugged me warmly, then rang the next day.

'Listen, I don't know how you feel about this, but if I could raise the funds, and get a motorbike, would you fancy some company on the Pan-American trip? I'm not gay, I just fancy an adventure.'

I laughed, and talked about it to Cate that evening.

'I'd feel a lot happier if you had company, love. It would be more fun, better security, and better writing, too,' she said as our cat, Kitten, appeared and with an ear-shattering yowl announced that he had finished his evening nap and was now ready for supper, after which he would have his late evening nap to prepare him for bed.

I phoned Clifford the next day, told him that if he raised some money, he was welcome to come, and invited him to a weekend barbecue.

He turned up with half an organic cow from the community freezer, flung his arms around me, gave me a smacking great kiss on the neck, and said: 'Bloody good decision. This is going to be a great adventure.'

The best thing about Clifford, I decided after several more beers that night, was that he was mad.

A month later, the sponsorship from Nambarrie arrived. I got half, the paper kept the other half, and the Arts Council came up with some. It was far from ideal, but it was better than nothing. I phoned Clifford to let him know.

'Let me talk to Camphill, and see if they'll come up with something. Anyway, if we run out of fuel five miles from Deadhorse, I'll just carry you over the finishing line, like Don Quixote and Sancho Panchez [sic],' he said. A day later, he called back.

'Right, I'm pretty confident I can raise four grand, maybe five if I mug my mum. My brother's promised to come up with an Aprilia Pegaso 650, the Camphill insurance expert reckons she can insure everything, including us and the bikes, and I've bought a digital camera so we can send back photos,' he said.

It could only be a matter of time before he phoned to say he'd learnt to fly and borrowed a 747 to get us there, I thought as I hunted out a copy of *Bike* magazine to see what it had to say about the Aprilia. 'Stylish single, GSOH, enjoys commuting, seeks miser for days out in town. Also enjoys country jaunts,' it said.

Country jaunts. I liked that.

As I was putting the magazine away, a piece of paper I'd been using as a marker fluttered out and butterflied to the floor. I picked it up. It was a blank sheet, with the letter N and an arrow on it. A waiter at the Big Texan Steak Ranch in Amarillo had drawn it and given it to me when I was riding from Chicago to Los Angeles on Route 66 for the previous book.

'Here,' he'd said. 'Just keep this pointed north wherever you go, and you'll never get lost.'

And north was exactly the way we'd be going. It was a good omen.

I went to bed, and slept the whole night through for the first time in months. Then woke the next morning, and realised two things almost simultaneously. Firstly, that if this thing came off, in a few months, I would be riding a motorbike over half the length of the planet. Secondly, that I knew nothing about the motorbike. Or any motorbike, come to that.

There was only one solution: phone Clifford.

'Don't worry, Don,' he said. He had taken to calling me Don since he had become convinced that the entire trip would be a heroic recreation of the journeys of the Spanish knight and his faithful servant Sancho Panza. I hadn't had the heart to remind him that Don Quixote was a hopeless romantic who spent his life chasing impossible dreams. Probably because it was all too accurate. 'All you need to know about motorbikes is that they go until they stop. Then you take them to a mechanic.'

'But Clifford, we're starting in southern Chile, and the nearest Triumph dealer is in California. God knows where the nearest Aprilia one is, for your bike.'

'Good point. We'd better do a basic course in bike maintenance,' he said, showing a disturbing flash of common sense. I put down the phone and rang Robert Sinton at McCallen's in Lurgan, the Triumph dealership run by former race ace Philip McCallen.

'An idiot's guide to Tiger maintenance? No problem. Come down on Monday morning,' he said.

So it was that on the following Monday morning we found ourselves standing in McCallen's workshop looking at a Tiger, the bike I'd be taking on the trip. Also looking at it, and a lot more wisely, were mechanics Paul Truesdale and Ronnie McCallen, who was no relation to Philip, apart from being his brother.

'Right,' said Clifford, obviously thinking he should ask some sensible questions, 'are all the bolts metric on this?'

'They are,' said Paul. 'You'll need a pair of vice grips; 8, 10, 12, 13, 14, 17, 19, 22 and 27 sockets; 17, 19 and 22mm combination spanners; 4, 5 and 6 Allen keys; and a Torex T30, T40 and T55.'

'Good grief,' I said, wondering what on earth a Torex T55 was. It sounded like a Russian jet, and far too big to fit in a pannier. 'Is any of this in the bike's standard tool kit?'

'Not really. Look,' said Ronnie, unrolling the tool kit in question to reveal what looked like a toothpick and one of those things you used to get in the *Innovations* catalogue for scratching the bit of your back that you can't reach otherwise.

'What do we do if the engine breaks down?' said Clifford, scratching his head.

'Nothing. You're buggered. The good news is that they don't tend to. You shouldn't even need to change the plugs,' said Paul.

'What about the tyres?' I said suddenly, surprising everyone, particularly myself.

'Well, if you're planning to do a couple of hundred miles a day, and you take it easy, you should get 8,000 miles out of a back one,' said Paul. 'How far is it from where you start to the first Triumph dealer?'

'About 8,001 miles.'

'Never mind. We can just carry it the last mile,' said Clifford optimistically. 'What about punctures?'

'Well, if I was you, I'd buy a couple of cans of that foam which reflates the tyre and seals the puncture until you can get it somewhere it can be fixed,' said Ronnie.

'Buy puncture foam thingy,' I wrote carefully in my notebook.

'And what if the radiator or oil cooler gets punctured?' said Clifford.

'You can repair both of them with epoxy resin, or Radweld, but only for smaller holes. You can even use egg white, because it congeals on contact with air. Or you can just crimp off the holed bit, if it's not too big, but my advice would be to fit radiator and oil cooler guards, as well as crash bars for the engine and twin relays for the headlights. You'll also need spare throttle and brake cables, and a complete set of spare fuses and bulbs. And a high windscreen. A Scott oiler with a touring-size oil reservoir would be good as well,' said Paul.

I brightened up. A Scott oiler was something I'd actually heard of. It was a tank of oil which fitted under the number plate and kept the chain constantly lubricated.

'Do the eggs have to be free range?' I said.

'Only if you want a free range,' said Clifford.

'No need, we've already got an old one in the kitchen at home,' I said, writing 'Buy eggs. And Scott oiler.' into the notebook.

'What if the starter motor packs in?' said Clifford, who was showing worrying signs of pessimism.

'Shut up, Clifford. You're making me want to go home, sit in an armchair, read a Biggles book and give up the whole idea,' I said.

'The good news is that it shouldn't. If it does, just put the bike in second gear, rock it back until the compression stops it, then take a run at it,' said Paul. 'Right, let's get the tank off and show you what's underneath, although if you get to that stage, all hope will be lost anyway.'

'You're even worse than Clifford, Paul,' I said.

For the next couple of hours, we undid bolts, unscrewed nuts, took wheels off and got most of them back on. Well, half of them, anyway.

Splendid. We shook grimy hands with Paul and Ronnie, and I drove back to the office and emailed Andrea at Triumph to see if we could borrow some tools and get all the accessories fitted – only for her to reply:

Sorry, but we simply don't have the tools to lend, which probably sounds bizarre. However, we build the bikes rather than service them, so the tools we have are geared to production requirements (e.g. air tools that can handle endless repetition). While our development workshop has hand tools, they only have a set per person, and if we loan them to you, someone won't do any work for two months! You will need to obtain the extra tools you need yourself. If you gather together what you need, I'll arrange for it to be collected and packed with the bike. Note though, we will have to include all the tools and spares on the carnet and this can sometimes hold up the bike clearing customs. If you have a few days' grace at the start of the trip in Santiago, it might be more sensible for us to UPS all the ancillary items direct to your hotel.

Regarding accessories, we do not make, and therefore cannot fit, for product liability reasons, crash bars, radiator and oil cooler guards or a Scott oiler. We will fit our higher screen, twin relays (if possible) and supply a complete set of spare fuses, bulbs and cables.

Kind regards,

Andrea

Good grief, I thought, and mailed Clifford.

'Listen, a tool kit is the least of our worries. Neither of us knows how to use it, anyway,' he wrote back.

Seriously, to be honest I would rather gather up our own kit – then we know what we have. I have many sources from where we can beg, steal or borrow a comprehensive tool kit. We should just carry a CD-ROM on basic Triumph/Aprilia maintenance in Spanish – if we break down we just let the local garage boys view it while we check into the nearest motel, watch a video of *Long Way Round*, down a few tequila shots, sleep it off and collect the repaired machines, ready to ride off into the blazing afternoon sun – Pancho Sanchez cooled by the magnificent shadow cast by the heroic and brave Don Quixote. By the way, I've discovered a worldwide orphans' charity called SOS which I think we should use the trip to raise money for. We can just publish their website with a donations link every day. Speak to you soon. *Buenas Noches*. Which reminds me, I don't know where I am going to fit in my Spanish lessons.

Oh well, I thought. At least I have a socket set at home that I bought in B&Q's bargain section. And an adjustable spanner, or monkey wrench as my dad used to call them for no known reason, although it probably explains why we never saw a monkey around the place.

That, and the fact that we lived in Tyrone.

5

Here is a handy hint for anyone who wishes to preserve their sanity, although if they lived in Belfast as I do, they would not have any left after years of trying to simultaneously understand the weather and the politics.

Do not apply for an American work visa.

I know, for I was that man, and I write this to you now from the secure wing of Purdysburn, Northern Ireland's finest mental institution, in the section reserved for baffled gentlefolk, where I am being fed a daily diet of fresh mackerel in the hope that it will restore my shattered nerves, although to be honest, a nice glass of wine would do the trick just as well. After all, do not the French say 'A muscadet keeps the doctor away'? Well, maybe they don't, but they ought to.

Anyway, where was I before I managed to interrupt myself? Ah yes, American visas. A few months previously, I had received a missive from the British Guild of Travel Writers to say that several members arriving in the States on assignment had been stopped at immigration, asked where their work visas were and then, when they failed to produce one, strung up by the dongles and made to sing 'The Star-Spangled Banner' in a quavering falsetto until the clock struck midnight. Then they were packed onto the next plane home, their fountain pens firmly capped and their stories decidedly unwritten.

Since it would be a bit of a shame to make it all the way from Chile only to arrive at the California border and be strung up by the dongles, I grabbed the nearest *Yellow Pages* and looked up the number of the US Consulate in Belfast. However, it was not that simple. It was not to be that simple for quite some time. The number I had to ring was a visa information line costing £1.30 a minute, and none of the phones in work would let me. I finally gave up trying and called on my mobile, paying more for the call than the actual trip was likely to cost. Still, at least it would help George Bush pay for the war in Iraq. You know, the one that left the country in ruins and sent all our oil and gas bills through the roof.

I finally got through to a pleasant girl called Cherry, and she said that confirmation of an appointment at the Belfast Consulate would be in the post. It arrived two days later as promised, complete with a list of demands which would have tested the patience of Job, Mrs Job, all the little Jobs and It's More Than My Job's Worth.

First, I had to complete two separate on-line visa application forms. The first one needed all my personal details and ended with the questions with which anyone who's travelled to the States and been handed a green immigration form will be familiar – like whether I was a criminal, drug dealer, fraudster or terrorist, had been involved in Nazi persecutions, genocide or kidnapping, had a dangerous physical or mental disorder or displayed an inclination towards moral turpitude. Whatever that is. I imagine it's something disturbing involving turpentine and fifteen-year-old lap dancers.

After toying briefly with the thought of writing 'Actually, now that you mention it, I did murder my granny in a psychotic blackout when I got back from handing Osama the proceeds of the cocaine haul. As if it wasn't bad enough scorching my SS uniform when she was ironing it, the old bat started on at me again about sleeping with my sister's goat,' I thought better of it and ticked the No boxes.

The second form, meanwhile, wanted to know details of how many countries I'd been to in the past ten years, what I'd had for breakfast on March 3, 1979, my inside leg measurement and the name, address and phone number of everyone I'd be staying with in the States, plus the numbers of any phone boxes I might happen to be passing on the way.

After I'd done all that and printed all the forms out, I had to go and lie down in a darkened room for a while, but my ordeal was far from over. Next was the photo, and if you think a standard passport photo would do, I can only admire your gadabout optimism. The photo, you see, had to measure precisely 50mm square. The head, naturally enough, should measure 25 to 35mm, with the eye level 28 to 35mm from the bottom. Heavens, I can't imagine how we've existed this long with rectangular photos which just show what you look like.

I sighed deeply and set off for McMullan's Pharmacy on the Lisburn Road. After three days, and the taking of 4,868 photos involving a variety of permutations and distances from the camera, including one unfortunate occasion when I tried standing in the middle of the road, only to be knocked down by the Finaghy bus, thankfully resulting in only mild concussion and a bill for a broken headlight, I returned to the office with a photograph, took a deep breath, and read the next requirement.

It involved, naturally enough, handing over more money: £60 in cash to the nearest branch of Barclay's bank, to be precise. Now, there were two problems with this. First of all, I can't remember the last time I saw £60 in cash, and secondly, the nearest Barclay's bank to Belfast is somewhat to the north-west of the city, in the area known as Glasgow.

Still, never one to be put off by a little geography, I read on and discovered in the small print that I could actually pay at a bank in Northern Ireland but they'd charge me for the privilege. Once I'd done this and got a receipt, I then had to go to a post office and get a stamped, self-addressed Royal Mail Special Delivery envelope so that my passport could be sent back to me if my application was successful. If I hadn't died of old age by then.

Not only that, but I needed a letter from the boss stating my title, length of employment, salary and reasons for leaving a perfectly safe desk to put my life at risk for three months. Oh, and recent bank and mortgage statements to prove I was solvent, plus a previous passport with proof of travel to show that I wouldn't frighten the natives by turning up with a pith helmet and shooting stick and asking the nearest policemen for a lift to the Colonial Club.

I will trouble you no more with the details, but suffice to say that a week later I arrived outside the US Consulate in Belfast at the appointed time of 9.45 a.m., dragging behind me a large suitcase bulging with documents. Only to find a queue of about a dozen people waiting outside the security hut. After forty-five minutes, I was finally shown in, given a pass and invited to walk through a scanner which presumably detected and removed any traces of Islamic fundamentalism I'd picked up through growing up in Tyrone.

It was only then that I was allowed to walk up the path to the Consulate, a fine Victorian building which was once the home of an Italian wine merchant. Inside, I found all the people who had been in the queue in front of me, and it was another forty-five minutes, thankfully enlivened by the wittiest doorman in the world, before I was finally called up to have my fingers scanned and be interviewed by a charming girl from northern California.

'So what's the purpose of your trip, sir?' she said pleasantly.

'I'm hoping to ride a motorbike from Chile to Alaska for a newspaper series and a book.'

'Wow. You'll pass pretty close by my home town,' she said.

We then spent a minute chatting amiably about her home town and the weather, and she told me my visa was approved, and would be sent out in the post. It was as painless a conclusion as the process had been difficult, and I hope you can see now why it has left me in a secure wing at Purdysburn, although hopefully only temporarily.

Now, if you'll excuse me, I'll just go and have a word with Cedric, one of my fellow patients, who thinks he's a light-bulb, and spends his days hanging from the ceiling.

I have to take him down, you see, since it's bedtime, and I can't sleep with the light on.

I picked up the phone for no other reason than that it was ringing, and found Clifford on the other end.

'Listen, bad news about third-party vehicle insurance. Our insurance expert at Camphill has phoned every travel insurance specialist in the country to get cover, and they just laugh at her when she tells them we're going to Colombia. Not to mention El Salvador.

'Don't worry about it. Paddy Minne and I couldn't get insurance for the Delhi to Belfast trip either. We'll just have to be careful, and if we hit anything short of an armed policeman, just keep going,' I said.

'That's all right, then. On a more important note, is Don Quixote's mate Pancho Sanchez or Sancho Panchez?'

'Good question. I've seen both.'

'Me too. I think I prefer Pancho. That way I'll forever remain anonymous when signing autographs on the streets of Medellín, Quito and Kilkeel, amidst thronging hordes of *Way to Go* readers eagerly anticipating the publication of your latest masterpiece – Chile to Alaska on half-budget, no insurance and no sentimental bloody rabbit.'

'Listen, don't be nasty about Jim. He's very sensitive. As rabbits go.'

'I know, I shouldn't be. I used to have one myself. By the way, I see that Ewan McGregor is off again with Charley.'

'Oh? Where?'

'There's a piece in the *Sunday Times* saying that they're planning to ride from the top of Scotland to the bottom of Africa in 2007. But listen to this: there's a quote from the silly bugger saying, and I kid you not – hang on till I get the paper – "We live in such comfortable and easy times that it doesn't do yourself any harm to go and test yourself and survive with just the bare essentials."'

'What: the bare essentials like millions in the bank, research staff, free bikes, tools and flights, satellite phones, two huge trucks following you, fixers in every country and a BMW support crew on permanent standby – those sort of bare essentials?' I laughed.

'Aye, those must be the ones he's talking about.'

There. Having sorted out the important things like Ewan and Charley, that only left a few minor details to arrange, like getting us and the bikes out to Chile. Since Zoom had agreed to get us as far as Toronto, I emailed Air Canada to see if they could get us from there to Santiago. As a back-up, I asked Varig, the Brazilian airline, if they could just get us from London to Santiago direct.

They both swore on their grandmothers' graves that they would come back with a great deal. That was in July. It was now the first week of December, seven weeks before we were due to set off, and in spite of 4,386 increasingly desperate phone calls, emails and manila envelopes stuffed with threatening haddock, they had utterly failed to tell us whether the great deal was two for the price of one, one for the price of two or Scotsmen go free on Fridays except when Thursday falls on a Saturday, in which case the answer is a deep-fried Mars bar.

In exasperation, I emailed Carson McMullan of All-Route Shipping to see if he could at least get the bikes out. A few days later, I was driving through Belfast in the pouring rain, wondering yet again why I didn't live in California, when Carson phoned.

'Listen, I think we can go with this,' he said.

'Carson, if I wasn't a happily married man, I'd propose to you on the spot,' I said.

'Thanks. There's only one problem, though.'

'What, you're happily married too?'

'No. I mean yes. I mean with the bikes. Because they're going by sea, I'll need them by next week. And I'll need the carnet documents before they're shipped.'

'But I haven't even got the log book from Triumph yet, never mind getting the bike re-registered in my name, and even after that, the RAC said it would take a month to produce the carnet,' I wailed as I went under a bridge and the line went dead, leaving me sitting in the car in the rain wondering why I hadn't taken on a simpler project, like organising world peace, or getting Ian Paisley to do a Full Monty with Gerry Adams for the Save the Dalai Lama's pet rabbit charity appeal.

However, I always find that as one door closes, another slams shut in your face, and the next day I managed to get laryngitis and lose my voice. Honestly, you wouldn't believe how difficult it is miming: 'Listen, if I get the log books from Triumph tomorrow, persuade the vehicle licensing people to fast-track the re-registration and get the lot to you by the end of the week along with the Ulster Bank customs indemnity for £21,000, which means I'll have to sell the bloody house if the bike gets hijacked in Colombia, how soon can you get the carnet back to me?' Especially over the phone to the RAC.

So the next time you get *The Unbearable Lightness of Being* in charades, count yourself lucky.

'Mary, I'm not taking you to Alaska on a motorbike, and that's final.'

6

Suddenly, after months of delay and frustration, everything began to happen very quickly. A week before Christmas, Larry Dillon from Varig phoned with a half-decent price for flights from London to Santiago.

'There's only one problem. I need a decision right now,' he said.

'Honestly, Larry. First you keep me waiting for months, then you want an instant answer.'

'I know, I know.'

I took a deep breath, and reached for my credit card. The adventure, which up to now had seemed like a hypothetical exercise in complex logistics, had suddenly become real.

The days hurried by, wrapped up in great overcoats and carrying presents. On Christmas Eve, pottering about the book-lined study at the top of our house, I opened a drawer in my old oak roll-top desk and came upon my first passport. Good heavens, I thought, opening it to find a much younger me looking back with the same expression of boyish optimism I still possess, if only because I've put so much work into it.

What would this young man have thought, I wondered, at the way he had turned out?

He would have loved this house, with its book-lined walls, the firelight reflected on its wooden floors and the ancient model biplane hanging from the ceiling. Since he was the sort of chap who looked up every time he heard an aeroplane, and still was, he would have been delighted to discover a pilot's licence in the flight bag in the hallway.

And, most of all, I thought, as Cate called up the stairs to say that the fire was lit, supper was ready, the wine was open and the TV was ready for our traditional Christmas Eve viewing of *It's a Wonderful Life*, he would have been very, very pleased with his future choice of wife.

Indeed, it was for that reason that, as the weeks crept ever closer to departure, the thought of being without her for three months became almost impossible to imagine.

'Oh love,' she said one evening as we sat down to a Sunday night curry, old movie and bottle of wine, 'it's going to be so strange waking without you every morning.'

'I know, I know,' I said, 'but if you come out for a week in the middle, say up the west coast of California, then at least that'll split it into two spells of six weeks, rather than one of three months. Even better, if we spend the first three weeks looking back at being together, then the next three weeks looking forward to meeting again, then after California three weeks looking back on that, and three weeks looking forward to me coming home, then it'll just be a series of three-week breaks.'

She looked almost convinced.

'We'll just have to try living in the eternal now of Zen,' she said, pouring me a glass of wine as Kitten appeared and expressed an entirely impractical interest in my lamb madras.

The next day in work, I picked up the phone and found Dean Pittman, the US Consul, on the other end.

'Hey, I've just read that piece you wrote in the paper about applying for an American work visa,' he said.

'You're not going to ban me for life for slagging the system, are you?' I said nervously.

'Sure thing. We want you to hand your visa back, and never darken our doors again,' he laughed. 'No, just calling to say we all had a good chuckle, and to wish you the best of luck for the trip. Keep your head down in Colombia, and give us a holler when you get back, then come up here for a coffee and a doughnut and tell us all about it.'

I promised I would, then put down the phone and thought, not for the first time, that there are more decent people in the world than the other sort. At least I hoped there were: that afternoon I logged onto the official Alaska state website and found my article in the section on terrorism.

The next day, I got an email from a reader asking if I was planning to go through Winnipeg. I mailed him back saying there was no reason to go to Winnipeg other than to see if the corner of Portage and Main really was the coldest, windiest spot in Canada, and since I had already done that, and it was, there was little point in going back.

The worrying thing was that he was the second person, after Simon Calder, who thought the Pan-Am went through Winnipeg.

My only fear was that in a year or so, when the book came out, I would be preparing to give a talk at the Royal Explorers' Club when some old duffer in a tweed jacket with leather elbows would come pottering up and say in a voice cultivated by a lifetime of Claridge's finest claret: 'Is it really true you didn't go via Winnipeg, my boy?', then give me one of those looks with which Englishmen have struck down natives at a range of half a mile since time immemorial, or before the Queen Mother was born, whichever came first, turn on the heel of a well-polished Church's brogue and stalk off, leaving behind only a faint aroma of breeding, damp tweed, even damper dogs, ancient leather armchairs and Old Throgmorton's Ready-Rubbed Pipe Tobacco for Gentlemen, by Royal Appointment.

34

In the meantime, my only other fear was leaving Cate for three months, no matter how much I divided it into three-week segments.

'I don't know why I worry so much these days. I never used to be filled with this nameless dread, endless low-level anxiety and early-twenty-first-century angst when I was younger. Like about three,' I said, wandering around the kitchen grumbling to myself one evening.

'Listen,' she said, turning away from where she was making supper, 'I love you more than anything in the world, and I'll miss you hugely. But the most important thing is for you to go on this trip and enjoy the things you love doing, like getting up every morning to think, write and ride a motorbike off down the open road. And know that you'll be coming back to someone who loves and supports you, as I know you do me. After that, everything else is just stuff.'

She is, I thought as I looked at her in the firelight later, the most remarkable person I have ever known.

The days crept by, emails hissed to and fro, and the reality of the trip loomed ever larger. On the night of 18 January, at one minute to midnight, Clifford stepped out of his house at the foot of the Mourne mountains, stood beside the little Zen garden which he raked every day, looked up into the starry night at the full moon, then rang the Japanese bell which hung at the edge of the garden. The single chime rose into the clear, cold air, hung there for a few diminishing seconds, then was lost in the night, leaving only the pure and hopeful silence at the end of all unspoken prayers.

In Belfast, Cate and I stood in our garden, looked up at the same moon, and raised a glass of Laphroaig each.

For what the three of us knew was that at this very moment the keel of the SS *Oluf Maersk* was kissing goodbye to the dockyard wall in Felixstowe, that it would not touch land again until it sailed into the harbour of San Antonio, Chile, on 4 February, and that deep in the echoing dark of one of the containers on deck were the two motorbikes that would, not long after that, take us over half the length of the planet on the longest road in the world.

'Good luck, chaps,' I said to them as they sailed off into the wine-dark night.

'And God speed. To them, and to you,' said Cate.

The next morning, leaving the house, I looked to the west. Somewhere out there, the bikes were sitting in a cold, dark container, wondering why they weren't in a showroom in Essex like all their mates. The Aprilia was, almost certainly, muttering: 'Mamma mia, Sophia Loren, rigatoni and linguine, but I'm freezing and I haven't seen the sunshine for a week. What is to become of us?' And the Triumph was undoubtedly replying: 'I do believe we're on our way to darkest Chile for a grand adventure. Now buck up, there's a good chap.'

I got into the car and drove to work, before any of the neighbours spotted me talking to two motorbikes that weren't there.

Geoff's Uncle Fred in a photograph that was later used in a police recruitment poster.

7

By now, there were only three weeks to go before the great adventure, and everything seemed to be proceeding disturbingly smoothly.

Until I made the mistake of checking out the Foreign and Commonwealth Office travellers' advice website. I wish I hadn't, for what it said was that the risk of kidnapping in northern Ecuador and most of Colombia was so high at the minute that at any given moment you were liable to be pottering along admiring parrots and minding your own business when several large, hairy men in combat trousers and the sort of green forage caps favoured by the young Fidel Castro would leap out from the trees, produce a veritable arsenal of machine guns and kidnap you. Then they would chop off your dongles and refuse to return them until your granny handed over her pension.

Since both my grannies were dead, this was a worrying development, and after thinking about it for some time, I decided to do something sensible for a change, and contact the

British Embassy in Bogotá to see just how dangerous the situation in Colombia was.

The reply finally arrived the day after we left and was forwarded to me by Cate. If it had arrived the day before, I don't think I'd have left at all, for this is what diplomat Andy Stainton had to say:

> You are obviously intent on doing the trip and probably nothing anyone can say would prevent you from going ahead, but you will be going through some extremely dangerous parts of the country.
>
> The highway between the border and to the south of Cali is still notorious for illegal checkpoints, where people can be kidnapped if thought worthy.
>
> I would suggest that you cross the border early enough in the day to make it to Cali, Armenia or Pereira. Once out of Cali the road is very good and fast to the *zona cafetera* and the major towns are reasonably safe. Going north from this area through Risaralda, again there have been recent kidnappings.
>
> As an example, an Italian cyclist was kidnapped recently, but on the other hand a British Oxfam worker visiting from UK was held at a FARC checkpoint for two hours and then allowed to proceed. So it is definitely a grey area. The idea is, if you are stopped, try and prove you don't have anything worth being taken hostage for and definitely don't advertise your trip prior to coming. Make sure they know you are not American.
>
> There are a number of precautions you could take: 1. Get a boat from Ecuador to Buenaventura then by road to Cali. This road is not 100% safe but you are minimising the risk considerably; 2. Fly to Cali from Quito and head north by road, thereby avoiding the most dangerous part of the route; 3. You could hire a couple of armed motorcyclists to escort you through the danger areas. These guys would ensure you don't stray off the beaten track and could advise you of places not to stop and where is safe. There are a number of security companies that should be able to do this; 4. The police may be able to provide a similar service, but they are a target, so it is probably not the best idea; 5. Take your own chances.

Your trip goes against the information provided by the
FCO, so I am duty bound to tell you that.

Having painted a totally black picture, the good news is
that the Colombian people are friendly and certainly in the
more remote areas would be extremely interested and
inquisitive about the two gringos on motorbikes. Good luck
with your trip: as a fellow motorcyclist I'm extremely
envious, and if you were going through Bogotá it would have
been interesting to meet a couple of loonies from Belfast!

In the meantime, I managed to squeeze in another mistake by
logging on to Amazon to buy a couple of copies of *Way to Go*,
since we had given away the last copy in the house to a friend
from Vermont who came to dinner. There, I discovered the
good news that it was one of Amazon's recommended reads;
and the bad news that recommended along with it was *Two
Wheels Through Terror: Diary of a South American Motorcycle
Odyssey* by Glen Heggstad.

Glen, according to the blurb was 'an adventure motorcyclist
who seeks out and rides the most rugged places on the planet.
He has been a Marine, a Hell's Angel and a martial arts
competitor, but no amount of training or experience was able
to prepare him for what he became while riding to the
southern tip of South America: a prisoner. This book is the
shocking travelogue of Heggstad's journey and his capture by
Colombia's rebel ELN army. Heggstad is ripped from his
motorcycle, robbed of everything, and forced to march
through strange jungles with assault rifles in his back. He is fed
only small amounts of rice and water and is forced to carry
heavy equipment, heavy packs, and heavy doubts about his
future. Even with all the hand-to-hand and sophisticated
combat training Heggstad possessed, it was his shrewd
thinking, precise planning, and a "do-or-die" last act of
desperation that eventually secured his freedom. Glen
Heggstad has spared no detail from this account. He has stated
that writing this book and reliving his tragedies was as painful
as suffering through them the first time. Read this first-hand

account of an ambitious motorcycle journey that gets horribly, and violently, detoured.'

Mmm. After reading that, I did the only thing a grown-up, mature, courageous man would do: went and cried in the toilets for a while. Then I phoned Clifford, who had mentioned the week before that he had dug up a couple of useful contacts in Colombia.

'Here, contact them and see how safe the place is at the minute. If it's not, ask them if they can come up with an armed escort across the country. Or a ferry ticket from Ecuador to Panama,' I said.

Vikings – who took omens so seriously that if one of them fell off his horse or dreamed of a three-legged rabbit with a lisp before they were due to set off for a spot of pillaging, they would call off the adventure immediately – would have told me to light the fire, lock the doors and sit inside drinking ale and telling ghost stories until it was safe to go out again.

There were only three problems with this. First of all, the motorbikes were already halfway across the Atlantic on their way to Chile. Secondly, peat briquettes were so crap that it was almost impossible to light a fire with them these days, and thirdly, when I tell ghost stories I frighten myself so much I can't sleep. Not that I was finding it easy sleeping these days anyway, what with worrying about kidnappings, wondering how I was going to manage without Cate for three months, and wondering even more how she was going to manage for the same length of time with only Kitten for company, even if he was a great conversationalist, as long as the subject was food or sleep.

At least the thought of leaving her behind made me appreciate the sweet and gentle blessings of everyday life with her all the more, to the extent that even something like putting out the bin and coming back into the house to see her cooking in the kitchen made me come over all funny.

In the fortnight before we left, I had only had two positive conversations about Colombia. The first was with Wilmer at

Provincewide, the motorcycle dealers who had offered to give me a very nice Roof helmet for the trip. Wilmer was a man who knew about surviving in tough countries, since he had spent nineteen years in Nigeria as Coca-Cola's head of quality, although you might think that an oxymoron, like military intelligence or Scottish football.

'Colombia?' he said. 'No problem. Just remember: when you stop at a restaurant, ride past it first, then ride back the other way and stop. That way they'll think you're heading south, and set up the road block that way.'

The other conversation was with Dave in work, who said: 'Listen, if you and Clifford get lonely on the trip, just remember that homosexuality is illegal in Colombia, but apparently if you're on top, they don't treat you as the gay one.'

Making a mental note to tell Clifford, I suddenly had the bright idea of checking what the Foreign Office website had to say about Pakistan, which Paddy Minne and I had gone through on the first Nambarrie Run. Basically, it was as bad as Colombia: the advice was don't go there, whatever you do don't go to Baluchistan, and whatever you do twice over, don't take a train to the Iranian border.

All of which we did, without a problem.

See? Things are never quite as bad as you think. Or, as Paddy was so fond of saying: 'How hard can it be?' Mind you, that was just before he hit the sheep in Bulgaria, I thought as I opened my email to find a comforting message from a mate called Paul Wilson to say that was he just back from playing golf in the Himalayas before being chased off the course by furious monkeys.

> Just thought I'd wish you good luck for the trip. *The Rough
> Guide to Travel Survival* says if you get attacked by a guerrilla
> the best thing to do is go for the eyes or try and stick your
> finger up its bottom … Sorry, that was a gorilla I was
> thinking of. What it actually says is that to avoid kidnapping
> you should vary your routine, stay out of the local media,

hire a bodyguard and get kidnap insurance. However, if you are kidnapped:

Take a deep breath and flex your muscles when being tied up. When you relax, you may be able to struggle free (and face the 1000km barefoot jungle hike to civilisation, alone).

Comply with the kidnappers (it's lucky homosexuality is illegal in Colombia, isn't it?).

Speak to the kidnappers without anger.

Keep your mental edge (whatever that means).

Study your captors' habits and routines for a possible means of escape.

I tried all these methods while held captive in journalism, although clearly they're not that successful, as it took me five years to get out.

Seriously, all the best with the trip, and take care and all that; I hope not to hear any stories of a 6' 7" man found wandering semi-naked on a deserted highway with only a waterproof map to keep him company.

I made a mental note to hold my breath until we got to Alaska. Then I wondered why everyone was obsessed by homosexuality in Colombia.

That evening, Paddy Minne, the world-famous Franco-Belgian motorcycle mechanic who had been a close friend since we had ridden two Royal Enfields from Delhi to Belfast seven years before, called around with the little digital video camera from that adventure that he was lending us for this one.

'I am so green with envy of you going on this one,' he said. 'Are you excited about it?'

'Aye, half excited, half nervous, half thinking I'm going to miss Cate like hell, half wondering if I can still be funny after a year of being a gloomy bastard,' I said, vaguely aware that that was probably too many halves.

'Don't worry, you were a gloomy bastard before the last one, and you were funny then,' he said comfortingly.

In a way, he was right: I remembered that the months before the Delhi to Belfast ride, in which an impossible bureaucratic or logistical problem seemed to arise every single day, had left me so close to going hopelessly gaga that I swore at the time that if I got back safely from it I would give up adventures, fill a pipe with Old Throgmorton's Ready-Rubbed, don a pair of slippers and spend the rest of my days in an armchair by the fire reading a good book.

Aye, right, as they say in Belfast.

Ironically, about a month before that trip, I'd met Cate, now my wife, on the Lisburn Road in Belfast. Her beloved dad had died two years before, and she'd just returned to Belfast to resume her academic career after caring for her mum since then.

Since we knew each other slightly through Caitriona, a mutual friend, we stopped for a chat, most of which I apparently spent moaning about the almost impossible difficulties of organising grand adventures.

'Honestly, you really shouldn't complain so much. It'll be wonderful,' she said. She was, of course, right, but she was so embarrassed about telling off someone she hardly knew that the next time she saw me, she hid in an alley rather than speak to me.

We still laughed every time we thought about it.

And so the precious days slipped by, bringing with them, even at this late stage, surprises from the road we were going to travel: a week before we left, I was at a party hosted by Cliff and Bernie, two friends I'd known since we were at university together in 1846. The university was still being built in those days, which is probably why Cliff is the only person alive with a degree in Bricklaying and Philosophy.

Halfway through the evening, I was just saying to Bernie: 'You know, it's weird. Just when we had the route settled, along comes a copy of *The Rough Guide to Chile* last week which says that the Pan-American now starts in Quellón, 100 miles south of Puerto Montt.'

'Oh no it doesn't,' said a middle-aged man who just happened to be passing. 'It starts in Ushuaia, at the southern tip of Argentina. There's a pub on the main street called the Ideal

Bar, where if you tell them you're Irish, you get a free drink.'

Fortunately, Bernie went off to get another glass of wine at that moment and I was able to drown the cad in the hot tub.

But this was bad news: not just because Cliff and Bernie wouldn't be able to use the hot tub for a while, but because Clifford and I had missed a free drink.

Talking of whom, he called the next day.

'The good news is I've got my traveller's cheques. The bad news is they're all in $20 denominations. They're going to take up most of my luggage space,' he said.

'Here, you don't fancy lending me your Enfield for a few days? I just want to try out my new helmet and gloves.'

'Aye, no worries. The bike could do with a good run, since it's been sitting there all winter.'

He turned up the next day to find me checking the oil and tyres, dusting off the cobwebs and cleaning the spark plug.

'I hope you've included a full tank of petrol in that free service,' he said with a grin.

'Absolutely, sir,' I said as he started it up with a well-practised kick, climbed aboard and pottered off down the avenue with a cheery wave.

'He's a good soul,' said Cate.

'He is. I'll be glad of him,' I said, giving her shoulder an empathetic squeeze and thinking as we walked back to the house that there were many more good souls in the world than the other sort.

It was a lesson Paddy Minne and I had learnt every day on the Delhi to Belfast trip, and it was a lesson I learnt again when I went into work the very next day to find an email from Peter Rolston, an Ulster expat now living in China. The year before, he'd written me a very kind letter to tell me how much he'd enjoyed *Way to Go*.

He'd just read the column I'd written in the paper saying how afraid I was that the moment I rode into Colombia, I'd be kidnapped and strung up by the dongles, and this was his response:

44

> Dear Hill,
>
> Have just read your latest dispatch, fear you may be going
> soft. Stop blubbing, man, and pull yourself together. After
> 6,000 miles in the saddle, your dongles will be useless anyway.
> Dib dib,

The Major

Brilliant. And he was right. Biggles would have breezed
through Colombia without a thought in the world, I thought,
sending Peter back a promise that I would pull my socks up
and stop worrying about my dongles.

For Cate and me, the months had become weeks, the weeks
had become days, and suddenly it was only four days before I
left. We clung together, unwilling to let go.

'Listen,' I said, 'why don't you just come along for the whole
three months? Tell work you're nipping out for a sandwich,
and when you get back in May, walk in gaily and say: "God,
you wouldn't believe the queue in that shop!" Oh, and don't
forget the sandwich.'

She laughed, but only just.

I must be mad, I thought, leaving the woman I love for so
long.

Then, the next day, Murphy's Law struck, as it does: she got
a call from Edinburgh to say that her mum had taken a turn for
the worse. Once a leading chef and pillar of the community,
Ann had been in a home there for several years. In her beautiful
mind, what was once a *son et lumière* display of creativity and
energy had become a few flickering candles in the long dark
night of her decline. The last time we had gone to see her, we
had sat with her through a summer afternoon, drinking tea and
holding her hands, so delicate we dared not even squeeze
them. Once, she had looked out of the window at a shaft of
sunlight on the roses, then turned to Cate and said, suddenly
and heartbreakingly: 'Catherine'.

This time, I drove Cate to the airport to fly over and see her,
thinking of my own uncle Fred, a former motorcycle policeman

who had been the finest of men, and who had gone the same way. The next day, I met my wife, her face brave but edged with strain, off the plane. Her mother had only spoken once during the long hours she sat with her. 'I just want to go home,' was what she had said. How hard it is, I thought, to say goodbye to those we love, whether it is for three months, or an eternity.

The night before I left, I phoned my own mum and dad to say goodbye.

'Hope you get nice weather, son. Don't forget to keep an eye on your oil levels,' said Dad.

'Do be careful of those bandits, dear,' said Mum – the same advice she'd given me before riding from Delhi to Belfast.

Early the next morning, Sinead, a researcher from RTÉ's Ryan Tubridy show, phoned about a last-minute interview they wanted to do.

'And do you have any family?' she said.

'Cate, my wife,' I said.

'And is she a woman?'

Cate and I carried my bags downstairs afterwards, half laughing and half crying.

Enzo and Elias. Geoff is the one in the middle.

8

It is sometimes difficult, even for a chap who is used to adventuring, to pinpoint the moment when an adventure actually begins.

For Scott of the Antarctic, it was probably when he picked up the phone, rang Lillywhites of Piccadilly, and ordered three dozen Small but Sturdies from the pony department.

For Biggles, it is usually when Air Commodore Raymond steps through the door with the news that there is a spot of bother in Bongo-Bongo Land, and there is only one man who can sort it out. Looking up and catching a glimpse of himself reflected in the window as he reaches for his cigarette case, Biggles realises that the chap in question is, yet again, him.

For me, it probably began when I closed the front door of our house for the last time in a long time, and drove to the airport with Cate. Earlier, we had exchanged our last tokens of farewell as I set off on the longest and most dangerous journey of my life: from her, a tiny silver box containing a flower for inspiration, a key for improvement, a shamrock for luck, a heart for love and an angel for protection. My gift was silver too: a vintage RAF sweetheart badge, one of the little brooches in the shape of pilot's wings which wartime flyers gave to their loves before they, too, headed off on dangerous missions.

We were, as you can imagine, in a bit of a state when we arrived at the airport.

'Buck up, old thing,' said Cate as we got out of the car. 'You'll be turning into Ewan McGregor if you're not careful.'

'Just a bit of dust in my eye, dear,' I said, pretending to blow my nose in a manly sort of way.

However, I was soon to be even more in a bit of state when a quick tour of the departure lounge revealed that a small but essential element of the trip was missing: Clifford.

He had said he'd be there early, but after half an hour, with the flight about to close, there was still no sign of him. The photographers had come and gone, saying they would use library pictures of him for the local newspapers. Just as I was beginning to wonder if I had told him the wrong airport, or if I had actually imagined organising the whole expedition, he came sauntering down the stairs without a care in the world.

'Ah, it's yourself,' he said gaily. 'It's amazing how you can get lost to the world when you're enjoying a nice cup of tea.'

'Bloody hell, Pancho, don't do that. You'll give me a heart attack. Have you got your passport, money and bike documents OK?' I said.

'Got the passport and the money. Never got the bike registration document in my name back from Swansea, but I've got a letter confirming that the bike's mine.'

I looked at him, aghast.

'Pancho, you won't get through a South American border without the original bike registration document,' I said.

'Ach, the letter will be fine. Don't worry about it, Don,' he said blithely.

I had my doubts, but it was too late to do anything about it now, I thought as we carried the bags to check-in. A few short minutes later we were hugging Cate's mate Edelle, who had turned up for moral support, and I was saying a tearful farewell to a wife I would not see until she joined us in Los Angeles, two months away. I must be utterly doolally, I thought as we climbed the steps and I turned to give her one last wave, leaving the love of my life for so long.

As our flight to London climbed into a leaden sky, I thought of that scene from *The Dambusters*, where the camera pans around the room of a man who did not come back from the raid, then pauses at the hairbrush and the ticking clock on his bedside table. I imagined her driving back to our empty house and walking around, looking in the same way at the unsung icons of our harmony: the cards on top of the fridge, the half-read book beside the bed.

I phoned her that evening, from the departures lounge at Heathrow.

'Just remember,' she said, 'if you die on this trip, I'll kill you.'

'Don't worry, dear,' I said, 'I'll keep my wits about me. The half I have, that is.'

I put down the phone, a knife turning in my heart, to find Clifford digging in his jacket pocket.

'Fancy a Werther's, old chap?' he said.

I took it, and sat back in my seat. After two long years of planning which had almost removed what little sanity I had, the grand adventure had finally begun.

Clifford went off for a wander, and I bought a sandwich and was making some notes when a Scottish voice said: 'Here, aren't you Geoff Hill?'

'Stop messing about, Clifford, you know I haven't a clue,' I said without looking up from the ham sandwich I was giving my full attention to, if only out of respect for the pig. Then I remembered that Clifford had just gone off for a potter.

The voice, in fact, belonged to a wildlife guide and ornithologist called Duncan, who with his girlfriend Clare and a copy of his great-grandfather's *Book of Australian Birds* was just about to set off for a month's twitching in the outback.

'You see,' he said, 'in my spare time I work in a bookshop, and last year so many people came in asking for *Way to Go* that I thought I'd better buy a copy. Then when I saw the Nambarrie T-shirt, I thought: "There's your man off somewhere again", so I thought I'd come over and find out where,' he said as Clifford reappeared and introduced himself.

'What part of Scotland are you from, then?' said Clare.

'Near Dalbeattie,' said Clifford.

'Och, I cut my teeth in Dalbeattie. Do you know Jenny Smith?'

'Know her? She drives the Post Office van,' said Clifford mysteriously. 'And I used to go horse riding with her until I fell off.'

So the next time someone tells you it's a small world, tell them they don't know the half of it, I thought, leaving them to the joys of Dalbeattie and returning to my ham sandwich and the fascinating but intractable problem of my keyboard.

You see, to write stories about the trip and keep me in a job, I had been furnished with a personal digital wotsit which did everything short of making tea. This was supposed to be linked to a neat folding keyboard by what I believe is known in the trade as a wireless bluetooth connection. In theory, all I had to do was hit the right buttons, and the two would rush into each other's electronic arms like a digital version of Cathy and Heathcliff.

However, what actually happened was that when I asked the wotsit to find the keyboard, it went off like a nun at a disco and flirted outrageously with every bluetooth device within range, so that after a fruitless half hour, I had connected only with fourteen mobile phones, three laptops, two PlayStations, one video arcade game and a passing ambulance, not to mention setting off the fire alarm. Fortunately, just as I was about to throw it in the bin, haul out my old faithful notebook and pen and borrow a pigeon from Duncan, if he stooped to such a common species, our flight to São Paulo was called.

'Here, let's have a look at your passport,' I said as we queued at the check-in desk.

'Why?'

'Because they say if you look like your passport photo, you're too ill to travel.'

He laughed and handed it over.

'No, you look just as ugly as in real life. What does the *F* in Clifford F. Paterson stand for?'

'I'm not effing telling you,' he said, snatching it back.

'Is it … Francis?'

'I'm not bloody telling you. You've three months to guess.'

Two hours later, having completely failed to blag an upgrade by telling them we were personal friends of Larry at Varig, we climbed aboard, and the plane trundled across the bejewelled plain that is an airport after dark.

And then stopped. And trundled all the way back.

It seemed that a passenger at the back had gone berserk, locked herself in the toilet and refused to come out. She had either been working too hard and just wanted some time off in loo, or had had a horrifying presentiment off the in-flight meal, a chicken whose unhappy life was echoed in the karma of its korma. Perhaps she was worried that flying with Varig would give her varigose veins.

After a while, several cheery policemen boarded the plane and escorted off the plane a small Japanese woman who wished everyone a polite 'Bye bye' as she was led away. She looked disturbingly like Yoko Ono.

Finally, as the clock struck midnight, our plane rose into the cold and starry night, turned south across the ocean and sailed on through the moonlit dark, clouds flowing around it in the same way that, miles below, ghostly convocations of baffled plankton parted and then closed around the inexorable progress of whales.

At dawn I woke from a fitful sleep to a roseate sunrise over the port wing and a sudden, liberating realisation: that I would not have to go into the office for the next three months and spend every single day racking my brains for a story to write. That was what I was escaping from; that relentless, de-motivating stress which had turned a joy into a drudgery.

This time, the stories were out there, all along the open road to Alaska.

I slept again, glad that I had remembered, in that moment of revelation, why I loved travel. Mind you, when I say slept, I really mean struggled to sleep in a seat which made me regret giving up my subscription to *Contortionists' Weekly*.

Thanks to the delay caused by the Yoko Ono lookalike, we were now running two hours late, and landed at São Paulo at 9.10, with a 9.30 connection to Santiago in Chile. Amazingly, not only did we make it, but we even had time for a quick coffee at the little bar in the corner. After all, not to would have been like going to Blackpool and not buying a Kiss Me Quick hat.

'That must qualify for the shortest ever visit to Brazil,' said Clifford as we ran up the steps to the plane, 'but at least we contributed something to the economy.'

For the third time in twenty-four hours, we rose into the air, turning west over the sprawling mass of São Paulo.

'How's your Spanish coming on then, Don?' said Clifford.

'Spanish? We're in Latin America, lad. It's verb declensions I've been working on: *amo, amas, amat, tequila, tequilam, tequilorum,*' I said, gazing out of the window at a landscape, not of wild and woolly jungle, rife with jaguars and fierce marmosets as I had expected, but gently rolling fields which looked more like Sussex, or a giant golf course. Which is much the same thing, now that I think about it. After a while, this gave way to mildly parched flatlands. Once, we passed over a vast flotilla of tiny white clouds, each one towing its black shadow east across the arid plain in search of the blessing of water.

And then, suddenly, the Andes, as if the earth had been overcome by a sudden and violent ambition to reach the sky.

It was across these jagged mountains in the harsh winter of 1817 that José de San Martin led his revolutionary army, surprising the Spanish, who were all sitting around warm fires in woolly pullovers, and securing Chilean independence with the seizure of Santiago, the city to which we were now spiralling down just in time for lunch.

On the airport immigration form, our three choices of status were Single, Married or Widowed: since divorce is still a touchy subject in Chile, a bride and groom will often deliberately misspell their names on the wedding certificate in case they should later feel an annulment coming on.

Not that that seemed to be a problem for Clifford and me: after a whole day together, we were still getting on fine as, stuffed with beef and dazed with lack of sleep, we staggered into the arrivals hall to be met by the welcome sight of Elias, the driver who was to take us to Valparaiso, near the port of San Antonio where the bikes had hopefully arrived and were being held ransom by customs until we arrived to sign the release documents.

We had originally hoped that Elias's boss, the translator and renowned fixer Enzo Tesser, could do this for us, saving a three-hour diversion, but the day before departure, it had become mysteriously and irrevocably impossible.

Thank heavens, then, for Enzo's wife, Martina, who had met Enzo at a disco in Valparaiso thirteen years before and fallen instantaneously in love with him, and he with her. Being German and therefore phenomenally efficient and helpful, Martina had rustled up Elias and a car as quickly as she had fallen in love with Enzo. Not only that, but she ran a guesthouse where we could spend the night before going to the port in the morning.

'Ah, this is the way a chap should arrive in a country,' I said as I sank back into a soft car seat and Clifford and Elias began a lengthy discussion about which South American women were the best. Since Elias looked like Jesus's younger brother, this was a mite disconcerting, like when you're walking down the street minding your own business and a nun comes up and starts snogging you. I hate it when that happens, especially the older ones who should know better.

Anyway, where was I? Ah yes, women: the eventual outcome was that Argentinians had the best bodies, Brazilians were the best dancers and Chileans made the best wives.

Oh, and Colombians were the best at shooting you when you asked them why exactly the garage was full of unmarked boxes of what looked like soap powder.

There. Having sorted that out, we pulled up outside Enzo and Martina's house, a towering hundred-year-old wooden neo-romantic edifice painted in all the colours of the rainbow.

'Enzo thought that if the local kids were going to cover buildings with graffiti, they may as well make themselves useful,' said Elias by way of explanation, attempting to lift the biggest of my bags out of the boot and almost giving himself a hernia.

'Sorry. I seem to have accidentally brought a lot of books,' I said as he gave up and carried my helmet in instead. Inside, we found Enzo, Martina, several hundred children, a matching number of trolls, a collection of ancient typewriters and barber's tools and a languid spaniel called Bicho.

Within five minutes, we were sitting at a scrubbed wooden table in the courtyard with a hot coffee, a cold beer, supper on the way and the promise, after forty sleepless hours on the road, of a cosy bed that night.

Thank you, Lord, for this day, I said to myself, raising my glass to the sun as Bicho leaned against my leg and placed his wet nose with infinite tenderness in my palm.

However, my state of nirvana did not last long, for as Clifford went for a bracing swim, I typed three stories into the wotsit then tried to send them back to the paper.

Only to find that the wotsit, which only the day before had been running around like a mad tart flirting with every electronic device in Heathrow, was now sulking in the corner and refusing to speak to anyone.

In the circumstances, I did the only thing possible: had a beer and went to bed in a tall room which had been painted by a small man, so that the fetching shade of turquoise only reached two thirds of the way up the walls. Clifford wandered in just after and fell into his own bed, only to discover the centre of the mattress missing, so that he spent the rest of the night with his head on the pillow and his bum on the floor.

Next morning at nine, we set off in Elias's car to see a man called Rodrigo at the customs office in San Antonio, with Enzo in the back seat tightly clutching a pile of documents which would have choked a whole squadron of donkeys, never mind one.

The reason he was clutching them so tightly was because Elias was a man who drove with a combination of consummate skill and a handsome disregard for death, overtaking and undertaking, sometimes at the same time, and all the while telling Clifford that Colombian women were possibly even more beautiful than Argentinian ones.

In between women and overtaking, he talked, too, of the Pinochet years, a subject which all Chilean conversations invariably come back to, like picking at a scab.

'None of my family were tortured or murdered,' he said, 'but you still see many women on the streets, asking for justice for those responsible for the Disappeared. Or just even to know where their husbands or brothers are, so they can bury them and be at peace.'

Compared to that, perhaps being separated from your wife for three months isn't so bad, I thought, reminding myself to count my blessings more often.

Soon we were in San Antonio, a down-at-heel kind of place in which mangy dogs roamed the streets and a solitary policeman tried in vain to control the traffic jam. Or possibly caused it.

'No policeman, no problem,' said Elias succinctly as we stopped outside the customs office.

Inside, we found Rodrigo sitting at a desk. On the wall beside him, naturally enough, were two photos of George Best in his prime. His playing prime, not his drinking prime, that is.

'You are from Belfast also? ¡Estupendo!' he said with a broad grin as Enzo placed his pile of documents on the desk in front of him.

'Right,' he said, 'we'll let Rodrigo sort through those while we go and find the bikes.'

We followed him through the organised chaos of the docks, getting directions from several stevedores who looked like they chewed razor blades for fun, until we came to a giant warehouse. And there, right at the far end, were two bike-sized crates, one marked Hill/Triumph and the other Paterson/Aprilia.

Inside my chest, my heart started doing funny little things at the thought that the two motorbikes we were going to ride all the way to Alaska were only a few feet away.

Since Clifford's bike was Italian, he rushed over and gave his crate a huge smacking kiss, but I simply gave the Triumph's a manly pat on the back, which seemed a more British thing to do.

'Well done, old chap,' I said, when I thought no one was listening.

We walked back to Rodrigo's office, and what seemed like several days passed as he typed, shuffled, stamped, stapled and collated. Somewhere in the interior, a small rain forest died to replace the paper he had consumed.

More time passed. His tie slowly went out of fashion. On the radio, Frank Sinatra sang of old loves for young women, and on the wall beside Rodrigo, George waited patiently, his left foot swung back eternally in the act of scoring the perfect goal. At last Rodrigo stood up and handed over, after all that, two solitary sheets of paper for us to sign.

We did so with a flourish, shook hands with him, walked outside to find to our astonishment that it was still daylight, and walked back to the crates to wait for the truck which would take them south to Puerto Montt. It arrived, they were forklifted aboard, and we waved them off, then climbed into the car and set off for the airport to fly south and wait for their arrival the next day.

Halfway there, Enzo suddenly decided it was lunchtime, and Elias stopped the car at a village restaurant. We ate mashed corn and chicken stew, serenaded by two passing troubadours, while Enzo discussed the price of horses, mostly with himself.

By teatime, we were back at Santiago Airport and checking in for the flight to Puerto Montt.

'I'm sorry, *señor*, but you will have to pay excess baggage on this bag,' said the man behind the counter. 'What on earth is in it – gold bullion?'

'Books,' I said glumly, borrowing $80 off Clifford.

'Is the *F* for Fotheringill?' I said as he handed over his passport.

'Nope.'

'God, the women here are gorgeous,' Clifford said as the plane, laden with my books, lumbered down the runway for several miles before taking off. 'My project for the first week is to work on my chat-up lines.'

As we descended to Puerto Montt an hour later, I looked out of the window at a green and pleasant landscape which looked disturbingly like Ireland.

'Are you sure we're on the right flight?' I said.

'Don't mind, as long as they've cleared the penguins off the runway,' said Clifford.

We climbed into a taxi and asked the driver to take us to the Hotel O'Grimm, for no other reason than the name. Tragically, it was full, so we ended up at the Colina, a rambling seafront hotel where for twelve quid we got a cosy room with en-suite genuine fake marble bathroom and a bar downstairs in which sat several rough looking men drinking from vast pitchers of beer.

In the circumstances, it seemed only polite to join them, particularly to celebrate the fact that after months of looking at Puerto Montt on a map, we were actually there in the middle of the living, breathing reality of it. Not to mention celebrating bikes on their way, bags dumped in the room, us showered and shaved, shirts and socks washed, comfortable beds for two nights, cold beers in front of us and ham and cheese toasties on their way from the kitchen.

In fact, only one thing worried me as we wandered up the stairs at midnight, filled with beer, ham, cheese and goodwill to all men.

According to Enzo, Rodrigo had been doing that job for five years. It could now only be a matter of time before Chile invaded Peru to create storage space for all the paper he had produced. But then, we had a fairly good chance of getting across the border before fighting broke out.

After all, if it took an entire afternoon to import two motorbikes, it would take years to bring in enough guns to start a war.

A one-hundred-granny farewell from Quellón: mile zero of the Pan-American Highway.

9

'To awaken quite alone in a strange town is one of the most pleasant sensations in the world. You are surrounded by adventure.'

FREYA STARK

I slept the whole night through, and woke with that happy childlike sense of wonder at what the day would bring.

'Wake up, Pancho, you lazy ballix. Our bikes are arriving today. It'll be just like Christmas, except without the Brussels sprouts,' I said to Clifford, who was just stirring.

'That's a shame. I'm the only person in the world who actually likes sprouts,' he said, rolling over and going back to sleep.

'You're right, though,' he said when he finally woke. 'I'm just getting used to the idea that you can wake up and feel good every day. It just shows what unhealthy lifestyles we normally lead.'

He had a noisy cold shower, dressed and went off for a walk, humming 'Yellow Submarine' to himself.

Then, after breakfast, we strolled in the sun along the shore to Angelmo, the craft district filled with stalls selling everything from exquisite alpaca woollens to diving helmets, ancient spurs and stuffed wild boars. We were just wondering vaguely where the office of Juan Luis Moreno, the Navimag shipping agent who was taking delivery of the bikes, was when Clifford glanced casually to his left.

'Bloody hell, they're here!' he said.

We walked over, and were just congratulating the truck driver on his speed when Juan Luis came out and shook our hands. Before long, our trusty steeds were forklifted off the truck and trundled into the company workshop. Inside, several men were wrestling with a marine con rod the size of an elephant's leg. African, that is, not Indian.

We borrowed pliers and claw hammers off them, took a deep breath, and began dismantling the crates, feeling a bit like James Bond in that scene from *You Only Live Twice* in which Little Nellie is unveiled. Fifteen minutes of crashing and banging later, I had my first glimpse of the gleaming blue machine which would hopefully carry me to Alaska.

'KX55 NEO. Great registration. I'll have to get a pair of Keanu Reeves sunglasses,' I said.

'What are we going to call them?' said Clifford as we rolled his red bike out of the crate. 'I think mine looks like April the Aprilia, and a Tiger just has to be called Tony.'

'April and Tony it is, then,' I said, taking a deep lungful of air redolent with the smell of oil and grease, closing my eyes and feeling, in that moment, like a small boy in my father's workshop, watching in wonder and admiration as he rolled up his sleeves and set to work on a Norton, Rudge, BSA, Ariel or any of the pantheon of British makes of which Triumph was now the sole survivor.

We spent the long afternoon in the cool of the garage fitting windscreens, mirrors and luggage, then packing and repacking the panniers and top boxes, helped by a small, green-eyed boy called Leonidas who was just passing by. At last we were satisfied that we had made a complete cock-up of it, and stood back with the contented air of men looking at a job badly done.

'*Que te vaya muy bien*,' – may things go well with you – we said to Leonidas, shaking hands with him. He burst into a grin of delight and ran off as Clifford, rearranging spare fuel cans and oil filters in the top box, discovered a chocolate toolbox which his mechanic Andy had packed in a moment of whimsy. We called the Navimag mechanics over, handed out the chocolate spanners and hammers, and they stood around admiring our packing and agreeing that we could not have made a worse job of it.

'Just one more thing. My lucky teddy,' said Clifford, taking a small bear which a Japanese friend had given to him and wedging it between the handlebars.

Splendid. Everything except the bear would undoubtedly be repacked in a few days, but in the meantime we celebrated with an ice cream and a wander around Angelmo, where the air was rich with a strangely appealing blend of fish, honey and cheese. Vermilion wooden buildings teetered over the water, and for a few pesos a fisherman rowed us out around the wooded islands of the bay, each one dotted with extravagantly turreted homes.

We sat for a few minutes in the sun, then he started the outboard with an asthmatic rattle.

'Sounds like a Triumph,' said Clifford.

Still, I'm sure he enjoyed the long swim home.

At three in the morning, I was awakened by a large motorbike hurtling down the road outside.

'Ah, that's a good omen,' said Clifford at breakfast, reaching for another pastry from the table where they were covered by two large lace umbrellas, like Dolly Parton's bra.

'After I won the Isle of Man TT in 1978, I had a dream that I was going to die there.'

'And did you?'

'No, I never went back.'

We walked down to the Navimag offices, said goodbye to Juan Luis and loaded the bikes, not helped by a small dog who couldn't decide whether he wanted to have sex with my ankle or pee on it. Still, since I never know whether I'm coming or going either, I empathised with him.

At last we climbed on the bikes, as happy as boys, and half an hour later were riding onto the ferry to Chiloé, the island south of Puerto Montt.

And if you are wondering why we were heading south when we wanted to get to Alaska, the answers are simple:

a) Any Irishman knows that the longest distance between two points is a straight line.

b) Further checking with *Rough Guides* confirmed that the Pan-American Highway had indeed been extended 150 miles to Quellón on the southern tip of Chiloé.

c) Don't mention Winnipeg.

We leaned on the rail watching leaping dolphins, sunbathing penguins and a family of pelicans slide past as we chugged to Chiloé. The island is famous for dried fish and wet weather, but fortunately we found neither, even if the air did pong a bit of cod liver oil and rain.

It had, I just realised as we rode off the ferry, been at least six months since I'd been on a bike, but it's a funny thing, riding a bike: you never forget how to do it. Someone should really make up an aphorism about it.

And apart from almost falling off several times through admiring my new Roof helmet in the mirror, I was enjoying the smooth, powerful balance of the Triumph.

Compared to the Enfield's single-cylinder engine, which sounded like a heartbeat, and the Harley's big V-twin, which was like two flatulent hippos making love underwater, the Triumph's triple sounded like a giant sewing machine, which was rather appropriate, since it would sew the thread of my destiny over the next three months.

But, like all bikes, it had this glorious truth about it: it forced me to exist in the moment; the perfect endless moment of the wind rushing past, the road beneath my feet, the smell of the green woods and the sights all around of roadside milk churns waiting for collection and farmers making hay while the sun shone.

We took to the coast road for a while, a winding roller-coaster past wooden shingle houses and matching churches, and stopped for lunch in a tiny fishing village.

'Lord, it's so good being out in the world,' I said, munching a meat pie and looking out at bright boats dancing in the bay.

'This is the real world, not the one we've left behind,' said Clifford as we were approached by three small girls who told us they were on holiday, then politely quizzed us on how old we were, whether we were brothers, what we were at, if we were married and how many children we had.

'*Mi esposa se llama Catherine, pero nosotros tenemos solo un gato negro y blanco que llama Kitten,*' I said, probably in Spanish so bad even I hadn't a clue what I was saying.

'*Ah, Catherine. Un nombre bueno,*' said the smallest of the three.

It is one of the lovely things about travel, I thought, that in years to come, when these three girls meet for cocktails after work in Santiago to jokingly complain about their husbands and the price of shoes, one of them will suddenly say: 'Hey, do you remember those two guys on motorbikes that day at Quemchi? I wonder if they ever made it to Alaska?'

Lives that meet and part, blessed by moments of shared humanity.

As for when we got to Alaska, never at this rate was the answer, I thought, looking at my watch and realising that it was the middle of the afternoon and we still had a hundred miles to go today. We said goodbye to the girls, their mothers and pretty much everyone in the village, and rode on to Castro, the island capital.

Pastel coloured houses dipped the toes of their stilts in the sea, and by the woods and lakes beyond were little clusters of *cabañas*, holiday cottages painted lilac or terracotta, ochre or indigo, fuchsia bobbing in the warm breeze by their doors. They looked so entirely charming that it was all I could do not to stop, find a post office and write to Cate telling her we were going to live in one and have fifteen children all called Pedro, especially the girls. I could always get a job as a church shingler, or dried-fish motorcycle courier.

On we rode over hill and dale, exchanging cheery waves with passing bikers, farmers on horses, small children and goats, although the goats tended to fall over if they waved too enthusiastically.

By early evening we came at last to Quellón, the ramshackle seaside town which is the end of the world and the start of the Pan-American Highway, and found a wooden seafront inn which had been recommended by *The Rough Guide*, although from the stained bedclothes and the dead cockroach in the shower, only the rough bit held true.

The cockroach had, in fact, probably died of hypothermia, since further investigation proved that the shower had only two settings, Freezing and Would Suit Hardy Penguin.

While I sat down to write up the events of the day, Clifford went off exploring, and came back with the news that there was a party in the town hall. As we were walking there through the purple dusk, he clutched my arm and pointed at a shop window. There, in the dim interior, was an old man, carving a statue of Don Quixote and his trusty sidekick.

'You see. The day started with a good omen, and it's ending with one,' he said as we entered the town hall for what turned out to be more or less a ceilidh.

Grandmothers cooked the food, their granddaughters served it and then went off to snog their boyfriends behind the donkey shed, and on the stage, a bearded man in a black beret who looked like Che Guevara's dad sang songs of such revolutionary passion that by the end of the evening, we were all hugging each other and swearing undying devotion to the cause, whatever it was.

'Here, that was a grand day,' I said to Clifford as we climbed dubiously into our beds that night. 'What was the best bit for you?'

'When we came out of the restaurant at lunchtime and you put your helmet on backwards,' he said, then laughed so much I had to throw not one but both grimy pillows at him.

'Actually, the helmet's a bit noisy. I'm going to stick toilet paper in my ears and see if that cures it. Anyway, it looks good, and that's the main thing,' I said.

In any case, tomorrow we would finally start on the long road north.

You see, south may hold its languid charms, east its Oriental pleasures, and west may be the direction in which lovelorn cowboys ride off into the sunset, but it is north where manly adventure lies.

So tomorrow we would ride north, for adventure, and a noble, heroic life.

Which was, now that I think of it, a good time for a short history of Chile. If any proper historians want to complain about the lack of veracity or proper dignity in this history, let them complain to the third penguin on the left.

A short history of Chile

12000 BC and 30 seconds
Country populated by mammoths and giant armadillos.

12000 BC
Migrants arrive from Asia.

11000 BC
Fed up with diet of mammoth and giant armadillo, migrants become farmers and learn to cook. Subsequent civilisations noted only for inhaling hallucinogenic substances and sacrificing llamas.

1465 AD
Incas, owners of the largest empire in the world, arrive from Peru, build huge network of palaces, temples, fortresses and roads, then pass the time sacrificing children, supply of llamas having run out.

1538
Spanish arrive in form of Pedro de Valdivia, who tells Incas he's taking over country. Incas think about it, then pour molten gold down his throat, producing worst case of heartburn in history. Spanish take over country anyway, installing feudal system of rich landlords owning vast estates run by virtual slave labour.

1817
Virtual slaves get so pissed off they declare war on Spain. Spanish, confused by fact that Chilean revolutionary leader is called Bernardo O'Higgins and is son of Tyrone man, admit defeat. Chileans declare independence, and get drunk.

1817, the morning after
Chileans wake up with huge hangover and vow to improve quality of wine.

1830–1870
Wheat, silver and copper make country fabulously wealthy.

1876
Wheat, silver and copper recession makes country miserably broke.

1890
Nitrates boom makes country fabulously wealthy again.

1914
Nitrates bust makes country ... well, see 1876 for details.

1970
Salvador Allende abolishes feudal estates to make poor wealthier and happier. US Government, which thinks only rich should be happy, gives CIA $8 million to topple Allende government and install General Pinochet, liked only by his mum and Margaret Thatcher. Pinochet silences protests by vicious campaign of torture and executions.

1988

Pinochet forced out. Rest of world discovers Chilean wine.
Future looks rosé. And red. And white.

As the town clock struck eight the next morning, we stood at
the end of the earth, and looked south across the cold, grey sea.
That way lay 2,000 miles of ice and penguins, and the other
way lay 16,500 miles of road.

On our left was a soaring abstract sculpture to mark Mile
Zero of the Pan-American Highway, and a brass plaque
announcing the fact that it did run all the way from here to
Alaska, just to prove that I hadn't dreamed all of this up after all.

So if you ever see the chap I met at that party who claimed it
started in Ushuaia, Argentina, do give him a dig in the dongles
for me.

Oh, wait, I'd forgotten: he's floating face down in Cliff and
Bernie's hot tub.

I thought of the day, several weeks before, when I had given
a talk to the children of Knockbreda Primary School in Belfast
about the trip.

'Hands up who loves adventures,' I had asked them, and
every hand in the hall went up.

I turned to Clifford, who was sauntering slyly after a passing
penguin.

'For God's sake, Clifford, that's a male penguin,' I said.

'How was I to know?' he said, returning shamefacedly.

'Never mind. Right, hands up who loves adventures.'

We both put our hands up, and were just about to climb on
the bikes when half the town turned up to wish us well. The
men shook hands with us, the women kissed us, and we had
our photos taken with several thousand grannies.

At last we were ready. I climbed on the Triumph, although
not before I had yet again put my helmet on backwards and
made myself the laughing stock of Quellón.

I set the mileometer to zero, and took from my jacket pocket
the piece of paper the waiter had given me in Amarillo, on

which he had drawn the letter *N* and an arrow.

I attached it carefully to the tank bag, facing north, and turned to Clifford, who was sitting on the Aprilia with the engine ticking over.

'Ready, Pancho?' I said.

'Absolutely, Don,' he grinned.

'Grand job. Follow me. I'll be right behind you,' I said, and we roared off in the direction of the arrow to forge in the crucibles of our souls the swords of our manly destiny.

Until I hit a pothole fifty yards up the road and nearly fell off the bike.

'You all right?' said Clifford.

'Aye. I just collided with my manly destiny, that's all.'

'I hate it when that happens. Try sitting further back in the saddle.'

We rode on, through the cool, grey morning.

In the green and cottagey dales, mist whispered to woodsmoke that they would marry, and their marriage was blessed by the clouds with a gentle rain which brought forth from the forest the smells of pine and eucalyptus, mingling quaintly with cod liver oil. In a downpour we got off here and there and trudged to strange sights, like the ancient wooden village of Chonchi, home to the eighteenth-century timber millionaire Ciriaco Alvarez, who dressed in rags and sweated alongside his lumberjacks.

Or the shingled churches of the coast, their interiors a hymn to the carpenter as much as the Saviour, and the stars of their painted ceilings twinkling with hope in the damp darkness of the day.

Outside, we found the still and silent graves of men who had fallen from grace with the sea.

At noon we took respite from the rain in a trucker's roadhouse called the El Paso, eating eggs and raspberry pie as all around us men devoured lamb chops and the several dozen varieties of potato grown on the island while watching a Manchester City game on the TV in the corner.

At Ancud, the Fort of San Antonio is all that is left of the last outpost of the Spanish Empire in South America. Here, in January 1826, the lonely and demoralised garrison fled from a Chilean attack into the forest, bringing an end to a colonial presence which had dominated the continent for three hundred years. Today, low ramparts and seven soggy cannon, guarded by a small woman shyly selling superannuated chocolate, are all that is left of all that cruel swagger.

By nightfall, we were in Puerto Varas, a town looking across a lake at twin volcanoes. Naturally, the rain stopped the moment we got in the door of our inn, a clean and friendly place run by a clean and friendly woman from Hamburg.

It had been a hard first day, 200 miles in the pouring rain, but at least it had taught me one useful lesson.

Tucking your trousers into your motorcycle boots may look cool, but it sure lets in a lot of water.

And anyway, what if it had been hard? We were men of steel, and if these things were easy, everybody would be doing them, as my granny was so fond of saying as she assembled nuclear warheads in her armchair by the fire of an evening.

Over a breakfast of cheese and plums in our little German-Chilean inn the next morning, we met a charming elderly couple from Santiago, who gave us their address and 4,527 suggestions for our route that day.

We thanked them kindly, then went the way we had originally planned, luxuriating again in that wonderful feeling of packing and heading up the open road every morning, unencumbered by possessions other than the ones you can carry with you.

Even an act as simple as sitting on the ground with your back against the wall of a petrol station, drinking a coffee in the sun, becomes something deeply satisfying.

Many Germans, of course, felt the same way when they settled here just after the Second World War. As a result, along the road you will regularly see signs for places like the Eva

Braun Bierkeller, where you will be served foaming steins by a waitress with a blonde wig and a Charlie Chaplin moustache, or the Gasthof Himmler, where a strange, silent little man with steel-rimmed glasses will take your details, then ask whether you want to pay in gold or cash.

Many other Europeans have settled here too, drawn by a landscape much like home, so that if you walk into any shop, you will see wurst hanging cheek by jowl with chorizo, or Camembert nestling next to Cheddar.

As for the Pan-American, today it was a symphony of curves, sweeping sinuously through rolling meadows in which plump Aberdeen Angus grazed contentedly, and woods of oak and elm, all under a sky as blue and warm as yesterday's had been cold and grey.

Once, magically, I passed a vintage Citroën Big 15 which had been painted bright yellow and stuck on a pole outside a restaurant.

We had planned to treat ourselves to a night in the venerable Continental Hotel in Temuco, whose cobwebs had not been touched since it was built in 1890, in honour of the fact that presidents Cerda and Allende, and Nobel Laureates Pablo Neruda and Gabriela Mistral had stayed there. Sadly, after a day on a motorbike you tend towards the wild-eyed desperado rather than the poetic head of state look, and the clerk took one glance at us, another at his register, and announced that the hotel was full for the foreseeable future, and some time beyond.

With the wonderful serendipity of travel, though, we ended up at heaven on earth: a wooden hillside inn overlooking a lake and the obligatory volcano, run by American teachers Glen and Beverley Aldrich, who had come to Chile for a holiday seventeen years earlier and never left.

'You guys better be careful,' said Glen as I lay on a hammock on the porch petting both their dogs. 'We had a German biker called Gunther here twelve years ago who was riding from Chile to the States, although not as far as you two. His bike broke down three times, he took five months instead of three, and he got so depressed at being cooped up when he got home that he had to give up his job.'

'What sort of bike was he riding?' I said.

'A Triumph.'

Clifford laughed his leg off, then told me to get out of the hammock and do some work so he could get in and continue the epic existentialist poem he was composing to a woman he hoped to woo back home. What a fascinating character he was, even in the short time I had known him, I thought as I trudged back to the room to see if I could get a connection with the digital wotsit.

A Christian who drank, a Buddhist who enjoyed a good steak. A former TT winner who enjoyed pottering along at 60mph. A man who never wore a watch, yet regularly asked me the time. A deeply spiritual being with the libido of a deranged alley cat. A man who loved women, yet had been tortured by them, and whose search for a soulmate had left behind a string of marriages, affairs, broken hearts and children who may or may not have been his.

A sort of combination of the Dalai Lama and Casanova. Typical Gemini, in fact, unless you take the same view of astrology as Paddy Minne, who had once memorably said: 'I'm a Sagittarius. We don't believe in that crap.'

After the privations of the ride from Quellón, it had been the best of days, I thought later as, after a meal of salmon soup, fine steak and home-made raspberry ice cream washed down by an Errazuriz Merlot, we lay in the hot tub in the garden watching the sun go down.

Just out of interest, as I had a last glass of wine on the porch overlooking the lake before I went to bed, I hauled out my battered copy of *By Pan-American Highway through South America*, the account by the intrepid American explorer Herbert C. Lanks of his travels in Silver, a converted station wagon, on the newly built highway in 1942.

In it, he described how he and his travelling companion

Paul Pleiss had camped on the shores of this very lake, in a grove of majestic beeches.

'Across the lake, a mountain cone of snow cast its image in the waters. The sun set behind us in a canopy of red, the clouds sank down, blanketing Villarrica for the night, and overhead the stars appeared one by one. It was the perfect end of a perfect day,' he wrote.

A perfect day for both of us, I thought, looking up at the same stars and raising my glass to the ghost of Herbert.

A perfect day, whatever the future may bring.

But then, as any South American Zen Buddhist will tell you, you shouldn't spoil the Chile of today by worrying about the Colombia of tomorrow.

Paradise always has its price.

In spite of the guidebook's promise that a room at Las Colinas, the hillside inn where we spent the night, was $21, it was in fact, four times that, though worth every centavo.

Indeed, it was not the first time the guidebook had led us astray: it had described our hotel in Quellón as the plushest in town, and it had turned out to be a fleapit that no self-respecting flea would have been found dead in.

'We're not the only ones,' said Glen over breakfast. 'Last year it was $40 to climb the volcano, this year it's $80.'

Chile, it seemed, was discovering the value of itself.

Still, such surprises were part of the joy of travel, I thought as we shook hands with Glen and Beverly, gave the dogs one last pat and rode north in T-shirts through fields of freshly mown hay glittering in the sun.

As we rode into the shade of roadside trees, it was like plunging into an icy pool from which we emerged, aglow with gratitude, into the sun again.

In a car, of course, you see the passing landscape through a glass darkly, but on a bike you feel everything, and are at one with that landscape: with the daisies and primroses nodding in the verge, with that little garden bright with primulas and petunias, with that stern young man trotting a horse through a lavender field, with that stork rising from the mirrored lake and, miracle of miracles, with that elderly couple waving from a passing car, who turned out to be the ones from Santiago we had met at breakfast the day before, hundreds of miles from here.

Mind you, they were not the only ones waving: car drivers were forever hooting, waving and giving thumbs-up signs as we rode along.

Possibly because of our astonishing charisma, of course, but more likely because, loaded up and riding north, we were symbols of those two great feelings of modern life.

First, the sneaking suspicion that there must be more to life than sitting behind a desk to pay a mortgage.

And second, that longing to just pack up and go.

I'm sure you have felt it, too: that moment of truth when, arriving at work in the morning, you are filled with an overwhelming urge to drive past and just keep on going.

Unfortunately, I was so busy coming up with theories about early-twenty-first-century angst and feeling at one with the world that I almost became at one with a sailboat. Not because I was way off course, but because it was being towed by the car in front, which had braked suddenly.

Still, it would have made an interesting insurance claim, unlike the incident later in the afternoon when an insect the size of a hummingbird who was pottering south down the Pan-American on his way home to Mrs Bug and the little Bugs had a sudden, unexpected and irrevocably fatal meeting with my windscreen, leaving a large crimson splat.

However, since it looked rather pleasingly like a swooping Bird of Paradise, I decided to leave it on. By the time we got to Alaska, he would be the most travelled bug in the history of buggery, even if he was too dead to enjoy the experience.

A bit like St James the Apostle, after whom Santiago, for which we were already seeing road signs, was named. As is Santiago de Compostela in Galicia in north-west Spain, where his bones are allegedly buried. James, son of Zebedee and

Salome, arrived there in a stone boat in 44 AD, after a rather pleasant cruise from Jerusalem. Sadly, the apostle enjoyed the experience as little as the bug had enjoyed meeting my windshield, since he had just been beheaded by Herod.

However, that was enough thinking about Santiago, for we would not be there for a day or two, and by now it was late in the afternoon and we still had not found a bed for the night. We finally tracked down a *cabaña* outside Chillán as basic as last night's accommodation had been luxurious, and settled into our already familiar routine, like a couple who had been married for years.

I washed socks and T-shirt, showered and sat down to write up the events of the day, and Clifford went outside to sunbathe and compose his epic poem of seduction.

And then we went to find some dinner in Chillán, which today may be an unremarkable industrial town, but was once the birthplace of a man who was much more important to the history of Chile than any saint.

His name was Bernardo O'Higgins, and no matter where you go in Chile you will see statues of him, looking vaguely like Liberace. The most revered man in the history of the country, he was, of course, the son of a Tyrone man – Ambrose O'Higgins, an engineer who came to Chile in the service of the Spanish crown in the early 1760s.

To be fair, Ambrose has been claimed by both Meath and Tyrone, although I suspect he came from the latter. Not just because I do myself, but for three reasons.

Firstly, he is most famous for inventing the weatherproof shelter, and as anyone from Tyrone knows, we have more weather there than we know what to do with.

Secondly, he single-handedly saved the national postal service, an act that could only inspire a man from Tyrone, where there is little to do but write letters, mostly about the weather.

And thirdly – well, I'll get to the third reason in a minute, since you wouldn't want to use up all your reasons at once.

Anyway, after his first harrowing journey from Argentina

over the Andes during the winter of 1763/64, Ambrose arrived in Chile, wrung out his socks, decided he was never doing that again, and came up with the idea of a chain of weatherproof shelters.

By 1766, thanks to his efficient execution of this plan, Chile enjoyed an all-year overland postal service with Argentina, which had previously been cut off for several months each winter.

With his feet dry and the post secure, Ambrose's thoughts turned to other things, and he fell irretrievably in love with Isabel Riquelme, the daughter of Spanish nobleman Don Simón Riquelme y Goycolea and his wife Doña María Mercedes de Mesa y Ulloa.

On 20 August 1778, in the small town of Chillán, Isabel presented a shocked Ambrose and her stunned parents with a little surprise in the form of a very red-haired and very illegitimate baby. This was Bernardo. His father, dealing with the situation in a mature and responsible fashion which will be familiar to Tyrone men everywhere, took one look and ran away.

Isabel's parents sighed deeply, and within two years had arranged her marriage to Don Félix Rodríguez, with whom she had a daughter, Rosa Rodríguez Riquelme.

As for Bernardo, his early years were spent in obscurity as his natural father continued to rise in his profession, ending up as Governor of Chile and Viceroy of Peru. And although Don Ambrosio, as he was now known in South America, rarely saw his son, at least he made sure he was baptised and educated.

When Bernardo was twelve, he was sent to Peru for his secondary education and, at seventeen, to the leafy borough of Richmond in England, where, after finishing his history, geography, music, French and painting homework, he would wander down to the local coffee shops of an evening to meet the several leading Latino political activists of which Richmond has long been a hotbed. Among them was Sebastián Francisco de Miranda y Rodríguez, a young Venezuelan who had established a secret Masonic lodge whose members had sworn to fight for the independence of Latin America. In 1799, Bernardo moved to Spain, where he became friends with José de San Martín, later the liberator of Argentina.

As Bernardo tried to return to Chile in 1800, his ship was turned back by the British, who were then fighting the Spanish and French, and he returned to Cadiz suffering from yellow fever, and only made it home in 1802 to find that his father had died a year earlier.

So the next time your flight's delayed for half an hour, do stop moaning.

His father having left him the family estate near Chillán, Bernardo settled into the life of a gentleman farmer. Then, in 1808, the opportunity for which he had been waiting arose: Napoleon invaded Spain and left Spain and its colonies in a vulnerable state. Throughout Latin America there was a wave of revolutionary movements, and in Chile a *junta* in Santiago ousted the governor. By 1811 Chile had its own government, but by 1813, Peru had invaded, forcing those in power to regroup in Argentina.

Even worse, the Peruvians were followed by the Spanish, who had regained power at home and were now determined to do the same abroad.

In 1817, with O'Higgins at their head, the Chilean army scaled the Andes through four passes and in a series of dazzling victories sent the Spanish packing. Chief among those who fought alongside him was Juan MacKenna, a young engineer turned soldier who in 1796 had arrived in Chile with letters of recommendation to Ambrose O'Higgins. MacKenna's Spanish training had been arranged by Count Alejandro O'Reilly, an influential Irish officer in Spain who was related to MacKenna's mother, Eleanor O'Reilly.

During the ensuing struggle with Spain, MacKenna sided with the pro-independence forces of Bernardo O'Higgins. Rising to the rank of general, he was widely conceded to be the real military brains behind O'Higgins's success on the battlefield until his career was cut short in 1814 when he was killed in Argentina during a duel with a political rival of O'Higgins's.

The man acting as second to his opponent was William Brown, a man from Mayo, which brings me to the third reason why I think Ambrose O'Higgins was from Tyrone.

First of all, Juan MacKenna was from Clogher, the sleepy village in that very same county, which would naturally commend him to Don Ambrosio.

And secondly, a Mayo man would naturally want to assist in the demise of an opponent who had made his way up through the ranks with the help of a Tyrone connection – if only because Brown was jealous of the fact that when our post arrives, it is always dry.

In any case, the O'Higgins clan left behind them in Chile an unparalleled legacy.

Don Ambrosio left a chain of roads, bridges, schools, factories and mills throughout the country, not to mention his grandson Benjamin Vicuña MacKenna, one of Chile's most distinguished historians; among the hundred books he authored is a biography of his grandfather.

And Don Bernardo left behind the nation itself. In 1817, he was elected Supreme Director, and immediately established a national navy, under the command of British admiral Lord Thomas Cochrane, to attack the Spanish in Peru as part of his ultimate goal to free Latin America. His success complete, though, he was then presented with a rather large war bill, and the taxes he imposed to pay for that led to so much discontent that in 1823 the former hero of the nation was forced to step down.

'The talents which constitute the great generals, like the great poets, must be born with us, and I am discerning enough to know that I lack these,' he said as he left for Peru, where he lived until his death.

Today, there is little in Chillán to mark the fact that O'Higgins was born there, apart from a few faded murals and a statue of the Liberator in the plaza which on the morning we visited had sitting on its head an unpatriotic pigeon doing its worst, although it was later taken away and shot for treason.

But then, Bernardo would not have really wanted all that much fuss over his birthplace. He was, after all, a Tyrone man, and we are very proud of our modesty.

Anyway, where was I? Ah yes, in the plaza of Chillán having breakfast with Clifford beneath the statue of Bernardo.

'Here, I've just had a brilliant idea,' said Clifford. 'I'm going to take a photo of every beautiful woman we meet along the Pan-American Highway, and publish it as a book.'

'It'll probably do better than mine,' I said, helping myself to more scrambled eggs and ham. 'After all, the biggest seller I've written so far is *The Ulster Joke Book*.'

'In fact, I think I'll start with that girl in the ice-cream parlour over there. What's the Spanish for: "Can I take your photograph for a book?"'

I told him, and two minutes later he was back.

'God, she's drop-dead gorgeous,' he said, inspecting the result of his handiwork with the digital camera. 'In fact, I think I'll write her a poem.'

'I thought you were writing a poem for this other woman back home?'

'Aye, but that's serious. This is just for practice.'

He thought and wrote for a minute, then said: 'What about this?

For Claudia
Not by chance, the fleeting moment of our glance
It gave our hearts the opportunity for a dance
I am glad that we met today, in a happy sort of way.
Shall we meet again? God alone can say!'

He walked across the street to deliver it, and came back with a smile on his face.

'Well, when's the big day?' I said.

'In an hour. I've booked the priest and the cathedral. Now all

I have to do is find her a helmet so we can take her on honeymoon to Alaska.'

Sadly, a close inspection of the bikes revealed that there was no room for his bride-to-be, so we set off as normal, passing several little hotels on the way out of town which were, naturally, a million times better and cheaper than the shack we had stayed in last night.

At lunchtime, we stopped for a coffee in the plaza at Curico, under one of the sixty giant palm trees which make it the most beautiful in all of Chile. The waiter was a charming multi-linguist who had travelled all over the world, and from his habit of disappearing with the change, we could see how he had afforded it.

'Och well, it was only 50p,' said Clifford as we walked back to the bikes.

'Are you sure you're Scottish?' I said suspiciously.

Soon we were in Chile's wine country, seeing signs for Errazuriz and Santa Rita. It was like walking into a strange house and finding it full of old friends. All the wineries around here offer tours, but having seen around vineyards several times, I would rather enjoy the result than inspect the process. And besides, we had a hacienda to visit.

Los Lingues, just off the highway north of Fernando, was one of the oldest and best preserved haciendas in Chile, dating from 1575, when King Philip of Spain gave it to the family who still own it today. As well as being their home, it was also the finest and most expensive hotel in Chile, costing so much a night that to stay there would have meant not only blowing the entire budget for the trip and the advance royalties for Clifford's book of Pan-American beauties, but selling both bikes and the house back home.

'I wish I'd brought Claudia here for the honeymoon instead,' he said wistfully as we wandered past a swimming pool, through gardens alive with songbirds and past stables filled with pure-bred Spanish horses, wooden verandas blessed with sleeping retrievers and a framed letter on the wall confirming that the wife of Don German, the owner, was a distant relative of the Queen.

'Can I help you?' said a polite voice behind us, and I jumped and turned to find a dignified looking man with a shock of elegant grey hair.

'Listen, I'm terribly sorry. I'm a journalist writing a newspaper series and book on the Pan-American Highway, and we just popped in for a quick look. We'll leave immediately,' I said.

'Nonsense, nonsense,' he said in perfect English. 'You are very welcome. Is that your Triumph parked outside?'

'It is.'

'Nice bike, although you'll have trouble finding mechanics for it in Chile. That was my BMW you saw as you came in.'

He paused for a moment as another, equally elegant chap walked up.

'Can I help, Don German?' he said.

The paterfamilias of this ancient and revered family, for it was he, paused, then looked at us again.

'I tell you what. Why don't you have dinner and stay tonight, as my guests? Dieter here will give you a quick tour, then find you a room,' he said.

'Good heavens. That's extraordinarily generous of you,' I said.

'Not a bit. Actually, I'm glad you called by. We're collaborating with Rothschild on some new wines, and I've been looking for an excuse to taste them.'

We followed Dieter in a daze through a chapel with a crucifix donated by Pope Pius IX, Louis XVI mirrors, Ming vases, sedan chairs and family portraits sitting on a table once owned by Bernardo O'Higgins, until we came at last to a vast and ancient bedroom complete with en-suite Labrador and Victrola gramophone.

'Here we are,' said Dieter. 'Famous room, this. Argomedo was born in that very bed.'

'Good heavens,' I said, wondering who on earth Argomedo

was, then surprising myself by remembering that he was a member of the very first Chilean parliament in 1829.

At eight, we donned our finest T-shirts, put on socks in honour of the occasion, and found ourselves leaning on a bar made of two-thousand-year-old alerce wood, watching Dieter mix three perfect *pisco* sours. Well, that was what I was doing: Clifford was showing his photo of Claudia to Luis, Don German's younger brother.

'Lovely,' said Luis, who turned out to have a Kawasaki 1100 parked around the back. 'You two don't fancy taking me to Alaska with you, do you?'

Some time later, we sat by a tinkling fountain under the stars with Dieter and the family as white-gloved waiters brought us a feast, washed down with Don German's new wines, which were a happy marriage of the discretion of the old world and the exuberance of the new.

Herbert Lanks, who had camped beside a farmhouse near here in 1942 and been invited in for dinner, had had an equally civilised evening.

'After our meal we went to the living room, where auntie, who had been a concert performer in Santiago, entertained us with the music of Chopin, Strauss and Liszt,' he wrote.

Heavens, what a day it had been, I thought, falling asleep accompanied by the Dalai Lama, Casanova, two golden retrievers, a Siamese kitten and the ghost of Argomedo.

Having grown up on the large estate of the big house where my grandfather Edward was the butler, it was the hardest thing in the world to say goodbye to the family, the dogs and the cats of Los Lingues next morning.

Or perhaps we were just feeling the effects of Don German's hospitality, but I was feeling decidedly melancholy as we rode north through the cool, grey morning towards Santiago. Beside us ran the railroad tracks, those familiar friends from the Route 66 days.

Santiago is famous for its smog, and today was no exception

as we clattered through the narrow streets, peering at cathedrals, plazas, shoeshiners, photographers and the house where Pablo Neruda lived with nine thousand books and his wife.

Suddenly, in the window of a tourist office, I spotted a sign saying 'Biplane flights over the city'.

Hurrah, I thought, going inside to phone them.

'How much are the flights?' I asked the man on the other end.

'Eight hundred dollars for six people,' he said.

Since we had neither, I sighed, put the phone down and got back on the bike.

I tried singing 'If You're Going to San Francisco' for a while to cheer myself up, but that only made me think of Cate, who I wouldn't see until California. Then I tried a few catchy Leonard Cohen numbers, and finally settled on alternating between 'Take it Easy' by the Eagles and Simon and Garfunkel's 'El Condor Pasa'.

We stopped for coffee at noon, meeting by chance Rodrigo and Luis, two Argentinians who were touring in the country in a 2CV fitted with a turbo light on the dashboard, which they switched on when they wanted to think they were going faster.

Around us, the landscape was changing before our eyes, from lush river valley to semi-arid mountains, so that the salt smack of the sea was a welcome surprise. Not as much a surprise, though, as what happened next: parking the bikes on an incline to take a photo of the view, we were just walking away when they simultaneously rolled off the side stands and curtseyed gently to the ground. Awarding them 5.9 for artistic merit, we strolled back to inspect the damage: slightly twisted handlebars for April, and a broken indicator cover and scratched pannier for Tony.

'Sorry, chum,' I said, patting him apologetically.

'Don't worry. Makes him look more rugged,' said Clifford helpfully.

By nightfall we were in the tiny fishing village of

Pichidangui, glad at least that we had missed the days when this coast was notorious for highwaymen and pirates such as the Englishman Lord Willow.

However, even he was not the most notorious villain of this area: that dishonour belongs to Doña Catalina de Los Ríos y Lispergeuer, or La Quintrala. At twenty-three, she murdered her father with a poisoned chicken, then seduced and killed a knight of St John and forced a servant to confess and be hanged for the crime. By the time she was finally brought to justice, she had whipped and tortured to death thirty-nine people on her estate.

Personally, I blame the parents: her grandmother had murdered her husband by pouring mercury into his ears as he slept, and her mother had whipped a stepdaughter to death and tried to poison the governor of Chile. Today, small children all over Chile are still warned: 'Be good, or La Quintrala will get you in the dark.'

As you can imagine, after being very bad to my motorbike on only the fifth day, I spent a troubled night.

Or maybe it was just the chicken I had for supper.

'What a day,' said Clifford, flinging back the curtains of the beachside *cabaña* where we had spent the night. 'I think I might celebrate with clean underwear.'

'Pancho, we've been on the road for over a week,' I said.

'I know that. I brought one pair for each month. You did tell me to pack light,' he said sheepishly, then wandered off for a swim singing: 'Oh, the Lord is good to me, with the sun and the rain and the apple trees.'

'You know,' he said over breakfast, 'I lead such a complicated life, being a director at Camphill, a manager, a musical instrument maker, a fund-raiser and a social worker, that just doing one thing every day is such a blessing to me.'

He gave a deep sigh, finished his coffee and went off for his morning meditation in the little chapel on the beach while

I went off to phone Ronan Kelly at Radio U105 and give my weekly broadcast to the nation.

'I gave thanks to the Benedictine monks in Rostrevor who are praying for us every day,' said Clifford when he came back with a clean soul and matching underwear.

How could we not have safe passage with so much goodwill around us, I thought as we set off, although not before I had checked that my own trinity of salvation was safe in my jacket: wallet, notebook and Cate's little silver box of love tokens.

As the road winds north here, with the mountains on the right and the ocean on the left, you pass, from time to time, hoardings advertising everything from lingerie to holiday homes – a far cry from the days when Francis Drake buccaneered up and down this coast. On the hoardings, though, the girls or happy nuclear families smiling out at you are invariably Nordic, or at the very least undeniably European.

Lanks had noticed the same thing when he passed through here in 1942, and I had asked an old man about it in a bar the night before.

'Ah, *señor*, we always want to be what we are not,' he had said wisely, then, even more wisely, ordered another *pisco*.

At lunchtime, we stopped at a roadside shack for our usual coffee and Clifford wandered around the bikes with an unidentified piece of metal he had picked up at the scene of our little accident the day before.

'Aha,' he said at last, 'it's the end of your footpeg. Do you want to keep it?'

'Not really,' I said. 'If there was no room for Claudia, there's hardly room for a bit of broken footpeg.'

He dropped it in the sand, and I imagined a child finding it, days or weeks from now, taking it home and wondering for years where it had come from, or if it had been left there by aliens.

'It's funny you should say that,' said Clifford as the waitress appeared with two fresh melon juices. 'When I was a child, I had a recurring dream that I'd been kidnapped by aliens.'

'That wasn't a dream, Pancho.'

'Listen, don't knock it until you've tried it. God, she was gorgeous,' he said, going off to take a photo of the waitress for his book of Pan-American beauties.

The area we were passing through was famous for two things: *pisco* and stars, although if you drink enough of one, you will inevitably see the other. *Pisco*, the distillation of the muscatel grapes on the stony hills around us, is claimed as the national drink of both Chile and Peru so passionately that if you ever feel like ending it all, an easy way is to walk into a Chilean bar and say loudly: 'Hey, buddy, gimme one of those famous Peruvian piscos.' Or vice versa.

They are commonly served as *pisco* sours, a fluffy combination of pisco, lemon juice and egg white as bitter and insubstantial as Tracey Emin, although with more artistic merit.

The stars, meanwhile, are viewed here through numerous mountain-top observatories that take advantage of permanently clear skies. The only disadvantage is that the stars are upside down in this part of the world, but the astronomers get around that by building the observatories backwards.

In much the same way that, after our break, I put my helmet on backwards. Again.

Blasted by wind and baked by sun, we rose into the mountains in great, sweeping curves, then fell to the arid plain, leaving as we did what Chileans called El Norte Chico, the little north, and entering El Norte Grande, the start of the vast Atacama desert, which stretches all the way to Peru and would take us three days to cross.

But that was tomorrow. Today, we descended through the mauve dust of the desert to the oasis town of Vallenar, found a nice little hotel and went out for dinner, walking through streets alive with courting couples, strolling musicians drifting in and out of bars and dissolute dogs.

Lanks, too, had come to this little town in the desert, and found it enchanting.

'When we came to its green meadows and rows of willow and eucalyptus trees, we drank in great gulps of their fragrant odour,' he wrote. 'Water gurgled through the irrigation ditches at our side, and the town itself had concrete pavements, fine commercial houses and a large plaza shaded by magnificent trees. We dined in the cool patio of the Bernabe Hotel on fruit salad, soup, meat pie, garbanzos, steak, lettuce, bread, grapes, cold beer and a demi-tasse of coffee. Out of a side room, over whose doorway hung a Rotary Club sign, filed a group of American businessmen, all puffing black cigars.'

Sadly, the Bernabe Hotel and the American businessmen had long gone, but we tucked into tender lamb and potatoes at a little corner place which had plastic tables and chairs and a TV in the corner, but which was proud enough of itself to boast bow-tied waiters and a wine list as long as the distance we had come today. We finished with a *pisco* sour, to celebrate the fact that earlier in the day we had passed the thousand-mile mark since starting the journey in Quellón.

Not only that, I thought as we fell into bed that night, but we had discovered an infallible way to keep our money safe in Colombia.

Just hide it in Clifford's old underwear.

Here, the next time someone tells you that deserts are hot, give them a dig in the dongles.

For we were frozen next morning as we sped north across the first stretch of the northern Chilean wilderness.

Personally, I blame the Bolivians. Ever since they lost their access to the sea in the late-nineteenth-century War of the Pacific, they have had their revenge with the annual curse of the so-called Bolivian winter, an icy wind which sweeps across the sands every February.

Still, it doesn't matter how cold and wet you are as long as you're warm and dry, as a man from Fermanagh once said to me, and we donned our Nambarrie fleeces and sped on, surrounded by sand dunes and blasted by freezing wind, our hands blue with cold and drips hanging precariously off the ends of our noses.

It was just like summer holidays in Rossnowlagh, except without the earwigs.

As for the desert itself, I couldn't decide whether it was endlessly fascinating or just fascinatingly endless, but at least it freed up my mind to think of the important things in life. So I rode on, thinking happily of apple crumble and custard, until we got to Copiapo, or Cup of Gold, named after the many mines in the area in which men still toil endlessly in the dark in the hope of that gleam of light which will save them.

Our tanks were emptying fast, so I pulled up alongside Clifford at the next lights.

'Do you want to fill up? According to the map, there's another station in an hour, but we'd look a bit stupid if it was closed,' I shouted across.

'We look a bit stupid anyway,' he laughed.

'Aye, but I'd rather look stupid with a full tank.'

Lanks and Pleiss had stopped here, too, to fill up the tanks of Silver, their converted station wagon, change money with a Chinese merchant, then lunch on *filet mignon* and a bottle of red wine for nine pesos, courtesy of the Yugoslavian proprietor of the Hotel Montan.

As we were filling up, a gaggle of Brazilian bikers roared in wearing bandannas and balaclavas, looking like a combination of First World War air aces and Wild West desperadoes.

'Chile to Alaska? Wow. We've only got twenty-two days around Peru, Chile and Argentina,' they said wistfully, giving us a handful of stickers.

'Brilliant,' we said, and stuck them all over the bikes next to the ones we'd bought that morning saying Maximum Load 4 Passengers and Please Fasten Your Seatbelts, then rode off quickly in case anyone looking thought we were immature or anything.

And then, a long, gloriously fast run through the early evening, chasing our shadows across the sand until at last they fell exhausted before us at Taltal, a little fishing village by the sea, as fishing villages invariably are.

Have these fishermen no imagination?

We found a pleasant and cheap little seafront hotel, unloaded the bikes, and Clifford went for a walk. An hour later, he was back.

'Listen, Don, I'm really sorry, but I've got a date. Woman from Calama. No spring chicken, but I'm meeting her in ten minutes down the street. Is that a real pain?'

'No worries, Pancho. Go for it,' I said, looking up from my guidebook.

'Cheers, man. See you when I see you.'

Half an hour later, I finished reading and went looking for dinner, but the entire village seemed to be closed except for an ancient shoe shop with glass cabinets and a creaking wooden floor.

'*¿Hay un restaurante por aquí?*' I asked the equally ancient proprietor.

'*Primera calle a la izquierda,*' he wheezed.

I walked down the first street on the left, but all was dark except for a dim light coming from a half-open doorway. I pushed it cautiously, and found a voluminous woman sitting in what looked like a living room. She looked up from her knitting.

'*¿Queréis pescado, señor?*' she said.

'*Sí, gracias. Y una cerveza nacional, por favor.*'

She went away, and appeared ten minutes later with fish and beer. When I had finished, she asked me for 4,000 pesos, or about three quid. I gave her five thousand and left, still not sure whether I had been in a house or a restaurant.

Back at the hotel, I was just brushing my teeth when Pancho rolled in from dinner.

'Well, how did it go?'

'Beautiful. Married with three kids, spoke no English, great karma, perfect evening,' he said, getting into bed and falling instantly asleep.

We had ridden a long and dusty 300 miles today for the second day in a row, but I felt strangely content as I climbed into bed myself. Perhaps it was because it was Friday, and I could relax and look forward to the weekend. Heavens, I might even take the bike out for a spin tomorrow, I thought as I fell asleep.

Unfortunately, we woke to find that the man in charge of the Triumph had left the keys in the ignition all night with the lights on. As a result, the battery was as dead as the several dozen dogs we passed on the roadside every day. And, indeed, as flat.

Not only that, but after Jaime, the hotel owner, had jump-started it, the same man then stalled it, requiring the seat to be laboriously taken off to get at the battery, and the whole process started over again.

Honestly, what an idiot. If you see him, give him a good kicking for me. Tall chap, with a moustache, writes books. Can't miss him.

Still, at last we got it started and loaded up. I went back into the hotel to write all this down, only for Clifford to come running in ten minutes later.

'Listen, you're going to cook your engine if you leave it idling in that heat,' he said. 'We have to go, and I mean now.'

We set off. Only for everything to go dead at the first junction. We wheeled it back to the hotel, Jaime started it again, and we set off. Then the engine warning light came on.

Now, the normal drill when this happens is to stop immediately and phone the nearest dealer. Except the nearest dealer was in California, so I did the next best thing and phoned Philip McCallen's in Lurgan. At first there was no answer, because it was Saturday afternoon back home and they were either busy or had gone to the pub. Then there was no signal.

'Don't worry,' said Clifford. 'The light's probably on because the alternator is still charging the battery. It should go off when it's fully charged. Let's head on.'

I got back on, and we rode into the Atacama Desert, which

is the driest place on earth, apart from Ian Paisley's drinks cabinet. Not to mention the roof of my mouth, as I rode a motorbike with the warning light on across the most inhospitable wasteland on the planet. But then, I had no choice. I was sitting on the only way I had of getting across it.

The warning light was still on 120 miles later, when we stopped at a roadside *cantina*. The acid test now was whether the battery was charging, or whether the light meant the alternator had packed it in. I took a deep breath, switched the engine off, then, with my heart in my mouth, turned the key.

It started.

Silently, I gave thanks to the Lord, Biggles's sainted aunt, the seven sisters of Constantinople and the monks at Rostrevor.

'There you are. It's starting and it's going,' said Clifford. 'What more do you want?'

He was probably right, but I couldn't shake off the suspicion that I had done some permanent damage to the sophisticated engine management system, either by letting the battery run flat or by letting the engine overheat. Two hundred miles later, the light was still on, but Tony the Triumph was still going as we turned off the highway and rode thirty miles down a dirt road to find the only place to stay in the area, a simple hostel in a village by the sea. The showers were cold or cold, and our room came with an en-suite cockroach.

'I don't mind cockroaches,' said Clifford. 'I shared a bed in Scotland with twelve mice once, and that was worse.'

At eight, the generator flickered into life, a woman bent almost double with age brought us fish and beer, and we took out the Triumph manual and, like all blokes, read the instructions as a last resort.

'I don't know if I should read you this,' said Clifford. 'It says the light means that the engine management system's on the blink, and that you should contact the nearest Triumph dealer as soon as possible.'

'I will. As soon as we get to San Diego,' I said.

'The good news is that the bike will still run, but fuel

consumption and power may be affected. Oh, and listen to this. The bike is now officially in limp home mode.'

Limp home mode. For 8,000 miles. I took a long swallow of beer and tried not to worry.

'Nine o'clock,' said Clifford as we finished breakfast. 'We might actually get away early this morning, if you don't do too much footering about.'

'It's not footering, it's poggling. You can't set out for the day without a good poggle. Anyway, at least I took the key out of the ignition last night,' I said, hurt.

At this point, I should explain what poggling is. It's when you're just about to leave the house, and you wander about scratching your head, sure that you've forgotten something. Finally you leave the house, lock the door, then change your mind and go back to check if you've put the dog out. Then you realise you don't have a dog.

As I say, it's crucial before you set off anywhere.

We wheeled the bikes out of the yard where they had been guarded overnight by two chickens and a pig, and I pressed the starter button, uttering a silent prayer as I did so.

It started. Then, a mile down the road, it coughed and sputtered, and almost died. My heart sank, and I held my breath, as it hesitated again, then settled into a steady rhythm.

Come on, Tony, old chum, just one mile at a time, I whispered to my motorcycle.

After an hour we were at Baquedano, once a major railway depot for the now defunct nitrate industry, now a sleepy one-horse town beside which ancient steam locomotives sleep at sidings, dreaming forever of their days of glory.

We clambered aboard, pretending to be Casey Jones, a-steamin' and a-rollin' at the throttle of the Cannonball Express, then set off again into the relentless desert wind.

Strange things happen, in this endless wasteland. You stop for animals crossing the road, then get closer to discover they are just bits of shredded tyre dancing in the heat.

Or entire cities rise from the shimmering horizon, then vanish.

After a while, you begin to think you are going mad, then realise you were that way to start with.

Dust devils danced by the roadside, mocking us with their insubstantial grace as we rode on, and on, and then discovered there was even more on after that. Clifford ran out of fuel, and had to refill from our jerry can.

'Shame you don't have a bigger tank, Pancho,' I said, holding the funnel.

'Size isn't everything, Don,' he said, just as the howling wind splashed stinging fuel into his eyes.

'Honestly, you're worse than Ewan McGregor. Anything for a cheap thrill,' I said, digging the Optrex from the medical kit and sloshing it into his eyes.

Two miles later, the road turned to dirt. To make matters worse, there was no sign of the filling station which, according to the map, should have been there by now. We crawled on across the burning sands, running on fumes.

Then, a splash of colour. Was it a mirage? No, it was the filling station. We almost hugged the old man who came out to fill the tanks. As he did, you could feel the bikes gulping it thirstily, as glad as we were.

At last, after 340 long, hot, dusty miles in the saddle, we found Pica, an oasis, and a restaurant with a credit-card sticker in the window – just as well, since the desert had been disturbingly short of banks, and we had run out of pesos.

We were served spaghetti and beer by a waitress called Marie Luise, who was beautiful, charming and no more than three feet tall.

'Are those your children?' said Clifford, pointing to a boy and a girl who were waving at her from a birthday party in the corner.

'Yes. They have no fathers, which is a blessing,' she said.

When the bill came, the credit-card machine would not work, and half the restaurant gathered around to sort out the problem. Then the entire population of the bar next door.

'Here, let me try your card in it,' said one man.

'No, let me try mine,' said another.

'The machine is bust. Ask them if they have dollars,' said the town drunk, making more sense than anyone.

'Do you have dollars?' said Marie Luise from somewhere around my waist. We did.

'What a day. What a night,' said Clifford as we tumbled into our beds.

He was right. If adventure was what we were seeking, we had certainly found it this day.

I woke at seven, and finally got through to Nick at McCallen's in Lurgan to ask about the warning light.

'It's just saying there's a minor malfunction, but if the bike's starting and running, you're fine,' he said. 'If it's a major problem, the system will stop the engine completely.'

Which is exactly what it did, on the way to the village petrol station after breakfast.

With a sick feeling of dread in my heart, I pushed it into the forecourt, and tried the starter. Nothing.

Clifford came over, looking worried for the first time in the trip. As well he might. We were in the middle of the desert, 7,000 miles from the nearest Triumph dealer. We tried it again, and after a few attempts, it finally coughed into life.

'Ride it up and down the road a couple of times. If it settles down, we'll go. We can't really do anything else,' said Clifford.

It did, and a nervous hour later we were in Iquique, now a sorry-looking port, but once a place where more champagne was consumed per head than anywhere else in the world. The reason was nitrates, which in the late nineteenth century made Chile fabulously wealthy.

Then, after the First World War, the Germans developed synthetic fertilisers, and today the vast palaces of the nitrate barons of Iquique are empty, as are the dusty streets of ghost towns like Humberstone down the road. In the white terraced houses, curtains whispered in the wind, and an ancient copy of *Vogue* fluttered on a table. The swimming pool and the rows of seats in the theatre were empty, dust blew through the lobby of the hotel and a child's swing creaked in the breeze.

We tiptoed away, so as not to awaken ghosts.

It is not the nitrate barons for which this region is most famous, however, but the last stand, just off the coast, of one of the country's most enduring heroes, the splendidly named Arturo Prat.

On 21 May 1879, Prat's tiny wooden craft, the *Esmeralda*, was rammed by a giant Peruvian battleship, the *Huáscar*. Refusing to surrender, Prat leaped aboard the enemy ship, sword in hand, and fought to the death. As a result, you will find avenues all over Chile named after him, and there is even an Arturo Prat University in Iquique.

What a wonderful thing it must be, I thought, to graduate with a piece of paper confirming that you are a Qualified Prat.

As for us, we had our own battles this day, in the teeth of gale force winds all the way to Arica, on the Peruvian border, where Tony's warning light went out just as we arrived at a hotel. I went to sleep praying that it was a good omen, for tomorrow we would cross our first border.

In any case, the struggles of the last few days had become worthwhile for Clifford this evening, since he had achieved his major ambition of the trip so far as we were walking through the town looking for dinner.

'Look, a Chile sticker for the bike!' he said, pointing to a street stall.

'Where are you from?' said the girl as she sold it to him.

'Scotland,' he said, then, holding his nose with one hand and an imaginary bagpipes with the other, did a very passable jig to the tune of 'Scotland the Brave'.

And then, naturally, took her photograph for his book of Pan-American beauties.

'Hello, is that AA home start?' Geoff on a truculent Tony, trying to get through to McCallen's in Lurgan.

10

A short history of Peru

12000 BC–1532 AD
See Chile.

1532
Francisco Pizarro arrives with two dozen soldiers and takes
on entire Inca empire in lunatic enterprise. Lunatic enterprise
succeeds. Pizarro offers Inca emperor Atahualpa freedom if
he fills biggest room in palace with gold. Atahualpa does so,
then is strangled by lying toad Pizarro. Spanish voted least
popular tourists of year by *Inca Weekly* magazine.

1532–1821
See Chile. Entire nation under feudal slavery, made even
worse by forced labour down mines which kills millions.

1821
San Martín declares independence. Huge guano exports make
country fabulously wealthy.

1879
Guano runs out, leaving economy in the shit, with not enough shit to get it out of the shit.

1879–1970
Country builds up huge fishing industry to replace guano.

1970
Fish run out, leaving country in deep guano again.

2000
Japanese-Chilean professor Alberto Fujimori elected president after promising to get country out of shit.

2000, some time later
After bribery and corruption allegations, Fujimori flees to Japan, leaving country back in shit.

'You know,' said Clifford as we walked to the bikes after breakfast, 'April had eight years of life before this trip, but Tony was just born, bunged in a crate, then woke up in a strange land. No wonder he's feeling cranky. He'll be all right.'

And he was. For, oh, at least the first two miles. Then the engine died completely. After several attempts, it started again, and got us as far as the border with Peru. We got off the bikes, and turned to say a sad farewell to Chile, which had been the most gentle, civilised introduction to South America possible.

Well, except maybe for the desert. If I never saw another desert in my life, it wouldn't be a moment too soon, I thought as we joined the queue in baking heat for the passport window. We got to it, soaked in sweat, after half an hour, got our stamps, and were told to go to the second floor of the building across the road and find the customs office. We did, and found only a large canteen.

'¿Lo siento, pero dónde está la oficina de aduana, por favor?' I said to the woman behind the counter.

'It is me,' she said, and handed us two forms to fill in.

It was quixotic, but at least it was efficient compared to the chaos on the Peruvian side. It was like crossing the border from India to Pakistan: on one side, order and tidiness, on the other noise, colour, lights, action, music, lunacy and an obsession with paperwork.

At first we joined an interminable queue to get our passports stamped, although when I say queue, I mean more a rugby scrum involving about a hundred people, no referee and no ball. We finally got to the front, then found we did not have the correct forms. When we filled those in, we walked across the road to the customs office to get our carnets stamped.

Except the man in customs had never seen carnets quite like ours before, and had to haul out a large book entitled *How to Deal with Crazy Gringos*. An hour passed while he read. The man behind us, fed up waiting, finally reached over, stamped his own documents, and walked out, eliciting only a shrug from the customs official.

Finally, he finished. Or so we thought, for he then handed us a new piece of paper, and told us we had to get five stamps on it, and come back for the sixth.

'Listen,' I said to Clifford as we wandered out into the heat clutching our pieces of paper, 'if there are only two offices, the police and the customs, where in the name of God are we supposed to get five stamps on these?'

'That's a very interesting question,' he said, looking up at a circling vulture.

We wandered around aimlessly for half an hour until a passing woman took pity on us and pointed out that the officials wandering up and down the road with hats on from different government departments such as agriculture, fisheries and illegal *pisco* imports were the ones we wanted.

Within thirty seconds we had all the stamps we needed, and were on our way.

Until the Triumph cut out completely after fifty yards, leaving us stranded on the Peruvian side of the border, our only prospect that of going back through the whole three-hour process and trying somehow to get back to Arica.

This is getting a little wearing on the nerves, I thought as Clifford got off April and came over.

'Same thing,' I said wearily, then tried several times to start it. Nothing. Not even a spark. Just the sound of the starter motor turning over in the endless silence of the desert.

'Bollocks and buggery,' I muttered, trying to stay calm, and completely failing.

'This bike's not going anywhere, laddie,' said Clifford.

'I'll try it again,' I said, more in hope than expectation.

Miraculously, it started. I gunned the engine a couple of times, and the revs held. I climbed on, keeping the throttle open, and after a run up and down the road, they were still holding.

'Go,' said Clifford. 'Go like a bat out of hell, and don't stop until you get to Moquegua. I'll catch you up.'

As I raced north through the burning afternoon, stopping for neither drink nor rest, I had fleeting glimpses of the new country we had found ourselves in: at first an hour of more desert, then suddenly sweet groves of sugar cane waving in the breeze, women in fantastic colours and even more fantastic hats, cowboys on horseback, and cows grazing peacefully in green fields.

In Tacana, the single town I sailed through, strangely beautiful traffic policewomen tried in vain to direct a tangle of hooting, weaving cars, from ancient American clunkers to Mexican-made Volkswagen Beetles, buses, taxis, communal minibuses and gaily decorated motorcycle rickshaws.

All of this I saw, but I did not stop once for 150 miles until I reached Moquegua, shot through streets lined with thatched adobe houses, swept through the picturesque plaza, shot past the ornate metal fountain designed in 1877 by Gustav Eiffel, and finally rode up a hill and pulled up outside the finest hotel in town.

I switched the engine off, and breathed a huge sigh of relief.

We unloaded the bikes beside a tree alive with hummingbirds, went for a swim in the blissfully cool pool, and then got on April and rode into town for fillet steak, the finest avocado we had ever tasted and a beer, for about six quid each.

'You know, Pancho,' I said from the pillion seat as we trundled back up the hill, 'we're breaking three of our rules tonight. We're riding after dark, after a beer and without our helmets on.'

But then, as Douglas Bader once said, rules are for the obedience of fools and the guidance of wise men. Indeed, if I could be sure that I wasn't the former, I would almost certainly be the latter.

Days like this may be character building, I thought as I went to bed, but I don't know if I can stand many more of them. In fact, tomorrow I think I may well phone the Triumph dealer and have a word, I thought as I fell asleep. Although not before realising that in all the excitement of the day, I had forgotten that Clifford had made it through our first border without the bike registration document for April.

Maybe he was right after all, I thought as I finally nodded off.

'I had a lovely dream last night,' said Clifford on awakening. 'I met this beautiful girl, and we had a kiss and a cuddle and exchanged addresses.'

'Have you still got her address?' I said.

'Bloody hell, I've lost it,' he said, hunting frantically around the bed.

He wasn't the only one who had lost it: I had lain awake most of the night thinking of the options with the Triumph problem.

The simplest was that it was something we could sort out ourselves.

If it wasn't, the next option was to get the bike to Lima on a truck, and pay to fly a Triumph technician from the UK or San Diego to fix it.

If that was impossible, the last was to ship the bike from Lima to San Diego, and I could either get there by bus, meeting Clifford at a pre-arranged spot every night, or buy a cheap bike in Lima and continue on that. Lima to San Diego on a Honda 90: how hard could it be, as Paddy Minne would say.

Tired to the bones, I phoned Chris Willis at Triumph as Clifford went off for a morning swim.

'Sounds like the battery's not charging fully, so it's fluctuating around the critical level, which is cutting out the fuel injection,' he said. 'See if you can get a voltmeter and test it, then put it on a trickle charge overnight.'

Clifford came back, got on the Aprilia and disappeared, and was back in half an hour with the news that he had found the finest mechanic not only in town, but Peru, with the trophies to prove it.

The boy's a genius, I thought as we went outside and got Tony more or less started. With the engine coughing, spluttering and cutting out every hundred yards, I followed Clifford down the hill, into the town and down an alley to Cesar's, a little garage of exactly the sort that both Clifford's father and my own dear old dad had owned, rich beyond measure with the aroma of oil and the bright tinkle of spanners on concrete.

We whipped off the seat, and Cesar brought out a voltmeter and connected it to the battery.

'Twelve volts. The battery is fine,' he said.

I sighed. That meant the problem lay elsewhere.

Clifford phoned Chris Willis and paced up and down nervously as they talked through the possibilities. I stood about helplessly, with a sick feeling in the pit of my stomach, as Cesar slowly took the bike apart and checked everything he could think of. He stood back, his chin buried in his fist, then picked up the fuel tank from where it sat in the dust, tipped the contents into a basin, then dipped his finger in it and tasted it, the way a farmer tastes dirt to see if it is good earth.

'Pah. *Contaminada*,' he said. 'There is diesel in it. Look at the colour.'

'But the problem started before this tank of fuel,' I said to Clifford.

He shrugged.

'Could be we've had dodgy fuel for days, and it affects Tony more because of the fuel injection system. We'll just have to flush this out, hope no damage is done, and watch what we put in the tanks in future. And pray,' he said.

It seemed that Tony was a civilised English gentleman with a preference for Château Lafite, whereas April was a fun-loving Italian gal who was happy with any old plonk. For now, though, Cesar nipped off to the local Grifo filling station, which he said guaranteed good fuel, refilled the tank, and started the engine. It sang without a hiccup, although the warning light was still on.

'Sweet as a nut,' said Clifford. 'You know, someone said a beautiful thing to me before we began this trip, that a journey is best measured in friends rather than miles, and this man is living proof of that.'

He was right, for although I set out with Kierkegaardean fear and trembling in my heart, Tony was like a child reborn, swooping and diving into bends without a care in the world.

Across desert, through mountain passes and along a fertile river valley ripe with tomatoes we soared, stopping for lunch at a roadside *posada* where we met a Pakistani second-hand car dealer, as you do. His name was Syed Nayar Karim, and he specialised in the ancient American classics we had seen trundling around Tacana.

'Give me a call if the bikes break down, chaps. I'll do you a good deal on a very nice '57 Chevy,' he laughed as we tucked into fiery soup and Inca Kola, the indigenous Peruvian soft drink that looks like lighter fluid and tastes like bubble gum.

We climbed into the mountains again, passing fuel station after station selling only 84 octane or diesel, until finally, with relief, we spotted our new special best friend, Grifo, and filled both tanks with 95, inspecting it carefully first for clarity like the instant connoisseurs of gasoline we had become.

Even better, as we rode off, Tony's warning light finally went out.

By dusk we were in Arequipa, a chaotic, anarchic cowboy town famous for pickpockets and strangle muggings, in which the victim is strangled until unconscious. In the circumstances, it seemed wise to pay a taxi driver to lead us through the tangled streets to the finest hotel in town, the Libertador. We pulled up outside in a cloud of dusty glory to be met by aghast looks from the well-heeled clients, but the uniformed commissionaire did not bat an eyelid as he led us inside to meet Christian the receptionist, who lived up to his name by halving the room rate from $225 a night.

To celebrate, we went out to dinner, eating grilled alpaca on a wide balcony overlooking the Plaza de Armas, a tropical garden of palms and fountains framed by heroic seventeenth-century architecture to create one of the most stunning squares in South America.

The Spanish may have ruined this continent, but they made some great buildings while they were doing it, I thought as we rattled over the cobbles back to our hotel in a tiny yellow Daewoo taxi, our pockets unpicked and our throats unstrangled.

We fell into the downy billows of our beds, and at seven the next morning, joined the nuns for morning communion in the Monastery of Santa Catalina. Over two hundred of them once lived in seclusion in this vast basilica, the holiest place in Peru, along with three hundred staff to iron their wimples. But today, the footsteps of only thirty nuns echoed through the exquisitely frescoed halls.

The young women of Peru had got out of the habit, you just couldn't get the staff these days, and the sisters were doing it for themselves.

As for Pancho and I, we returned to the hotel for breakfast, loitered as long as possible, and were finally dragged kicking and screaming from our palatial abode, although not before Clifford had grabbed a picture of one of the waitresses for his collection, and I had taken one of a baby llama in the grounds of the hotel.

Or it might have been an alpaca. Or possibly a vicuña. I never can tell with those overcoats.

For the first hour of the journey, we fell through mountains of silica sand so like snow that I suddenly caught myself humming 'White Christmas', although don't tell anyone if you see them, because I wouldn't want them to think I was weird or anything.

And then, more desert. Hurrah! Yes, love that endless sand, just can't get enough of it, I muttered grimly, thinking that I might well never eat another sandwich as long as I lived. No matter how much ham and cheese there was in it.

Since by this stage we seemed to be riding across an endless beach, it seemed appropriate to come at last to the ocean, with the sudden salt smack of blue that always surprises. We stopped at a *cabaña* for coffee served by the toothless proprietor, and looked along a strand which stretched all the way to the horizon, and on which the only person to be seen was the world's most optimistic ice-cream salesman. Even better, just down the road was a filling station sporting a figure which I suspected was to become as important as a winning lottery number for us over the next few weeks – 95 octane.

We inspected it carefully as it poured into the tanks, then inspected the bill even more carefully.

'Thirty quid?' said Clifford in disbelief. 'That's three quid a gallon, six times what it was in Chile.'

Now we could see why every vehicle in Peru seemed to run on low-grade diesel which left everything behind it, including us, covered in oily soot.

Still, nothing else for it, and we sped on through the most dichotomous of landscapes, with desert or mountain to the right, and the crashing Pacific surf to our left. For Clifford, it was biker heaven, a road of sweeps and curves similar to the one on which he had won the Isle of Man TT in 1978, and it was no surprise that for most of the afternoon, all I saw was the back of his helmet, disappearing into the far distance.

For me, though, the best fun of the day came from a convoy

of about forty identical new white lorries being delivered to Lima or somesuch. I would pass them one by one, then stop for a break, watch them sweep past hooting their horns, and start the whole process over again.

It was like playing tag with a herd of albino elephants.

'Brilliant. Best ride ever,' was Clifford's succinct verdict as I finally caught up with him outside a little seaside hotel of white walls and wooden floors. If there had been any Japanese-Scandinavian sumptuous minimalist bikers around, it would have suited them to a tee. Fortunately, just at that moment I spotted one in a mirror, and booked us in for the night. Particularly since it cost less than a tank of petrol.

In the evening, I was standing on the terrace watching the sun fall and a crescent moon rise when a small, excited dog rushed up and disappeared into the hotel through the door I had inadvertently left open. I spent ten minutes chasing him up and down the corridors, then he spent ten minutes chasing me, until finally we threw each other out.

Clifford returned from a walk on the beach, and we had a dinner of *ceviche*, fish marinated in lime. On our table all through the meal sat a giant moth, silent and still.

In the morning, I discovered a signal on the wotsit, and mailed Andrea at Triumph to let her know that things were looking up.

'By the way, can the bike run on 90 octane? We're finding it increasingly difficult to find 95,' I added.

An hour later, she mailed back.

'No, 90 is too low. You might get away with one tank, but any more will cause loss of performance and eventually damage the engine. You could try mixing 90 with aviation fuel if you're passing an airfield, or using 90, adding octane booster, and being careful not to overload the engine,' she said.

Making a note to look out for octane booster and airfields, we packed the bikes and set off for the Nazca Lines, spread across 300 square miles of the Peruvian desert.

Some of the Lines are giant human or animal shapes, and

others are simply straight lines which go up and down. They are not to be confused with the Nascar Races, which go round and round and are much more pointless.

There are several theories about why the Lines were created in pre-Inca times:

a) They were an astronomical calendar to help organise planting and harvesting. This was proposed by Maria Reiche after studying the Lines from 1946 until her death in 1998. Today, in the little village museum dedicated to her, you can see details of her theories, not to mention her flip-flops.

b) They point towards where the sun rises at the start of the rainy season, so you know when to get your wellies out. This was proposed after several years of study by Dr Anthony Areni, the world's leading archaeoastronomer. These are people who have their feet in a trench and their head in the stars.

c) The pre-Incas got so bored looking at all that desert that they decided to do a bit of decorating. This was proposed by me after thirty seconds of looking at the Lines from the top of a roadside tower, although I have to confess the theory had been germinating through several days of looking at the same desert and wondering if it would ever go away.

Still, at least I had a head to look at it with: there was a time when the tribes in this area thought nothing of taking home a few noggins as battle souvenirs. I know, because Clifford and I found ourselves later that afternoon in a museum up the road looking at a collection of heads whose owners were not attached to them, and had not been for some time.

'Here, that one in the middle looks a bit like you,' I said.

'Can't be. He's got hair,' he said glumly.

Not that Clifford was ever glum for long: why, only the day before he had spotted a giant wave breaking over a rock with a seal suspended in it like in a snapshot, and this morning he had gone swimming and found he had a sea otter for company.

The man standing beside us looking at the heads, meanwhile, turned out, naturally enough, to be from Anchorage, Alaska.

'Deadhorse?' he said when we told him our ultimate destination. 'Cool. It'll be just about defrosted when you get there.'

Cool, however, was a word we struggled to come to terms with as we rode through the baking heat to the oasis lagoon of Huacachina, where the locals have found an even more interesting thing to do with the desert: bury themselves up to their necks in it because of the recuperative powers of the mud there. According to legend, the lagoon was the mirror dropped by a princess who had stripped to bathe and caught a hunter watching her.

It was, almost certainly, Clifford adding to his collection of Pan-American beauties.

'Bloody hell, what a great spot,' he said as we rounded a sand dune to find the lagoon, waving palm trees, the local policeman and a man called Lucho, who told us we should stay in his hotel. He turned out to be right, and five minutes later we were sitting by the pool talking to several friendly Dubliners. From the north side of Dublin, naturally, where the women have fake jewellery but real orgasms. They had just arrived, and were so white that Lucho's daughter was later sent to bed with snow-blindness from looking at them.

Unperturbed, Lucho somehow persuaded me to try sand-boarding on one of the giant dunes ringing the lagoon. However, I turned out to be just as bad at it as at the snow variety, so I decided to stick to what I do best, and had a beer by the pool, accompanied by two large parrots and a small cat.

After all, I was only following in two great traditions.

That of the Incas, who, when a man approached fifty, gave him a break from sacrificing virgins with an early retirement package which included food and lodging.

And that of the Peruvian muralist Servulo Gutierrez, who got through a legendary quantity of *pisco* during his weekends at this very lagoon.

'I dreamed there was a dog under my bed,' said Clifford, waking and looking under his bed, to find a dog.

'How come the dreams about finding a beautiful woman in the bed don't come true, but the ones about finding a dog under it do?' he said over breakfast.

'One of the great mysteries of life, Pancho. Like why the slower cars are always in front of you, why things only break when you need to use them and why the Jim Carrey relaxation tapes never caught on. Anyway, you've got a fair maiden to look forward to seeing tonight.'

As he did: Jemina, a half-German, half-Peruvian former work colleague now back in Lima with her sister and parents who was by his own account a stunning *übersenorita*.

'You're right, I do,' he said, draining his mango juice, getting on his bike and riding off into the desert, the armour of his helmet bright and his imagined pennant fluttering in the breeze. I followed at length, wondering if we were ever going to see the colour green again.

We did: at first sporadic hardy trees, then entire fields. Green! It looked so luscious after the endless miles of sand that it was all I could do not to stop the bike, run off the road and roll in it. Then eat it.

Thankfully, I contained myself in a manly sort of way until we arrived in Lima, a teeming chaos of a place where the elite own Cadillacs and snort cocaine, and the rest own nothing and snort smog.

We found Jemina, Karina and their parents, Hugo and Roswitha, in an elegant home which they had built in the well-known German-Peruvian style in a leafy suburb.

It came complete with swimming pool, two servants and a guard dog whose *modus operandi* was to lick to death anyone who dared to cross the threshold. Roswitha, meanwhile, was as round, blonde and jolly as Hugo was dark, elegant and spare.

He was from Arequipa, and spoke the slow, beautiful Spanish of that city, so perfectly weighted and exquisitely modulated that I could understand every word, and later found myself having an entirely coherent discussion with him about breast implants. Mind you, the coherence could well have come from the very fine bottles of vintage Argentinian Malbec he kept producing from his cellars.

The reason we were talking about breast implants, since you ask, was that he was getting out of the construction business and into the reconstruction business, importing the products which at this moment lay on the dining room table in front of us like stranded jellyfish.

'Here, Pancho,' I said, picking one up and giving it a friendly squeeze, 'a couple of these would make very nice cushions for the long days in the saddle.'

He sat down to negotiate a price with Hugo and I went upstairs to sleep in the former nursery, surrounded by German jigsaw puzzles.

At noon the next day, the reflexology woman came, as she did every Sunday. She did Clifford's feet first, and the screaming was so bad that several ambulances called by hoping for business, followed by a confused fireman who was later sent off in the direction of a real blaze. When it came to my turn, the pain was, indeed, legendary, but I tried to keep a stiff upper lip to set a good example to Tony, who was sitting outside in the courtyard wondering why he wasn't being forced to cross a burning desert for the first day in two weeks.

'Right,' said Jemina, who had been translating, 'she says you have rigid tendons, a closed spine, varicose veins and problems with your testicles, circulation, kidney, prostrate gland and gall bladder. But the worst of all is your liver. She wants to know how much you spend on a bottle of wine.'

'About eight dollars.'

'She says it is not enough. You must drink better wine, or give up.'

As I was writing a note later to my doctor asking if I could get Gevrey-Chambertin on prescription for medical reasons, I happened to glance over at the bookshelves lining the living room and saw, to my astonishment, a copy of *The Kalevala*, the Finnish national epic poem by Elias Lonnrot. Good heavens,

I thought. Apart from myself, the only other person I knew who had a copy of that was Cate.

'Ah yes, interesting book,' said Hugo in his beautiful Spanish when I mentioned it to him that evening after dinner. 'It is my wife's. She believes in mythology and reincarnation, but I do not.'

He paused for a moment, his proud and noble face silhouetted against the setting sun.

'However, when I was seventeen, I had this most vivid dream of the girl I would marry. Exact in every detail, and even in the dream, I felt as if I had known her in a previous life. Then, the very next day, I came out of Mass in my Sunday best, and there she was, walking down the street towards me wearing a red dress. It was astonishing, like cold water to the heart. She was exactly the girl of my dream. I was so stunned that I could not move, or speak, just watch with my mouth open as she walked away down the street.'

'Did you meet her again?' I said, horrified by the thought that he had let her walk out of his life, then regretted it forever.

'Yes, I know what you are thinking,' he laughed, 'but yes, I did see her again. The next day, in fact.'

'And what happened?'

'We were together for a year, but it did not work out.'

He looked across at Roswitha, who was round and German and jolly, telling Clifford that she had once been a close friend of King Arthur's.

'No. It did not work out,' he said, then took a sip of his wine and looked up at the rising crescent moon, the expression on his face exactly that of a man who has somehow become an importer of breast implants, thinking of the seventeen-year-old he once was, who walked out of the chapel one day in his only suit, and saw, walking down the street towards him in a red dress, the girl of his dreams.

We went into the city, and bought some octane booster.

A simple sentence, yet buried within those few words lies an experience close to insanity.

The reason why we wanted octane booster, of course, was because we were beginning to have serious doubts about our chances of getting 95 octane fuel in northern Peru, never mind Ecuador and beyond. We thought Lima would be our best shot at finding some, and after breakfast mentioned it to Jemina, thus setting in chain a process of events which would lead to the destruction of what few brain cells we had left.

Jemina then mentioned it to Karina, who hauled out the phone book. After some searching and several fruitless calls by Hugo, who had now appeared on the scene, we tracked down a place within walking distance whose proprietor swore on the grave of his grandmother, and her grandmother before her, that he had exactly what we were looking for. Pleased that it had been so simple, which shows that travel had taught us nothing, we set off on foot.

It was only ten in the morning, but the temperature was already at the level at which steel melts.

Half an hour later, drenched in sweat, we arrived at the aforementioned premises, only to find the owner denying not only that he had octane booster, but that the phone call had taken place, or that he even had either a phone or a grandmother. Having said that, he went on, there was another place down the road which might have the ambrosia of our dreams. He wrote the address on a piece of paper, and we set off afresh, although I use the expression in its most ironic sense.

Some time later, we found ourselves wandering through the corridors of a generic superstore which seemed to be staffed entirely by one indolent youth.

'Octane booster?' he said. 'Never heard of it.'

Naturally, we ignored him, and Clifford finally tracked down what we were looking for at the back of the shop. We picked up half a dozen bottles and brought them back to the youth, who looked at them in astonishment, grabbed one, looked in vain for a price, then picked a figure off the top of his head which turned out to be no more than a couple of quid.

It was not, I suspected, their best-selling line.

Satisfied, we trudged to the Bar Cordano, a cool and ancient hymn in mahogany and glass near the railway station, for something cold.

'Well, it could have been worse. You could have been a chicken,' said Hugo enigmatically when we told him later about the ordeal.

'You see,' he said, 'there was a time, twenty years ago, when the Peruvian economy was very healthy, and we all ate meat. Now it is not, so all we can afford is chicken. Which is bad news for the economy. And the chickens.'

'Do the chickens get up every morning and read the financial papers to see if they will survive the day?' I said.

'Almost certainly,' he said, going to open a bottle of wine. I was growing to like Hugo more and more.

'What about the guinea pigs, then?' I said when he returned. I had heard that guinea pig, or *cuy*, was a national delicacy, and had read in Lanks's account how he and Pleiss had stopped at a lonely farmhouse one day, spotted a couple of the little darlings running around, and had them roasted for lunch.

We had even spotted some on the menu at Arequipa, but it had been eight quid and we had been running low on funds that day, so we had made do with alpaca.

I had been reminded of them again the day before, when we had spent a grimly happy hour wandering around the catacombs of the Monastery of St Francis in Lima, admiring artistic arrangements of skulls and femurs, although how anyone was expected to find their own bones come Judgement Day was quite beyond me. In any case, we had climbed the stairs at last to a vast and airy hall, at the far end of which was a heroic representation of the Last Supper, with a blessed guinea pig sitting proudly on every plate.

'Guinea pig?' said Hugo, dragging my thoughts back to the present. 'If we cannot afford meat, do you really think we can afford guinea pig?'

Indeed, he was right, I thought, taking a sip of the wine and noting with satisfaction that it was of a quality which would have satisfied even the most demanding reflexologist.

Just before I finally went to bed, I checked Lanks's book to see if he had actually mentioned what guinea pig tasted like.

He had.

Chicken, funny enough.

After two welcome days of languishing in the bosom of the Lopez household, we hugged them all farewell, wished Hugo good luck with his breasts, got reluctantly back on our bikes, plunged into the chaos of the city, and discovered that Lima drivers were divided into two schools of physicists.

There were the Newtonians, who understood that no two objects could occupy the same space, but were prepared to give it a go anyway, flinging their vehicles with gay abandon at gaps in the traffic into which you would be hard pushed to fit a blunt razor blade.

Then there were the Einsteinians, who knew that matter was composed mostly of space, and felt that if they drove one car fast enough at another, the resulting collision would merge the neutrons, protons and electrons into a new car which combined the best qualities of the two previous ones, in the same way that Flann O'Brien's policemen became bicycles.

As a result, we emerged at length on the other side of the city, half motorbike, half car and half alive, but only just.

'I don't know about you, chum, but I'm never going near another city like that as long as I live,' said Clifford when we stopped at the filling station down the road.

'I do know about me, and I'm going to leave it longer than that, just to be on the safe side,' I said, walking into the toilets and looking in the mirror to find myself the proud possessor of a dark beard and two swarthy arms: the result of only half an hour in Lima smog. This would take several days of determined scrubbing to remove, so that every time I glanced in the mirror, I saw Robert de Niro staring back at me.

'Are you looking at me?' I would say to him sternly, then strangle myself with my bare hands.

In the meantime, though, our saturnine expressions must have impressed two cheery traffic policemen, who pulled us over for a chat, cheerily helped Clifford top up his tank, cheerily posed for photos, then cheerily asked for a bribe. We gave them a couple of quid, telling them not to spend it all on sweeties, and proceeded to the one-horse town of Casma to find the entire population and a brass band lining the streets.

We were immediately mobbed by curious locals, some more curious than others, and even though we later found that the brass band was for a presidential cavalcade on its way to an election meeting, it seemed churlish in the circumstances not to stay for the night. We tracked down a pleasant hotel in a sleepy side street lined with trees, and Clifford went out to the market, returning with the news that they were doing a special offer on penguin, but of guinea pig there was no sign.

Mind you, it was hardly surprising: just up the road from here once lived the native healer El Tuno, whose diagnostic methods, still practised by his apprentices, involve rubbing a live guinea pig all over the patient's body, then splitting the animal open and removing its innards for inspection while the heart is still pumping.

You will not be surprised to hear, I imagine, that Peru had been voted the world's least popular destination five years running by *Guinea Pig Weekly* magazine.

The central plaza of Cajamarca was an unremarkable place.

As we stood there the next day, the sun was whispering in the low trees around it, the breeze was answering in the grass, and a small dog was chasing a large cat across it. But in this modest space, a vast empire once fell in a single afternoon.

Atahualpa, the last Lord of the Incas, had come to this city in the late summer of 1532, to take his imperial ease in the hot springs, when a messenger brought him word of Francisco

Pizarro dragging his weary band of sixty-two Spanish horsemen and 106 foot soldiers up through the mountains.

With his army of 80,000 warriors, Atahualpa could easily have had them slaughtered at once, but he was curious, and he waited until at last, on Friday, 15 November, the dishevelled band of Spaniards entered this very square.

The next morning, at the head of five thousand men, Atahualpa entered the square himself to meet these strange visitors. Eighty noblemen dressed in dazzling colours and singing a graceful lament carried their lord on a litter of silver, gold and brilliant parrot feathers. On his head was a crown of gold, and around his neck was draped a band of priceless emeralds.

Enter, then, the scruffy figure of Dominican friar Vicente de Valverde, who rudely thrust a Bible into Atahualpa's hand and told him that he was welcome to dine at Pizarro's table. When he was politely told that the Inca emperor would consider it if the Spanish would consider returning the objects they had already stolen in their short time there, de Valverde ignored Atahualpa and began a long and tedious sermon. Visibly angered at this rudeness, Atahualpa threw the Bible on the floor, and all hell broke loose.

The friar scuttled back to Pizarro screaming: 'Come at these enemy dogs who reject the things of God!'

Two Spanish cannon roared, and the horsemen charged the Incas, hacking their way through to capture Atahualpa. Stunned by the ferocity of the attack and armed only with small axes and slings, the Incas were chopped down in their thousands.

Atahualpa was taken, and promised his freedom if he filled a large room in his palace with treasure. When he did so, Pizarro reneged on his promise and murdered him, bringing to an end an empire which had once ruled twenty million people.

What Atahualpa, an experienced warrior, had failed to realise was not only how superior were the Spanish weapons of swords, muskets, cannons and horses, but how consuming was their obsession with wealth and power.

Not that the Spanish had a monopoly on empire building, of course: earlier in the day, Clifford and I had spent hours wandering around the vast ruined city of Chan Chan. The capital of the Chimu Empire, this complex of temples, citadels and graceful avenues had once stretched for miles, until the Incas captured it in 1470 by cutting off the water supply. Sixty years later, when the Spanish rode through it to wreak their own devastation in turn upon the Incas, it was already a ghost city, and today it was only a skeleton of heroic walls reaching up to the lost heights of their former glory.

So much that once was, I thought as we stood in this peaceful square which in a single afternoon had seen one of the world's most horrific massacres. And then I thought the same thing as I had thought when I once sat in the cockpit of a Second World War Spitfire. That it is a remarkable thing that something so great as destiny can be unfolded in such small spaces.

And then we turned and walked away, as across the square came the large cat, this time chasing the small dog.

More desert. Hurrah!

Still, it would be the last stretch until Mexico, for soon we would be climbing into the mountains of Ecuador, followed by the hot, steamy jungles of Central America. Until then, though, I rode along quoting lines from T.S. Eliot: 'sweat is dry, and feet are in the sand', that sort of thing. Then I decided that T.S. Eliot was a bored, middle-class, pseudo-intellectual fraud – great place for revelations like that, the desert – and switched to Neil Diamond, who wrote far better lyrics.

Halfway through 'Crackling Rosie', I was wondering vaguely what a storeboard woman was when I happened to notice that the truck ahead of me in the same lane was not, as I had thought, proceeding in the same direction as me, but overtaking another one and approaching me at a rate of knots.

Slamming on the brakes, I slid onto the hard shoulder, waved an angry fist at the driver, and got a cheery smile in return. Charming people, the Peruvians: even when they are bribing or trying to kill you, they do it with a grin. The funny thing was, though, that like everyone else on the trip so far, they had been endlessly helpful, patient, kind and friendly.

Only the day before, a man in Trujillo had cycled miles out of his way to show us the road out of town. Then, of course, he had warned us to be careful up north, because the people up there would steal the teeth out of your head, then come back for the fillings.

Mind you, people were forever telling us that the ones in the next street/village/town/country were a bunch of thieving, good-for-nothing vagabonds, and it was always nonsense, at least so far.

At noon we stopped at a flyblown shack for the worst coffee I have ever tasted, as bitter as a widow's curse. Over the door hung a coy watercolour of Jesus and Mary, above the words (in English) 'God Bless Our House', beside a calendar of a naked woman sporting a trident and a pair of diabolical horns. Below this dichotomy of good and evil lay a tortoiseshell cat, sleeping soundly through the coming and going of burly truck drivers, all of whom stepped politely over her, wished us good day, then sat down and ate half a sheep.

'God, that coffee's crap,' said one of them as he passed by on his way out the door to board one of the trucks. The cabs of these are generally emblazoned with the names of wives or sweethearts, religious devotions such as Virgin of the Desert or, once, intriguingly, the words Jim Reynolds. Was the driver a gay trucker who had fallen in love, only to have his heart broken when Jim went back to his wife and three children in Tucson, Arizona?

We would never know, just as we would never know the identity of the blond couple who cycled past in the middle of the afternoon, giving us a cheery wave in spite of the fact that their only excitement of the day lay in looking forward to the next corner, fifty miles away. They could only have been Dutch. No one else would have looked so happy cycling across such a flat landscape.

Nor, too, would we ever know the lives and deaths of the families who lived in the shacks by the roadside, constructions of brushwood tied with string in which they seemed to exist on sand, air and not even the bitter fruits of failed ambition, that peculiarly Western delicacy, but of no ambition at all other than surviving from one day to the next.

In these scattered desert communities, the middle-class families were the ones with two plastic buckets.

Making a mental note never to complain again about having to fix the roof, and to instead give thanks that I had a roof to fix, I rode on.

At Sullana, the landscape changed with shocking sudden-ness from arid waste to sub-tropical paradise. Palm trees marched jauntily along the horizon, paddy fields glistened iridescent in the sun and bougainvillaea blossomed both willy and nilly.

However, it was just the desert mocking us, for soon we were back to a vista so dry that had it been a martini, even James Bond would have refused it.

The only signs of life were lonely goatherds wearing traditional lonely goatherd Nike caps, and at one stage one of their cares took a mad fit and dashed across the road in front of Clifford. I held my breath, thinking that he was planning to recreate the spirit of the original Nambarrie Run so faithfully that he was going to replicate the incident of Paddy and the sheep, but the Aprilia had the brakes that the Enfield had lacked, and Clifford missed the beast by a whisker.

Soon after, we were stopped by a large contingent of the Peruvian army, complete with armoured car and machine guns, who wanted to check our documents.

At last, I thought, an opportunity to produce the Very Important Letter. This was of the type, covered in important looking signatures, stamps and bits of sealing wax, once carried by adventurous chaps to advise the natives that the bearer was a representative of Her Majesty's Government, and that any attempt to string him up by the dongles would result in a fleet of frigates bombarding their beach huts before they could say, *'Allah u Akbar'*.

However, since Her Majesty had completely ignored my hand-written note asking her to put the navy at our disposal, our Very Important Letter simply said that, rather than the pair of aimless vagabonds we appeared to be, we were, in fact, a matching set of knights in shining armour who were raising money for a worldwide orphans' charity.

It was passed around, heads were nodded, and we were sent on our way with handshakes all around rather than the usual request for a bribe.

Our Very Important Letter had passed its first test.

The temperature, which had been rising steadily throughout the day, was now at a level which would have been more at home in the core of a nuclear reactor, and it was with some relief that we fell at last through the blissful cool of early evening to Máncora.

Once a sleepy seaside village, this was now a trendy beach resort popular with young, hip surfers. And us, who were none of the above.

In the evening, the dudes gathered at the beach bars to talk about the wave that got away, and the locals gathered in the square to watch *The Ten Commandments* projected onto an old bedsheet.

We sat in the middle, caught between tithe and tide.

In fact, the dudes don't know what they missed, because when Moses did the Red Sea gig, it was, like, so the greatest rip curl of all time, man.

'I dreamed I bought a Triumph Herald last night,' said Clifford, sipping a fresh papaya juice at breakfast. 'White, convertible, 5,000 miles on the clock, completely original. Lovely car.'

'I'm getting worried about you, Pancho. You've stopped dreaming about women.'

'I was dreaming about women. No woman could resist a car like that.'

Unfortunately, when we went outside, the Herald was nowhere in sight; just the usual Peruvian ensemble of brightly coloured motorcycle rickshaws, Beetles and ancient American V8s. Still, at least the stall down the street was selling genuine fake Nike baseball caps with Alaska on the front.

With that good omen behind us, we set off down the coast, accompanied by soaring squadrons of elegant frigate birds, like the benign cousins of pterodactyls.

We took one long, last lingering look at the sea, for it would be the last time we would see it until the north coast of Colombia, and turned inland for Tumbes, the wild frontier town that would be our jumping off point for the border in the morning.

'Where are you from, *señor*?' the attendant asked Clifford as we filled our tanks at the station on the way into town. 'Ah, Scotland. And have you tried our famous Peruvian *pisco*?'

'Nonsense. *Pisco* is from Chile,' said Clifford.

'Ah yes, of course. Just as whisky is from England,' he laughed, then insisted on jumping in a rickshaw and leading the way to the best hotel in town, with a locked yard for the bikes and a handsome pool.

In the hot and humid evening, we had dinner in the square as first a large and excitable election procession, and then a small and quiet religious one made its way past, followed by a small grey cat who jumped onto my lap, fell asleep and spent the rest of the meal there.

Across the square, a pan piper played 'El Condor Pasa', that most haunting of Andean melodies.

It was, in all respects, a finer farewell to Peru than Lanks and Pleiss had had an arrival. Driving south from the Ecuadorian border in pouring rain, they had got stuck in the mud, and been rescued by a local mill manager who insisted that they accept his hospitality for the night.

'After an excellent dinner … he led us up a stairway on the outside of his great, rambling house to a balcony on the third floor,' Lanks wrote. 'There, he opened a door into a great bedroom with two beds that the servants had just made up. As the day had been particularly trying, we soon fell asleep to the sound of the rain falling on the roof.'

Their experience had been typical of Peruvian hospitality, and when it came to turning our faces the next day to the unknown delights and dangers of Ecuador, we would be as sorry to leave it as we had been to leave Chile.

11

A short history of Ecuador

12000 BC–1540 AD
See Peru.

1540
Pizarro's brother, hearing rumours that Amazon is rich in gold, sends Francisco de Orellana off in canoe. Orellana ends up floating down entire Amazon River through Brazil to Atlantic Ocean, never to return. Rumours that he ran aground in Cork and opened a little tapas bar in Kinsale remain unconfirmed to this day. While waiting in vain, Spanish enslave natives to pass the time.

1819–1822
Simón Bolívar liberates country and creates republic of Gran Colombia, including Colombia, Venezuela, Ecuador and Panama. Within ten years, Venezuela and Ecuador sue for divorce, citing irreconcilable differences and Colombia's drug habit.

1861
Fearsome García Moreno becomes president and forces

population to become poverty-stricken Catholics. After his death, fearsome liberal president Eloy Alfaro turns population back into poverty-stricken atheists.

1911
García Moreno overthrown by military, who kill him, drag body through streets, then burn it just to really teach him a lesson. Country plunged into fifty years of chaos, with thousands of deaths and almost as many presidents. Peru takes advantage of chaos to steal half of Ecuador, and is thrown out of South American Good Neighbours scheme.

1950s
Banana boom. Population discovers money under mattress of fortune.

1960s
Banana bust. Population sells mattress of fortune to passing Peruvian bed merchant and goes back to sleeping on floor.

1967
Oil discovered, but profits nowhere near enough to pay off huge national debt.

1998
Economic crisis. Entire country goes on strike. Inflation soars, banks collapse. Country switches currency to dollar, leaving everyone poverty-stricken, but in a different currency.

Beside the breakfast table on our last morning in Peru was a white wall and an arched window covered with a slatted cotton blind.

In the half hour we sat there, the rising sun threw on the blind a haiku of light and shade, changing yet eternal. I thought of how the heart lifts when you walk into, for example, a Japanese or Scandinavian room with a wooden floor, white walls and a flower. And how it sinks when you encounter a space into which no thought has been put, and no care subsequently taken.

Everywhere, the search for simplicity and beauty over the complicated and ugly.

Indeed, the Peruvian and Ecuadorian passport and customs officials seemed to have adopted the same principle, as amid a maelstrom of heat, noise, chaos, dust and hawkers selling everything from puppies to parrots, they passed us through as quietly and efficiently as Swiss bank clerks, except with personality and humour.

Since Lanks and Pleiss had had a nightmarish entry into Ecuador which took them a whole day, it all seemed too good to be true.

And, as it transpired, it was: at the Ecuadorian customs post ten miles down the road, the helpful, friendly officials told us in a helpful, friendly way that we were at the wrong customs post, and would have to go back to the correct one in the middle of the chaos.

Fortunately, a young boy who happened to be hanging around offered to hop on the back of Clifford's bike and show us the way, and half an hour later we had our carnets stamped and were on our way. We gave him a couple of dollars as thanks, he bought us a couple of ice creams as thanks back, and we were officially in Ecuador.

'Is it Farquarson?' I said, as Clifford put his passport away.

'Nope,' he said.

Within minutes, the landscape changed from desert into a lush vista of rolling hills with giant Technicolor butterflies lolloping about and, by my rough estimation, enough bananas to stretch all the way from Chile to Alaska and back.

As for the road, it had been patched so often that it had taken a gentle undulating quality which after a while was lulling me to sleep. Fortunately, there was an unlimited supply of giant kamikaze bugs ready and willing to keep me awake by hurling themselves with an impressive splat against my helmet. One, I could not help but notice as it obscured my vision completely by spreading its innards generously over my visor, was exactly the colour and shape of a fried egg. Sunny side up, that is.

Up and up we climbed all afternoon into the foothills of the Andes, being careful around every corner, since it would have been amusing but fatal to have slipped on a banana skin and plummeted into the rushing torrents hundreds of feet below. From time to time we were soaked by tropical downpours, but it was only like taking a warm shower with your clothes on, and within half an hour we were dry again.

Up and up more we climbed, through an impossibly verdant alpine landscape, like the love child of Donegal and Switzerland. It was a union which was even blessed by a rainbow as we wound our way past appropriately wooden chalets, on the front porches of which families were gathered for Saturday afternoon pig roasts.

All waved cheerily, except the pig.

As dusk grew near and the air grew cold, we clattered at last through the cobbled streets of Cuenca, a hymn to Spanish colonial architecture.

We found an ancient inn with simple rooms and wooden verandas around a courtyard bright with flowers, and then we went out for that most simple and beautiful of pleasures: walking through the streets of a new town as the sun goes down and the moon rises over the mountains.

We wandered, mildly agog, past balconies and courtyards until we came out into a central plaza so stunning that I was overcome briefly by Stendhal's syndrome, named after the writer who was so overwhelmed by the beauty of his first visit to Italy that he had to be revived regularly by copious draughts of the local brandy.

All around us as I sat outside a little café recovering with a small *pisco*, women wore colourful felt hats, shawls and skirts, and the men sported hefty trousers, braces and the fine Panama hats for which Cuenca is famous. They may be called Panama hats, after all, but only after their main centre of distribution in the nineteenth century, for it was always Ecuador where they were made.

And it is Cuenca where they make the finest: the exquisite

superfinos which take four months to create, and which can be rolled up, passed through a wedding ring, stored in their balsa cases and taken out years later without a crease.

Sadly, even in the town where they were made, they were well beyond our budget.

What was not, however, was a beer and a feast, at last, of guinea pig. We spent an hour walking up and down the street looking in vain for the only restaurant in town which served it, then finally found it down an alleyway, went in and placed our order. Bringing the beast took another hour, most of which was presumably spent chasing it around the back yard.

Unfortunately, when it was brought to the table roasted on a steel platter, it was in its entirety, lying on its back with all four legs in the air and its teeth bared in a last grimace.

We took one bite each, and ordered the soup.

'Well, we won't be doing that again,' said Clifford as we got up to leave.

'Nor will the guinea pig,' I said as we strolled back to our inn and fell into our beds.

After the long, hard days in the desert, we were, for tonight at least, in paradise.

In the morning, we flung back the curtains to reveal a fresh, bright day, wheeled the bikes out of the hallway where they had spent the night, and set off through the mountains.

Tony, having his first taste of the national fuel, 90 octane topped up with Lima *aditivo*, was, so far, coping with it admirably, much as I imagine chaps in the war had to make do with Spam enlivened by a dash of HP sauce. The fact that we were now at 6,000ft may even have helped, since the lean air and the lean fuel would probably match nicely, in the same way that slim people are attracted to each other.

Within an hour, we were in Ingapirca, the remarkably intact fifteenth-century Inca citadel which, like Cuzco in Peru, was run on a series of overlapping trinities.

Women, for example, were divided into teachers, weavers and virgins of the sun, whose job was sitting around being virgins until some noblemen came along and married them.

There were, too, only three basic rules of law: don't lie, don't steal and don't be a lazy bugger.

The penalty for all three was elegantly simple: you got flung off the nearest cliff.

'And it's still happening,' said the young man standing nearby when he overheard us discussing it. 'The people in my village did it to a woman six months ago.'

'What had she done?' said Clifford.

'She annoyed everyone.'

Making a mental note not to annoy anyone in Ecuador, we crept back to the bikes and rode off down the open road into the morning sun.

But not for long: within twenty miles the open road had deteriorated into a dirt track.

'This can't be right,' I said, and we rode the twenty miles back and asked at a garage.

Only to be told that the Pan-Am was being dug up, and this was the only way north. We set off again, riding through the same village we had already passed through twice, watched by the same pair of baffled veterans on the same bench, and had just re-covered the twenty miles when the rain started. Then the road climbed into the clouds, so that I could only just see Clifford's rear light, a few feet from my front wheel.

We crept along. From time to time, visions would appear at the roadside: women in bright hats and shawls leading cows, washing clothes or simply sitting there, their faces damp with mist and beautiful with the impassivity of a thousand years of acceptance.

Waterfalls splashed by the roadside, fog steamed off the road, and we crawled through an ethereal world, like the frogs who live in cloud forests. We took turns at the tiring task of leading, constantly weaving to avoid potholes, ruts, mud, huge rocks in the road from landslides, and trucks which were, impossibly, overtaking on blind corners made even more blind by the cloud.

Suddenly, we climbed so high that we emerged from it, although unfortunately this let us see just how bad the road really was.

It was now late afternoon, and it looked more and more likely that we would be hauling out our sleeping bags and spending the night in a wet hedge. But then, as mysteriously as it had worsened, the road improved. I looked at my watch. It was an hour before dark, after which it would be suicidal to drive in Ecuador. With luck, we might just make Riobamba.

Oh, the glory of that last hour, dipping and soaring through mountain passes with the speedo touching eighty, then across a golden moor and down into shires worthy of Middle Earth, with little houses, a little railway and elderly couples out for an evening stroll in their Sunday best, all sporting Panamas, fedoras, trilbies or cloches on their heads. In a world which had lost the wearing of hats, it was a heart-warmingly elegant sight.

It was pitch dark by the time we rolled into Riobamba and hailed a taxi to lead us to a hotel, outside which we climbed off, weary, sore and chilled to the bone, yet exhilarated and satisfied beyond measure. Incredibly, we had covered 200 miles that day, on the worst roads I had ever seen.

'What a day, Pancho,' I said as we unloaded the bikes in the hotel garage then chained them up for the night.

'What a day, Don. Best ever,' he said, then paused. 'By the way, you know the way I said a couple of days ago I was giving up drink?'

'I do. You've done better than I have.'

'Well, forget it. Where's the nearest bar?'

If the road teaches you one thing, it is that around every bend is another surprise.

While the day before we would have sold our grannies for even a few yards of moth-eaten tarmac, today we were granted a dual carriageway, of all things.

We were, as you can imagine, in heaven, particularly since Clifford had sorted out his goggles problem. They had been made, you see, of a sophisticated dual-lens design which was meant to stop fogging, but which actually created a clever trap for water and dust, the two of which then got together to form an impenetrable layer of gunge so bad that the day before he had dispensed with them entirely. Since we had been doing 80 all the way down the road into Riobamba, this had created the interesting effect of making his eyes so bloodshot that if he ever gave up the day job, he could easily get work as an extra in *Return of the Evil Dead*.

This morning, however, he had thought for a while, then taken out the lenses, torn them apart and thrown one in the bin.

'There. Sorted,' he said, satisfied.

The landscape, as we rode north, was everything from the Yorkshire Dales to the Scottish Highlands to the foothills of the Pyrenees between France and Spain.

All of this, and it wasn't even lunchtime.

After an hour of this ever-changing panoply, however, our idyll was interrupted when we discovered that the peasants were revolting. They had burnt some cars and blocked the way with rubble, and were now sitting by the roadside watching the army clear up the mess.

'What are they protesting about?' I asked the major who waved us through.

'The usual,' he shrugged.

In fact, it later turned out to be a planned free-trade agreement with the US which would hit local producers.

An hour up the road, we found another blockade, except this time it was an impassable wall of earth and rocks. A gaggle of policemen sat around in two shiny black Hummers, obviously waiting either for a sign from the Lord or for the army to turn up with more men and a bulldozer.

In front of us, all the cars and trucks turned and went back, until there was only us left, feeling a trifle conspicuous.

Particularly when two of the protestors came wandering over.

'Where are you going, *señores*?' they said.

'Alaska,' we replied.

'Then you must get through. Alaska is a long way to go,' they said.

Several of them rolled up their sleeves and manhandled the bikes up a steep slope to the railway track which ran alongside the road. Which only left the minor problem of how to get them down the other side of the roadblock and across a deep, wide drainage ditch.

As we were standing scratching our heads and thinking this was another fine mess we had gotten ourselves into, someone appeared with a plank, and five minutes of pushing, shoving and hauling later, we were back on the road.

Suddenly, there was a shout, and we turned around to find a black Jeep slowly trying to follow the route we had taken. The man standing beside me sprinted off, grabbed a chainsaw, and set to attacking the base of a lofty eucalyptus tree. It came crashing down, missing the Jeep by inches, and the driver shamefacedly reversed back down to the road and drove away. Our friend with the chainsaw came back, set it down and grinned.

'You are honoured today, *señores*,' he said.

'We are indeed honoured,' we agreed, shaking hands with all of them.

As revolutionaries go, they weren't a bad bunch, I thought as we rode off, straight into a torrential downpour.

It did not stop for the rest of the afternoon, during which we arrived in the capital, Quito, and discovered a political scandal even worse than what the peasants were protesting about. Whoever had been put in charge of Quito's road signs had spent all the money on beer, sweeties or women instead. Not only that, but they had lifted most of the manhole covers and sold them to a scrapyard, leaving gaping holes in the streets. Now, in these circumstances, we had found that the easiest solution was simply to hail a taxi and ask him to lead us to where we wanted to go, in this case through the city to the Pan-American north.

But Quito, the world's most linear city, was thirty miles long and only five yards wide, and from the look of the map only had one main road running through it. How hard could it be? We pulled in to a gas station to fill up, have a coffee and think about it.

'Here,' I said to the attendant as I threw in a splash of octane booster then checked that the fuel he was pouring into the tank looked clear, 'is it easy to find our way through town to the road north?'

'Absolutely. Straight road all the way. Even an idiot could do it,' he said.

That should have been our cue to hail a taxi. Instead, we set off with blithe optimism, and ran into a diversion after a hundred yards.

Three more of those, and we were hopelessly lost in the old town, riding through streets which were now a foot deep in water, under which lurked manhole-sized holes.

At some stage, as the rain poured relentlessly down, I became aware that the waterproof guarantee on my motorcycle clothing did not extend to Ecuador, and I was soaked to the skin.

Making a mental note to have a word with Mr Dainese and Mr Gericke the next time I saw them, I pulled over, got off the bike and squelched back to Clifford. At least I think it was Clifford. It was raining so hard it was difficult to tell.

'Listen, this is bloody crazy. If we had any sense, we would have got a taxi at the start,' I said.

'If we had any sense, we wouldn't be doing the trip in the first place,' he said. He had a point. 'But you're right. I think it's taxi time.'

I waved down a taxi, and asked the driver to take us to the start of the Pan-American north of town. We followed him around the next corner, and there it was. I looked at my watch. It had been two hours since we rode out of the filling station.

By now it was teatime, but with a good run we could just about make the pleasant northern town of Otavalo, and a guesthouse run by an American couple whose restaurant was allegedly superb. I could almost smell the food when, an hour later, we rounded a corner and ran smack into another roadblock.

Except this time there was going to be no talking our way through it, even with the Very Important Letter. Several cars were burning nicely by the side of the road, there was an angry mood in the air which had not been there further south, and the pleasant captain who came over to talk to us said there was no way we would get through tonight, or even tomorrow.

'However, one of my men will draw you an alternative route,' he said, and an eager-looking private stepped forward, put down his sub-machine gun, seized my notebook and, five minutes of ardent scribbling later, had produced a masterpiece of amateur cartography.

'Splendid. And how long will this take?' I said.

'Oh, at least three hours,' he said airily.

It was no use. That would leave us in Otavalo well after dark, and only the truly suicidal stay on South American roads at night.

'There is a little village down the road,' said the captain helpfully. 'They might have a *hostería*, if you're lucky.'

We turned, and five minutes later were riding through the single street of the *pueblo* he had mentioned, envisaging a fleapit run by a toothless crone. Which just goes to show you what expectations do, for after asking two housewives if there was anywhere to stay, we found ourselves rattling into the courtyard of a perfect little inn. Even better, it had a garden out the back with a pool, and five minutes later there was a blood-curdling scream as Clifford leaped in to discover that at 9,000ft, water is a lot colder than in the Peruvian desert.

Still, never mind. He did turn an interesting shade of blue, and had recovered by the time we had found a little *cantina* down the street serving steak and beer.

That night, looking at the map in bed, I noticed that at some stage in the afternoon we had crossed the Equator, but it had

been raining so hard we had not even seen the 100ft Middle of
the World monolith that marks it.

So if anyone asks you what it's like, you can tell them it's
cold and wet, just like home.

Strange that we hadn't even felt a bump as we crossed it,
mind you.

Still, at least it meant one good thing: the road would be
downhill from here on, I thought as I finally settled down to
sleep at the end of a day in which we had gone looking for
adventure, but it had found us instead.

Only for a dog down the street to start barking. He finally
stopped at 2 a.m., and it must have been, oh, a good hour
before the demented rooster started crowing.

'That bloody thing sounds as if it's right next door,' I
muttered darkly to Clifford at some stage in the night.

That's because it was: in the morning, we crawled outside,
bleary-eyed, to find that in spite of the fact that we were the
only customers, the owner had put us in a room with his pet
cockerel in a cage outside the window.

Still, at least there was some good news: Clifford phoned
home to find that his brother had sold his Enfield to a local
lord, which meant that April was now officially his.

'Yabadabadoo!' he said, whipping off his clothes and
leaping into the frozen pool to celebrate, then giving April a
soggy hug.

Yawning mightily and threatening to run over any roosters
we saw, we set off north with the aid of our hand-drawn
military chart from the day before. Our diversion, in fact,
turned out to be a fine mountain road, soaring and diving
through a sunspilt vista of little villages with cobbled streets,
farmers tilling their fields, young girls leading cows, old dears
sitting on their doorsteps watching the world go by, *caballeros*
on horseback and, once, a finch no bigger than the end of my
little finger, sitting on the road an inch from the front wheel.

It was such a glorious morning, in fact, that I offered up a
little prayer.

Thank you, Lord, I said to the mountains and the clouds and the morning sun warm on my face.

Thank you for this day. And for Pancho. And most of all for my wife, Catherine, whose ring I wear every day to remind me of her.

However, I had, yet again, spoken too soon. Not about Pancho, or Cate, but about the diversion, for when we got to the village of San José de Minas, it transpired that the good citizens had spent so much building a fine church that they had left nothing for the road over the mountain beyond. As a result, it soon disintegrated into the worst yet, with us climbing 10,000ft over cobbles, earth and gravel, then inching our heavily laden bikes down the other side through wet, rutted mud with a drop of hundreds of feet inches to our right.

I don't know what Clifford was thinking, but I was reciting the Shepard's Prayer.

Al Shepard, the early American astronaut, that is, when he said: 'Dear Lord, please don't let me fuck up.'

As indeed two trucks had up ahead, both completely stuck on a steep corner. As I was edging past them a foot from the precipice, a fly flew into my eye, almost sending me hurtling to my death.

'You all right?' said Clifford, getting off the bike and running back as I struggled to stop the bike sliding over the edge.

'I'm fine, I'm fine. A fly just flew into my eye.'

'Which one?'

'I don't know. All those flies look the same to me.'

An hour later, after almost half the day in first gear, we finally reached tarmac again.

'You earned your motorcycling spurs today, Don,' said Clifford as we got off the bikes and wiped the sweat from our brows. 'That was the worst I've ever seen, and that's saying something.'

However, like myself earlier, he had spoken too soon: ten minutes later, the heavens opened, and we pulled into a filling station to change into our wet-weather gear. I touched the front brake, not noticing that there was diesel on the forecourt, and the next thing I knew I was in the rarely used horizontal motorcycling position.

'Only you could ride that road today, then fall over on a flat bit,' laughed Clifford as we hauled Tony upright and I apologised to him.

'Still, no harm done. And thank God that rain didn't come on when we were up the mountain. Nightmare.'

'Rain's too kind a word for it, Pancho,' I said, as we stood and watched cows, horses and houses with entire families inside being washed down the road in front of us. In the circumstances, we had had quite enough for the day, and half an hour later we were checking into the Ali Shungu, Otavalo's finest establishment, run by an American couple called Margaret and Frank.

We handed everything we had that was dirty and wet to them, which was everything we had, for washing, then Clifford went off to look at a local beauty spot with a driver called Fabian. Fabian was driving an old banger because the week before he had been driving back from Quito in his brand-new car, and had stopped to give two well-dressed young men a lift. One of them had offered him a soft drink, and the next thing he knew, he was waking up twenty hours later in the ditch with the car gone.

'Yip, it's the Wild West out here,' said Margaret as we watched them drive off. 'Last year some rustlers stole four of our horses, and when some of our staff went to get them back, they got shot at. Still, could be worse. We could live in Colombia.'

I hadn't the heart to tell her that was where we would be in two days.

In the evening Clifford returned, and we had dinner with the only other resident, a gay judge from Toronto.

In the morning, several opinions reached us as to the state of the Pan-Am:

a) It was blocked until the afternoon.

b) It was blocked until hell froze over.

c) A fish.

However, c) turned out to be the opinion of the town surrealist, and was discounted.

In the meantime, we went for a walk to the local market, a famous affair to which people flock from all over the country to buy the fabrics and crafts for which the Otavalo natives have been renowned for centuries. When they're not blocking roads, that is.

Even on a weekday, the market was a tranquil riot of colour, so that we wandered around in a daze and emerged some time later clutching assorted wall hangings, shawls, hats and bracelets with no idea whatsoever how we would carry them on the bikes.

We arrived back at the Ali Shungu to find the news that the Pan-Am to the north was open again, and after a spot of judicious repacking, set off with that familiar feeling, half excited, half nervous, of leaving a safe haven for the unknown, in this case the dangers of northern Ecuador and southern Colombia, which the Foreign Office had specifically warned us not to go into.

However, all was peaceful and still as we rode through the mountains, past pastures being tilled by the descendants of the Negro slaves brought here by the Spanish.

Once, rather wonderfully, we passed an Anti-Stress Centre, presumably for anyone who had been talking to the Foreign Office. Even more wonderfully, when we stopped half an hour from the border at a hillside café for coffee, the mugs depicted Santa, Rudolph *et al.* dashing across a snowy landscape.

As I sat looking out across the rolling hills, carefully tended meadows, blue sky and fluffy clouds, I thought that you would need to have a very bad government indeed to make a mess of a country like this.

Unfortunately, Ecuador had had several: like most of the countries in South America, its history had been one of leaders as bad as the people were good. Not only had they failed to capitalise on a potentially stunning eco-tourism destination in the way that, say, Costa Rica had, but the current lot had signed a deal with the US to exploit the national oil reserves which meant only 20 per cent of the profits staying in the country. When the oil ran out in ten years, there would be nothing but a very uncertain future for a population who deserved much better.

By the middle of the afternoon we were in Tulcán, described by the guidebook as an edgy, dangerous border town.

And indeed, within minutes of arriving, I had been mugged and Clifford had been kidnapped.

Fortunately, it was me who had mugged myself: counting our dollars in the hotel room, I had then left them there and gone off to phone home from a *cabina telefónica*.

When it came to pay the bill, I had to leave Clifford as a hostage while I went back to the hotel to recover the $5 necessary to free the Ecuador One.

To celebrate his release, we found a motorcycle shop, in which Clifford bought an Ecuador sticker for April and I splashed out on a Castrol one for Tony for no other reason than that it reminded me of the metal sign which had once turned in the wind outside my dad's old motorcycle garage.

All stickered up, we explored the town's only other attractions, which seemed to consist of a topiary garden, 4,836 moneychangers and a shop selling nothing but air compressors and giant bottles of Grant's whisky.

In a little church, Clifford lit two candles for our safe passage over the next few days.

And then we had some supper and a beer and went to bed early, for tomorrow we would rise at dawn and ride across the border into the most dangerous part of one of the most dangerous countries on earth.

'Ouch, that hurt.' Geoff after the crash in southern Colombia, on the most dangerous part of the whole route.

12

'Don't go to Colombia.'

'For all reasons, Colombia is nearly every traveller's favourite country. The people deserve top awards for warmth and hospitality. Just lean back, relax and enjoy the merengue beat.'

A short history of Colombia

Pre-1525
Assorted tribes live happily in valleys and cloud forests.

1525
Spanish arrive. Happiness abolished. Spanish spend years searching in vain for mythical city of El Dorado.

1819
Simón Bolívar liberates country and creates republic of Gran Colombia, including also Venezuela, Ecuador and Panama. Within ten years, Venezuela and Ecuador secede, leaving Colombia not so Gran.

1830

Bolívar dies, plunging republic into seventy years of civil war. In ensuing chaos, Panama tiptoes out the back door.

1903–1948

Country pulls socks up and gets down to work producing coffee. Prosperity arrives, and happiness makes brief reappearance.

1948–present

Working-class demands for more pay lead to riots. Riots lead to La Violencia, a decade which leaves 300,000 dead and leads to rise of left-wing guerrilla groups such as FARC, ELN, M-19 and others, run by teenagers awash with cocaine and hormones and carrying Kalashnikovs. Opposing them are private right-wing armies protecting landowners. In middle is government, wishing it was running Switzerland.

At six in the morning, we were woken by an ice-cream van trundling through the square playing 'Rudolph the Red-Nosed Reindeer'. Northern Ecuador, it seemed, was obsessed with Santa.

At the border, the beautiful old customs post which Lanks and Pleiss had passed was abandoned and sleeping by a river. Still, at least they had made good use of the forecourt: the Colombians had built a volleyball court on it.

As for the border itself, it was as seamless as the previous one had been chaotic.

With a calmness of spirit which was probably both necessary and entirely inappropriate, we entered the murder, kidnapping and drugs capital of the world. Only the next few days would tell which of the two heroes of its most famous novel, *One Hundred Years of Solitude*, we would become: Arcadio, the one who died, or Aureliano, the one they could not kill.

'Is the Pan-American safe to the north?' I asked the border guard just before we got on the bikes.

He looked up the road, and shrugged.

'It is never safe. It may be all right in daylight, but never at night. Whatever you do, you must get to Cali before dark,' he said.

I looked at my watch. If we pushed on, we might just make it.

'May God go with you,' said the guard, handing back my passport.

I swallowed hard, and started the engine.

As we wound north through a scene of mountains, rivers and waterfalls, it was like being in a Lake District which had been taken over by an armed drugs cartel.

Actually, that's something the National Trust might like to consider. It would certainly make fund-raising a lot easier, although they would need a complete new set of wheelie bins, marked Glass, Paper and Bodies With Bits Missing.

From time to time, we were stopped by Colombian soldiers, which was good news, for if they were about, the guerrillas usually weren't. They all looked like schoolboys, albeit with machine guns, and had the usual questions. Were we mad? Was it cold in Alaska?

Yes, we said in answer to both, and rode on up a road which when Lanks travelled it in 1942 was one way one day, and the other the next. Even more archaically, at junctions you stopped and hooted once for straight on, twice for turning right and three times for left.

At lunchtime, we stopped for a coffee at a mountain café, and got talking to an old man about the world's perception of Colombia.

'Ah, don't believe everything you read in the papers, señor,' he said.

'I know. I'm from Belfast,' I said. And write the papers, I thought.

We got back on the bikes, and sped on, since it was already early afternoon, and it was crucial that we make Cali before dark. As we rode north for mile after mile, spurning rest in favour of speed, I thought that we had not seen a single drugs baron, guerrilla or assassin, and we had not been kidnapped or murdered once. It looked like it was going to be one of those rare days when I was glad that nothing exciting happened.

Little did I know that I was only seconds away from disaster.

Sweeping downhill into the next bend, I suddenly realised with a cold shock of horror that I was going a little too fast, then braked a little too late.

I may have hit gravel or a patch of slippery road, but the next thing I knew, I was bouncing down the road with my head banging rhythmically off the tarmac.

Thankfully, it was in a helmet, and the rest of me was still in my protective jacket and trousers, though Clifford had taken his off in the humid heat of late afternoon. If I had taken mine off, as I had been planning to the next time we stopped, if there had been a truck coming the other way, if the bike had landed on top of me or if there had been something in my path more solid than the ditch, my life would have ended there and then.

Even as it was, the damage, as I got groggily to my feet, was considerable: my left shoulder was in agony, and most of the skin had been stripped off my left elbow and forearm. On my right hand, the bones of my knuckles gleamed through the blood and bits of tattered flesh.

A few yards back, Tony was lying in the ditch with oil pouring from the engine, the forks twisted and the front fairing bent completely out of shape. Behind him lay a trail of wreckage and luggage, including the panniers and top box, which had been torn off by the impact.

As I sat down on the verge with my head in my hands, bleeding and heartbroken that tiredness and a moment's lapse of concentration had put an end to two years of planning and the adventure of a lifetime, Clifford got off his bike and came running up.

'Jesus, man, are you all right? Are you all right?' he said, his face a rare mask of worry.

'I'm so sorry, Pancho. I'm so sorry,' I said, my head in my hands.

'Never mind that. Bloody hell, look at that arm. We'd better get that dressed.'

'What about the bike?'

'Never mind the bike. The bike's fucked.'

He walked back down the road to retrieve the medical kit from the trail of wreckage, and had just finished bandaging my arm when the first of several drivers stopped to see if we were all right. One of them phoned the police on his mobile, and within ten minutes a dozen motorcycle cops armed with machine guns arrived just as a man in a truck stopped to see if he could help.

'Is there any chance of taking the bike in the truck to Cali?' said Clifford.

'Of course,' he said, without even raising the subject of money, although Cali was still hundreds of miles away.

The policemen put down their guns and hoisted the stricken Triumph into the back, followed by the wreckage. I climbed stiffly in behind, and we set off.

For hour upon hour we hurtled north at the insane speed typical of Colombian drivers, with even Clifford, a former racing champion, struggling to keep up. In the back of the truck, sitting in a pool of blood and oil, I gave up trying to find a way to sit or lie free of pain, and looked out at a landscape which was growing increasingly sub-tropical, and in which surreal tableaux presented themselves from time to time.

Once, a man sitting on a motorcycle outside his house being looked at sternly by his wife, one hand on her hip and the other holding aloft a fruit pie.

And once, a house which seemed to be populated entirely by goats, peering out of doors and upstairs windows with not a human owner in sight.

In spite of all our earlier efforts not to be on this road at night, it grew dark, and I watched with despair as the silhouette of Clifford and bike became only a flickering headlight. It was gone nine by the time we got to Cali and at long last found the home of Emilia, the Argentinian pastor who was our contact in the city.

'Thank God,' said Clifford, climbing wearily off his bike and going to ring the doorbell.

Only for a neighbour to open a window and shout down that Emilia had moved to a room in the church she was building in another part of the city. Then, in the umpteenth act of kindness we had been shown that day, another neighbour saw us standing outside and came out with his mobile phone and her new address. Half an hour later we were there, and Emilia came out to meet us, looking with her gold-rimmed spectacles and grey hair in a bun like everyone's favourite granny, and surrounded by other members of the church who had waited for us.

'Oh, you poor dears. Come in, come in, and don't worry about a thing,' said Emilia.

'We know a bike mechanic, a doctor, a tailor who can repair those clothes and the perfect ointment for those wounds,' said another.

We had, it seemed, landed among the most caring and competent women in Colombia. They rounded up some neighbours to lift Tony down from the truck, and both bikes were locked in the basement garage, where they would be guarded all night by the gatekeeper. We handed our endlessly patient truck driver a well-earned $100, and made our way up the stairs to the room Emilia had prepared for us.

I sat painfully on the bed, and immediately felt faint and nauseous.

'You OK, Don?' said Clifford.

'Aye, it's just a bit of shock,' I said, and promptly threw up in the sink.

'I think you should be in hospital, man.'

'No, really, it's just shock. I feel better after throwing up.'

He looked at me, his face a mask of concern.

'Actually, you have a point. You're talking as much shite after the crash as you were before, so there can't be any brain damage. Right, let's get this gear off you and see how bad the damage is.'

'Bloody hell, you did a job all right, Don,' he said when I had finally struggled out of my shredded and bloodstained clothes.

He wasn't wrong: apart from the injuries we already knew about, I had taken the skin off both hips, my right buttock and both knees.

'What a mess,' said Clifford as he covered the wounds with Emilia's miracle cream. 'Still, thank God you had the jacket on. Thank God there was nothing coming the other way, you didn't slide into anything and the bike didn't land on top of you. Thank God you're alive, in fact.'

We climbed into our beds and switched off the light.

'Pancho,' I said, 'do you think there's any chance the bike can be fixed?'

It was a lifetime of seconds before he answered.

'Well, I had a good look at it after we got it off the truck, and it's maybe not as bad as it looks. Maybe. If we can get that cover welded where it's leaking oil and get the forks straightened, we might get it sorted. We'll phone the local bike shop and see what they think tomorrow. And listen, don't worry about coming off the bike. We've all done it. Bloody hell, I used to do it every weekend.'

He fell asleep, and I lay awake in the darkness, my mind feeling as full of guilt and regret as Paddy Minne's after he hit the sheep.

And my body feeling like the sheep.

I woke the next morning, and for a dreadful moment thought I was paralysed. Then I realised I had bled so much in the night that I had stuck to the sheets. Making a note to set some money aside for Emilia's laundry bill, I hobbled downstairs and found her already on the phone to the local bike shop asking them to send a mechanic around.

He arrived at ten, and introduced himself politely. He was called Diego, as in Maradona, and was just as good with his hands. Within half an hour of arriving, he had the front end of

Tony stripped down, and we could get a good look at the damage. The forks were twisted, all right, but could be straightened. The front fairing and the frame holding the instrument panel were badly twisted and smashed, but could also be straightened. More serious was the aluminium plate covering the engine generator, which was badly cracked.

'Mmm, that's a tricky weld,' said Clifford. 'Might be no harm phoning Triumph and seeing if they can ship us some parts.'

Diego went off with a cardboard box full of shattered motorcycle parts, and I called Triumph UK, only to get the splendidly British answer that it was five on Friday afternoon there, and the parts department had gone home for the weekend. I called the parts department in Triumph USA, and got an answering machine. Then I called the nearest dealer, in San Diego, and they said they didn't ship outside the US because it was too complicated, what with all the forms and stuff.

Ho hum. It looked like we were on our own, and would have to make do with repairs until we got to San Diego.

'We'll manage. The worst that can happen is that it'll leak a bit of oil. It'll be just like riding an Enfield again,' said Clifford as Emilia appeared to give us a tour of the church she was building as part of the rambling edifice we were staying in.

Inside, workmen were cutting and bending fifty-year-old bamboo for a roof which was a sinuous harmony of curves, and others were preparing the mixture for the walls of bamboo, fibre and mud, which was basically the same as medieval European daub and wattle.

'Brilliant,' said Clifford as Emilia went off to prepare lunch. 'The only bad news is that we can't really bring beer into a building with a church in it.'

Beerless but impressed, we returned to our eyrie, a white cell in the attic complete with several resident cockroaches of impressive girth. One was relaxing by the sink from which I had just rescued him, an adventurous one was making his way across the ceiling, and another was halfway up the wall, not sure whether he was coming or going, a bit like the small dog in Puerto Montt.

'Here, Pancho,' I said, 'it says in the guidebook that Cali is famous for salsa and beautiful women.'

Inspired, I limped to the nearest shop, bought some salsa sauce from a beautiful woman, and came back to make a nice sausage and pasta casserole. As I unpacked the shopping, I noticed that the brand name on the sauce was PanAmericana. A good omen, but not as good as the news Clifford came through the door with.

'Emilia says no problem with beer, so I've sent the gatekeeper out for some,' he said.

Splendid, I thought as half an hour later we sat down to supper.

Near-death experiences are a lot easier to deal with if you can have a beer afterwards.

In the morning, Maria the tailor came to collect my shredded bag, jacket and trousers, to see if she could use the first to repair the other two. Next came Hidalgo the carpenter to take the measurements of my folding keyboard, which had stopped folding after the crash, so that he could make a bespoke box to protect it.

In the meantime, Emilia's ointment was working miracles on my tattered skin. My arm and hips still looked gruesome, but I was already developing scabs on my knees which any five-year-old would be proud of.

In the afternoon, we went out to find a new bag and buy some food in a supermarket nearby, rediscovering the small pleasures of the domesticated male, like finding where they kept the extra-virgin olive oil. Clifford turned out to be a random shopper, buying things he liked the look of and reckoning he would find a way to fit them together when he got home, whereas I was already planning dinner menus for the four or five days we were going to be there.

Heavens, we could even have what was left of the Escobar family over and ask them if they preferred wine or Coke with their meal, to hearty laughter all round.

'Hey Pancho, how do you fancy nice fresh green pasta with chorizo, Portobello mushrooms, anchovies and olives?' I said.

'Apart from the fact that I hate chorizo, anchovies and olives, it sounds fantastic,' he said, going off to take a photo of the checkout girl for his collection, then buy a watermelon for no other reason than that it was on special offer.

'Look, a real coffee shop!' he said as we emerged from the supermarket, passing a security guard who was no different from your normal supermarket security guard apart from the gun. Just in case anyone tried to sneak out with a special-offer watermelon down their trousers.

'It seems remarkable,' I said as we sat down to our first decent cup of coffee since entering Colombia, 'in a country which produces the finest coffee in the world, although don't say that in Brazil, Costa Rica or Jamaica if you value your nuts, that if you stride manfully into a café, sit down and say with gay abandon *"Perdón, camarero. Quisiera un café con leche, por favor"*, you are served, virtually without fail, a concoction which tastes like bogwater that has been strained through Ewan McGregor's jockstrap.'

'Listen,' said Clifford, admiring with satisfaction his photograph of the checkout girl, 'if that's the worst thing that happens to us in Colombia, we'll be all right.'

'You're right. And I will try to stay on the bike in future,' I said, looking gloomily at my arm, which now resembled a left-over special-effects limb from *Creature from the Black Lagoon*.

'Right,' he said, 'I'm going to tell you about every accident I've had.'

By the time he got to number 15, I was feeling slightly better.

We walked home, and he went out with Enrique the architect to the local Waldorf school, where I imagine children learn how to make salads and run hotels, then came back in the evening and went out to a salsa club, having discovered that the salsa I had produced last night was only a sauce.

'Oh, I've told Emilia we'll do some nosh for after Sunday

service tomorrow, then give a wee talk,' he said as he sailed out the door.

As for me, I was suddenly, utterly exhausted, even though it was only teatime. I climbed into bed and opened the guidebook at random at the page on crime. Every year, it said, there were 28,000 murders in Colombia, or three every hour, and 3,000 kidnappings.

Making a mental note to stop reading guidebooks, I fell asleep and slept right through to the next day.

We found ourselves up at dawn, feeling like two Church of Ireland farmers' wives as we made canapés for the after-service buffet.

'This was all your idea, Pancho,' I said as I trimmed the crust of my 400th triangular ham, cheese and tomato open sandwich.

'I know,' he muttered darkly, arranging several slices of special-offer melon into an artistic fan.

After the service, we sat in front of the assembled congregation and he gave a talk on the Camphill communities and lyre making.

'The lyre is a wonderful instrument. Even an idiot can play it,' he said, then handed it to me to prove his point.

'Bastard,' I muttered as loudly as you can in a church.

Astonishingly, after a moment of blind panic and several seconds of frantic fumbling, I amazed myself, and everyone present, by producing the first few bars of 'Auld Lang Syne', that authentic tribute to Scottish gibberish. Perhaps I was the world's oldest musical child prodigy, and should give up the day job to become the Mozart of the twenty-first century, except without the flatulence.

Or, even better, the world head of marketing for Emilia's miracle healing cream, since the husband and wife team who made it were here and had just presented me with another tub.

In the meantime, though, I gave a talk on my life as a motorcycle adventurer, right up to the point where I became a falling-off-motorcycles adventurer. Everyone looked fascinated, although possibly only because, as I discovered later, after washing a T-shirt earlier, I had carelessly rested it on my lap for a few moments, leaving a large damp patch on my crotch.

Still, at least I managed to embarrass Clifford by telling everyone about the time he had phoned me to ask if he could come on the trip, then added: 'I'm not gay, I just want an adventure.' He went a very fetching shade of pink, set off beautifully by the lilac wall behind him, and whispered under his breath that I would pay for this.

He was almost certainly right, but fortunately at that moment he was kidnapped for the second time in a week, this time by several attractive young women who wanted him to tell them more about lyres. Obviously spotting the chance to add to his photo collection, he seized his camera and left, saying that he would be back in an hour or so.

Knowing him well enough by now to know that this meant he would be gone for most of the day, I climbed the stairs to our eyrie, still feeling sore and woozy, and spent the afternoon reading through my early research notes for the trip. This made me so excited about the whole venture again that I could hardly wait to rush downstairs, leap on a battle-scarred Tony and roar north. But I was in no fit state for rushing, and Tony would be in no fit state for roaring for at least three days, particularly since this was a weekend and tomorrow was a public holiday.

At six, Clifford returned.

'Bloody hell, I've just been talking to a woman who's had five of her family kidnapped and says the road from Medellín to Cartagena is as dangerous as the one from Ecuador to Cali,' he said. 'But the good news is we're going salsa dancing with the church ladies, so get your trousers on.'

'Dancing?' I groaned. 'But I can hardly walk.'

Seven of us piled into a taxi, including Jhoana from Hanover, who had that afternoon moved into the room next door to our rooftop sanctuary. Obsessed by Iceland from the age of eight, she had gone there a week after graduation and spent a year helping to build a farm and learning fluent

148

Icelandic. She had then trained as a midwife, and was now learning Spanish and studying to be a priest.

She was twenty-five.

We decamped into a dim basement in which a crowd of people were flinging their partners around the room with passionate detachment, the hips of the young ones rehearsing for later that night, and the older ones echoing what they used to do.

The waiter, rather than asking us what we wanted to drink, plonked on the table a bottle of *aguardiente*, the national hooch, which was like Pernod on steroids. Clifford, naturally, danced with all the women in the room and proposed to half of them, while I discovered that the more *aguardiente* I drank, the more my aches and pains melted away, and the better my salsa dancing got.

As we all fell into the taxi back to the church, I thought back over the last few days.

Two near-death experiences, dinner with a gay judge and salsa dancing with a trainee priest. As weeks go, it had been a week and a half, or possibly even five-eighths.

At noon the next day, we walked around the corner to the friendly neighbourhood X-ray clinic to see why my neck was still sore five days after the crash. He did my shoulder first, and the good news was that nothing was broken, but as he hung up the first plate of my neck, my heart missed a beat.

For there, right across the third vertebra down, was a definite line.

He looked at it, tutted and scratched his chin, then left the room. He had obviously gone to get a spinal injuries consultant, and my mind ran wild. I had a hairline fracture, but could go on carefully. Or I would have to get treatment here, but it could take weeks or months. Or we would have to fly home, leave the bikes and gear here, and continue the trip in the summer, or next year. Or I was destined to spend the rest of my life in a wheelchair, or an iron lung. If they still had iron lungs.

All this in the couple of seconds before he came back in and said: 'Funny mark on the plate that, isn't it? I'll do another one.'

On the next one, of course, there was nothing.

That's the problem with having an imagination, I thought as I paid the bill. When it's positive, it makes great stories. When it's not, it gives you nightmares.

'Don't worry,' said Clifford as we walked back to the church, 'every time I get a headache, I think I've a brain tumour.'

Feeling relieved but still woozy, I took to my sick bed to read Emilia's copy of M. Scott Peck's *The Road Less Travelled*.

'As we negotiate the curves and corners of our lives, we must continually give up parts of ourselves,' it said on page 69.

You don't know the half of it, Scott, I thought, looking at my arm, which now resembled a crust of cooling lava.

At this point, Clifford came in with a cup of tea and announced that we had run out of food and had to go shopping.

'Can't, Pancho. I'm enjoying this chapter on delayed gratification too much,' I said.

Laugh? I thought he'd never start.

At two, Tracey, a volunteer from Australia, arrived for choir practice.

'Hey, I was just sitting outside this café when a guy came out and shot another one dead,' she said.

'Clifford, are you sure it's safe to go shopping?' I said. 'Or even outside the house?'

'I don't care,' he said. 'I'm going salsa dancing again tonight even if it kills me.'

At three, Georg the doctor came, clicked and popped a few vertebrae, said I would live to ride another day, and wouldn't take a penny. At four, Monica from Triumph USA rang to say she was sorry she'd missed my call, but that they would do anything they could to help at any time. At half past, it was the turn of Hidalgo the carpenter, who arrived with a beautiful cedar box he had made for my keyboard. He said he wanted no payment, but I gave him the equivalent of a tenner. Then, at seven, Katia the acupuncturist came to work on my shoulder, and also refused payment.

After the dark day of the disaster, the forces of good were gathering again.

Clifford, in the meantime, had been kidnapped yet again – would the boy never learn? – this time by another group of church ladies who wanted to know how to build lyres. He returned after several hours too knackered to fulfil his salsa-dancing ambitions, so we went out with Jhoana for beer and pizza instead, returning neither shot nor kidnapped.

Which is always a good thing in Colombia, as my granny was so fond of saying of an evening.

Although only after she'd finished her nuclear warhead quota, of course.

After breakfast, the city paper and radio station came around to interview us about our grand adventure, and its temporary derailment.

As someone who spent most of his working life interviewing people who did interesting things, it felt both strange and familiar to be on the receiving end, and to shake hands with journalists knowing that they would go back to city council meetings, and we would get on motorbikes and ride to Alaska.

Mind you, that depended on Diego. He had said he would arrive at eight, but turned up at noon with his boss, Hector. A flexible attitude to appointments is, of course, entirely common in Latin America: one of the many legacies of colonialism, along with wine, dancing with handkerchiefs, bullfighting and Churrigueresque architecture, which makes baroque look positively minimalist.

Fortunately, his welding was better than his timekeeping, for he produced the engine cover plate looking as good as new, not to mention a hand-made gasket, bolted it on, filled the engine with oil, reconnected the electrics and pressed the starter button.

Nothing happened.

Not for the first time on the trip, I felt the world turn upside down and lodge in my throat.

He switched around a few electrical wires, and tried again. Still nothing. He switched them back, and stood there scratching his chin.

Then I remembered. On Tigers, you need to engage the clutch before the engine will start. It had caught me out the first time I had ridden one too. I told him, and he tried again. After a couple of turns, the engine sang again, and my heart with it.

Diego grinned, and Hector said something to Emilia.

'The bad news is he says it won't be ready for two days,' said Emilia, but I didn't care. The journey would continue, and that was all that mattered. I spent the whole afternoon lying on the bed reading, a luxury almost unknown since childhood.

The book was still *The Road Less Travelled*, and the chapters the ones on leading a charmed life, and serendipity. For someone who had fallen off a motorbike at 60mph and was lucky to be alive, then ended up in the only place which could put body, soul and motorbike back together again, not to mention giving Clifford new inspiration for his spiritual life, they were particularly apposite.

Not that it stopped him going out that evening on a hot date with Sonia, a leggy and stunning black divorcee he'd met at our salsa night, mind you. I could tell he meant business, for he even changed his underwear. Since she spoke as little English as he spoke Spanish, he left at six armed with a phrasebook as his only chart to guide him through the straits and shallows of the night.

As for me, I was happy to read, cook some supper, have a beer, note with interest the progress of my arm, which now resembled pepperoni pizza, and wait for Maria the tailor, who came in the terracotta dusk with my jacket and trousers, repaired with bits of bag. They looked like Joseph's Amazing Technicolor Dreamcoat, except without the Technicolor.

But the dream was still there.

Part of that dream, of course, was called Alaska or bust.

But part of it was also to be found in the words of the seventeenth-century Japanese haiku poet Matsuo Basho, when he said that the journey itself was home. And he was a man who knew what he was talking about, since he once walked half the length of Japan because he had heard that the women in Honshu were the most beautiful in the country.

It was a motive Clifford would have approved of, I thought as I climbed the bamboo steps to the flat roof in the humid night, and watched an electrical storm gathering over the mountains. Before long, lightning split the sky and thunder rattled the window-frames, and then the rain came, a blessing on the faces of rich man and beggar, drug dealer and addict, murderer and victim alike.

I stood there, the warm benediction washing over my own face and wounds, and felt calm and at peace with the world, for the first time in a long time.

At midnight, Clifford returned home, threw the phrasebook on the bed, and threw himself after it.

'I think I'm in love,' he said, and promptly fell asleep.

We woke to find that we had accidentally become famous.

The city paper had run our story on the cover and devoted almost an entire inside page to us, with photographs, maps and extensive quotes.

'Here, Pancho, your Spanish is getting a lot better,' I said, reading through the things Clifford didn't know he'd said.

As a result of the splash, the doorbell and phone rang all day with a stream of national magazines, newspapers, and TV and radio stations looking for interviews. We had, in spite of ourselves, become Ewan McGregor and Charley Boorman, except without the moaning and farting.

Well, the moaning, anyway.

'It's amazing,' said Clifford as we had a cup of tea in the twenty-eight seconds between one film crew trooping out the door and the next one arriving, 'we've been on the road for over a month and had some fair traumas already, yet we haven't fallen out once. If I was gay and not madly in love with Sonia, I might even propose to you.'

'Too late, Pancho, I'm already spoken for,' I said, waving my wedding ring in the air and noticing that the crash had knocked two tiny chips out of the rim.

Still, it would be a lifetime reminder to me to go around corners more carefully.

Talking of which, I would pretty soon have to get my head around the fact that in a couple of days I would be climbing back on the bike and trying to stay alive among some of the worst drivers and most dangerous guerrillas on earth.

As opposed to the really nice guerrillas of, say, Surrey, for example.

Even in the few days we had been here in this haven, it had become normal to wake every day in the same bed, so that getting up and riding hundreds of miles on a motorbike seemed like something we used to do. I knew, of course, from previous experience that within a few days of getting back on the road, that rootless, vagabond existence would seem perfectly normal too.

As it did not, for example, for the ant which was wandering across the page of the copy of *Moby-Dick* I was reading. I had picked it up from the bedside table across which he and his mates had been marching earnestly, leaving him as lost as St John of the Cross, the thirteenth-century Spanish mystic who in *The Long Dark Night of the Soul* described the experience of purgatory as like wandering around in the dark, not knowing whether you were stumbling towards the light or away from it. Setting the book carefully back on the table, I let him rejoin his marching colleagues, since purgatory was a bit too much of a burden for such a small ant, no matter how earnest he was.

Splendid. Ant saved, we set off in a taxi for another TV studio, then returned to find that Sonia had invited us over for dinner. In the garden apartment she shared with her two leggy children, we ate potatoes, meat and veg and drank sherry. It only lacked a priest in the corner to turn it into an Irish social evening.

She was so tall, dark and charming that it was easy to see why Clifford had fallen head over heels for her. As opposed to me, who had just fallen head over heels. We took a taxi back through the hot, damp night. Like all Cali taxi rides with a driver who treated the experience as a video game, it was another near-death experience, but I was getting used to them by now.

'Here,' said Clifford as we were climbing into bed, 'if we're turning into Ewan and Charley, you'd better be Ewan.'

'OK,' I said, 'here goes: God, I don't know how we're going to get through this trip with only an unlimited budget, free bikes, huge research and back-up team, two support vehicles, satellite phones and a BMW service crew every five miles. Not to mention having to sign autographs for ignorant peasants in Baluchibackwardstan, or wherever it is we are. Actually, I haven't a clue where we are, since I never bothered to find out. Still, never mind. I'll just make an inane comment about it, then giggle like a sixteen-year-old and burst into tears because I'm missing home so much and it's so hard being rich and famous.'

I paused for breath.

'Right, now you be Charley.'

Clifford farted, and went to sleep.

When he woke, the first words he said were, naturally enough: 'I dreamed George Bush's wife found me in bed with their daughter.'

'What happened?'

'I got kicked out of the White House. Then I discovered a plot to kidnap the president, but no one would listen to me.'

'They were probably hoping it succeeded,' I said.

At eight we were called out for yet another photocall, and immediately set upon by a plague of bloodsucking flies which within thirty seconds had turned what skin I had left into a landscape of blotchy weals. So the next time someone starts telling you about the idyllic tropics, give them a dig in the dongles for me.

For the rest of the day, in spite of the application of several layers of Emilia's miracle cream, Clifford's tiger balm, antihistamine lotion and Crimean sump oil, it took the will of a Shaolin monk trained in the black arts of origami and ikebana not to scratch. Great Zen training, adventures, I thought as I tried for the 4,386th time that day to think of something else.

Fortunately, I was given something else to think about, when the bike shop called at four to say the Triumph would be ready at five.

Clifford, who had recovered from the confusion of having a Bush and a bird in the hand at the same time, and had spent the day teaching the carpenter to make lyres, returned half an hour later.

'Nothing I can teach him. He's better than I'll ever be,' he said.

We piled into a taxi and drove through yet another tropical downpour to the bike shop, which was called Supercali, as in fragilisticexpialidocious.

And there, sitting outside, was a reborn Tony.

They hadn't been able to reattach the sheared left mirror, but everything else was an astonishing job. They'd even re-assembled the several shattered and twisted pieces of the headlight fairing and resprayed it to look like new.

'Incredible,' said Clifford, walking around the bike. 'Absolutely incredible. Wonder what the bill's going to be for this lot. Bound to be at least 400 quid.'

It was, in fact, about 70.

'Incredible,' said Clifford again. 'I would have charged you 500.'

'Aye, but that's because you're a tight Scots git,' I said, putting my helmet on the right way round and climbing on the bike wondering just how nervous I would feel not only riding it, but riding it back home through the nightmare of Cali rush-hour traffic.

Not one bit, was the answer. It felt good to be back in the saddle.

I parked Tony back in the garage, switched the engine off with a sigh of relief, and gave him a little hug when no one was looking. I know he's a British chap, but there are times when a little emotion is not inappropriate.

Clifford went out for a last date with Sonia, and I set to tidying our attic sanctuary with mixed feelings. It had been a blessing for us, this past week of recovery and repair, but it would be good to be back on the road again, heading north with my shredded skin held together by Emilia's miracle cream, and my matching nerves held together by the gaffer tape of hope and the bungee cords of optimism.

I had a beer, packed my new bag and went to bed early before I became the first person in the world to die of terminal metaphoritis.

Early the next morning, I felt like my grandfather, Edward the butler, as I climbed the three flights of stairs from the pantry to our eyrie with the breakfast things. It was, then, rather appropriate that soon after we said a sad farewell to Emilia, who had become our favourite granny in the past week. Not to mention Jhoana, the farm-building midwife and putative priest who was already fluent in five languages and would almost certainly be the first female Pope by the time she was forty.

Outside, apart from the torrential rain, lunatic traffic and bottomless potholes, it was a perfect reintroduction for me to the gentlemanly art of motorcycling. Not that you could see the potholes, mind you, since the streets were submerged under a foot of water.

Still, after an hour the rain stopped, the road cleared and our spirits lifted as we rode through a landscape very like Wicklow: misty hills in the distance, cows grazing in lush fields, priests trotting to and fro with bottles of holy water or whiskey, depending on their disposition, and friendly policemen stopping us for no other reason than a natter.

'It's funny,' said Clifford as we stopped for yet another cup of dreadful coffee – according to Emilia, the reason was that they exported all the good stuff – 'but I've lost all the nervousness I ever had about Colombia. I'm sure there are bandits about, but the people are just great. Especially Sonia. What a woman. A true meeting of hearts, that.'

He had returned from his date with her the previous night at the very respectable hour of one in the morning, after an evening of dinner and salsa, and announced that they had fallen irretrievably in love with each other and he would be getting the first flight south to Cali from Deadhorse as soon as we got there, or if not the first flight from Kilkeel as soon as he got back home and worked up some holidays.

Splendid. In the meantime, we got back on the bikes and I followed him north through the dappled shade of umbrella trees.

It was one of those days that made you glad to be half-alive, even if I was, not surprisingly, hypersensitive to every imagined unusual sound from the bike, in the manner of pilots who listen with a keen ear to their engines over oceans, or nuns who have been too long at sea.

'I'm getting a strange whining sound from Tony,' I said when we stopped a couple of hours later at a little café beside a water meadow over which swallows swooped and dipped. Just in case we really did start thinking we were in Wicklow, the racket from the squadron of cicadas in the bamboo grove on the other side reminded us that we were in the tropics.

'What does it sound like?' said Clifford, sucking a soft drink called Colombiana through a straw, since we had been too fearful of the consequences of asking for Coke.

I thought for a moment.

'It sounds like the sort of whine you get from the transmission of a truck,' I said.

'It's probably a truck, then,' he said.

He was, of course, right. When there weren't any trucks around, the sound mysteriously vanished.

By late afternoon we were in the pleasant mountain town of Santa Rosa de Cabal, centred around a twin-spired icing-cake church and surrounded by coffee plantations.

As we got off the bikes in the square to ask directions, we were immediately mobbed by people who were either mentally deranged, on helium or both. It was like arriving at a convention of mildly psychotic Donald Ducks.

As we were trying in vain to make sense of them, a man wearing sunglasses leaned out of a passing car.

'Do not stay here. It is too dangerous,' he said.

Now, when the locals tell you, they usually mean it, so we gave up and hailed a taxi to lead us to La Finca, a ranch-style hotel in the hills out of town. We found it up a muddy track, parked the bikes on the patio, and wandered inside to find the vast place empty apart from us and the manager.

'Do you have a room free?' I said.

'We have all of them free,' he said.

'And do you have food and beer?'

'Lots of both,' he laughed.

'That's good enough for me,' I said, taking off my jacket to find that it had rubbed all the new skin from my left forearm, and I was back to square one. No wonder it had been stinging like buggery all afternoon.

Still, I had ridden 150 miles today and not fallen off once, which was more than I could say for the same day a week ago. It was strange, I thought, going to bed that night anaesthetised by beer and covered in Emilia's miracle cream: when we were off the road, it was as if we had never been on it, and now that we were back on it, it was as if we had never been off it.

Funny the way motorbikes get in your blood, as my dear old dad would say. Or did he say the way the blood got all over the motorbikes?

Then, at breakfast, I finally overcame the orphan problem.

You see, the Spanish word for orphans is *huérfanos*, three little syllables which you would think would be the easiest thing in the world to pronounce. And yet getting the emphasis and intonation right had proved as impossible as the time I attempted to say 'Bad cat!' in Cantonese to impress a Chinese friend and declared instead that the kitchen had exploded.

On every single day of the trip so far, I had attempted to explain to anyone who had asked why we were doing it:

a) We were mad.

b) It was for a newspaper series, book and interactive video game which would, I hoped, outsell even *The Pop-Up Joy of Sex*.

c) It was raising money for, as I put it: '*SOS, una sociedad benéfica por huérfanos*'.

At this point, whoever I was talking to would adopt a by now familiar blank expression.

'*¿Huérfanos?*' I would go on. '*¿Niños sin madre o padre?*'

'*Ah, huérfanos!*' they would say, then go away, gather up the rest of the family, the toothless granny and anyone else who happened to be passing by, then gather them around and ask me to say *huérfanos* again, just for a laugh. As I rode away afterwards with the entire populace rolling around the square clutching their sides, at least I could comfort myself with the fact that I had brought a little joy to the world.

But this morning, everything changed.

As the breakfast waitress brought our scrambled eggs to the table, she glanced outside to where the bikes had been parked overnight, guarded by two sleeping dogs.

Seizing my chance, I gave her the spiel.

'*Ah, sí,*' she nodded quietly, and went off to get the coffee.

At last, I thought, I've cracked it.

'Lovely girl, that waitress,' I said to the manager as we were checking out.

'She is, but quite deaf,' he said.

Oh well. Undeterred, I started Tony and followed Clifford north through mountains lush with coffee bushes.

Before the crash, we had taken turns leading, but I was now following him all the time because, with no left-hand mirror, overtaking on Colombian roads was a death or death chance, as I had discovered several times the day before, and until I found a replacement, he was doing the overtaking for both of us.

At our noon coffee stop, a café beside a brown and turbulent river, the tree beside our table was alive with cicadas, butterflies and hummingbirds, and two 3ft iguanas were having their morning nap on a branch over the fast-flowing water.

At Manizales, a 150ft wooden tower was all that was left of a remarkable cableway which had once brought coffee the forty-five miles down from the plantations. Every single tower had been made of steel in England and shipped to Colombia in the last years of the First World War, except for the tallest and the last, which went down when the ship carrying it was torpedoed by a U-boat. Undeterred, the locals built a replacement in wood, and here it stands to this day.

Lanks had actually seen the cableway in action in 1942, nineteen years before it ceased operating. 'Over our heads rose gaunt towers of what we thought were high-tension lines. But then the heavy cable between the towers began to vibrate, and suddenly a basket appeared travelling along the cable, followed by two more,' he wrote.

After five hours on winding mountain roads, we were only in Medellín, once infamous as the home of Pablo Escobar, the former used-car salesman who was the most ruthless of all the drug barons until he was finally killed in 1993 after being shopped by the citizens, at huge risk to themselves.

Today, they look very pleased with themselves and their bright modern city, as well they might.

As for us, already knackered by hours of mountain roads, we were wondering how on earth we were going to replace our depleted funds, then find our way through the chaos of the city, when yet another guardian angel appeared in the shape of Oscar, to whom we got talking through the window of his car at traffic lights.

'Just follow me,' he said, leading us to a cash machine, going completely out of his way to guide us through the city to the road north, then recommending a good place to stop for the night. An hour later, after a ride through stunning mountain scenery, we were checking into a hotel in the tranquil mountain town of Santa Rosa de Osos, then going out to celebrate two things.

As we were checking in, I had told the manager about the *huérfanos* and he hadn't burst out laughing.

And Clifford had set a new world record for riding along with his indicator on for twenty minutes. Astonishing. If only it was an Olympic sport, I could make some money out of him.

We spent the next morning toiling up the mountain behind an endless succession of lorries. By the roadside, either dug out of the rock on one side or hanging over the edge of a cliff on the other, families lived in shacks often made out of no more than plastic and wood. These were people who would have aspired to be dirt poor, and yet outside each home, a tot was sweeping the edge of the road and freshly scrubbed washing hung on palm trees to dry.

At last we climbed so high we were in the frozen clouds where the truly desperate lived, and the roadside visions became less benign: warped children appeared out of the eerie whiteness, their hands beseeching you for a few coins, or old men sat in wheelchairs, their useless legs inches from the thundering trucks.

It was like Dante's *Inferno* restaged in a fridge.

And so, having spent a tedious morning climbing, we spent a tedious afternoon descending, on a road so convoluted that only a madman would have dreamed of overtaking. Which sums up most of the drivers who shot past us, hurtling towards blind corners with only a plastic Virgin Mary dangling from their rear view mirror to protect them from certain death.

By two, I was ready to contribute whatever it cost towards the building of a new South American rail network, just to get the trucks off the road.

By three, I was ready to vote for the death penalty for lorry drivers. I mean, what were they all doing out on the road on a Sunday? Had they no homes to go to?

Thank heavens, then, for the fact that the road finally got as fed up of curves as we were, barrelling down a wide river valley for the rest of the afternoon. It was an idyllic transformation, enlivened briefly when Clifford, faced with a bus overtaking a lorry and being overtaken in turn by a car, was forced to make a dive for the hard shoulder to save his life.

In villages here and there, entire posses of horses were tethered under the trees in the square, their owners having ridden into town to cleanse their souls at church, then walked across the plaza to the bar to do the same with their palates. Merengue or mawkish ballads blasted out of speakers, bottles of *aguardiente* or beer were opened, unfortunate pigs were roasted, and all was well with the world, at least until Monday morning.

As, indeed, it was with us, for at half past four we decided we had had enough for the day and pulled over in the little town of Caucasia. After consulting the guidebook and a man on a scooter, we found ourselves five miles up the road in a splendid little hotel with a palm roof. We had a frog in the bathroom, two golden finches on the balcony and four cold beers waiting for us in the bar downstairs.

We had dinner under the stars, serenaded by the whispering wings of giant bats as we watched lightning flickering over the mountain to which we had earlier bid a glad farewell.

After a hard day's motorcycling, what more could a chap ask for?

13

Cartagena.

In the two years I had been planning this trip, that name had gazed out at me from maps on many an evening. Long before we left, the medieval walled city on the Caribbean coast had become a symbol for me.

For to get there meant that we had conquered not only Colombia, but South America. Not that Colombia had taken much conquering, apart from me conquering my apparent inability to go around corners without falling off.

It had, by contrast, conquered us.

There had been other milestones on the trip, of course, such as Lima: when Tony had been limping through the desert with a then unknown problem, I had hoped and prayed that we would make it as far as Lima and sort something out there.

There had been Cali, that dreadful day of the crash.

There would be San Diego, where we would be welcomed back into the safe, comfortable bosom of the Western, anglophone world.

But Cartagena had always been there. For getting there meant that only a boat trip lay between us and the road that ran unbroken all the way to Deadhorse, Alaska.

You can imagine, then, my feelings as we rode up the last

few dozen miles of South America, narrowly avoiding assorted cows, donkeys, goats and dogs who were so heartbroken at our imminent departure from the sub-continent that they flung themselves at random across the road in front of us.

As, indeed, did a young motorcyclist who came hurtling down the road oblivious to all around him, missed us by a whisker and ran headlong into a scooter carrying a family of three. They picked themselves up, miraculously unhurt, but he looked dead as we were waved on by the soldiers who had appeared immediately on the scene, since one is to be found under practically every tree between Medellín and Cartagena.

Sobered by the fact that someone else had suffered the fate to which I had come so close, we stopped to gather our thoughts, and rode on a little more carefully, conscious that even now, fate could still play cruel tricks on us.

And then, suddenly, the sea.

How my heart lifted to see it, for the first time since Peru!

Even Tony and April seemed to sense it, leaping on with a new sense of purpose as we clattered, exultant, through the narrow streets of Cartagena's old town and found a little hotel by the ocean with a sparse room which we shared with two pigeons and a ginger cat.

Watched intently by the cat, Clifford sat under the ceiling fan to write a letter to Sonia. I could tell he was in love, since he hadn't taken a photo for his collection of Pan-American beauties for days. As for the epic poem to the original girl, that was long forgotten.

As night fell, I walked across the road and down the beach, and stood in the pounding surf, looking west. Somewhere out there in the darkness was Panama, and tomorrow we would find a boat to take us there.

And so, the next morning, we took a taxi to the Club Nautico, where several sources had assured us we would find a rich yacht owner ready and willing to become even richer by taking us and the bikes to Panama.

Things did not begin well: halfway to the marina, our taxi

died. We got out and pushed it up and down the street several times, but its innards remained mysteriously inert.

'I am sorry. This happens all the time,' said the driver wearily, flagging down another one for us.

Soaked in sweat, we presented a sorry sight when we finally tumbled in front of the sailing club. To find, naturally enough, a man called John from Dundee.

'Afraid you lads are out of luck,' he said. 'They've just changed the law to stop private boats taking motorbikes on board. Your only chance is to get the bikes to Panama with a shipping company, and fly or take a sailboat yourselves.'

Oh well, no one ever said this was going to be easy, I thought, wondering what on earth we were to do, when a small, quiet man called Andres stepped forward and offered to give us a lift to the nearest shipping company offices. Naturally, when we got there, it had gone out of business, but Andres was not to be deterred. He was not, in fact, to be deterred all day. Hauling out his phone, he called Annabella Suarez at Herman Schwyn, another company.

'You two are famous. She said she'd read about you already in *El Tiempo*,' he said when he put the phone down. 'She said she'll see what she can do and call back after two. Now, in the meantime, let's have a coffee and I'll give you a tour of the city.'

Andres, it seemed, had adopted us.

Over coffee, we got talking to Ed, a Swiss-born photographer now living in San Francisco, and we all ended up piling into Andres's car for a whistle-stop rattle around a city which was once the storehouse for all the plundered Inca gold waiting to be shipped back to Spain.

Not surprisingly, it attracted the attention of a host of pirates, including Francis Drake, who between them besieged the city five times in the sixteenth century alone.

The only time it came close to falling, though, was at the hands of the English admiral Edward Vernon, who attacked it with 25,000 men, 2,000 cannon and 186 ships.

Facing him was one of the most remarkable heroes of any

age: Blas De Lezo, who as a young officer in the Spanish navy had already lost his left leg, his right arm and his left eye in three separate battles. De Lezo had a mere 2,500 men, including natives armed with bows and arrows, and so confident was Vernon of success that he had already minted victory medals. Feeling it ungallant to defeat only half a man, he had ordered the medals to be cast with all of De Lezo's bits reinstated.

Remarkably, Blas won the day, although at the cost of a fatal wound in his remaining leg, and today a statue of him stands, although only just, at the foot of the fortress of San Felipe, having cost the city an arm and a leg less than it might have done. It was, in retrospect, possibly a good thing that he died when he died, for had he continued in the same vein, he would almost certainly have died of old age and loneliness as a solitary ear.

In any case, our real hero of the day was Andres, who got a call from Annabella at four to say we should go immediately to the docks. There, we were shown politely into the office of a vivacious brunette called Judith.

'Didn't I read about you two in the papers?' she said, then picked up four phones and began talking into all of them simultaneously.

'Right,' she said when she had finished. 'Go to the customs office and get your carnet documents stamped first thing in the morning, then come here at ten. I will have a price and a shipping date for you then.'

Colombia, I thought as we agreed with Andres on the way out that we would pay him $100 a day for his services and he drove us back to the hotel room we shared with two pigeons, the cat and a small lizard who had arrived that morning, would never cease to amaze me.

In the evening, we met Ed for dinner in a little square, then wandered through cobbled streets lined with elegant buildings of faded terracotta, ochre or periwinkle, all glorious with balconies and bougainvillaea. Behind us trailed a diaspora of hawkers and shoeshine boys, and in front of us we found on a corner a man called Fernando, a colourful character with matching shirt.

'Ah, motorbikes,' he said. 'Have you heard of Gregory Frazier?'

I had indeed. He was an American who had written a book about motorcycling to Alaska called, rather imaginatively, *Motorcycling to Alaska: How to Motorcycle to Alaska*.

Still, I was hardly one to criticise, since when I was a child I had named two pigs, a goose and a hamster Pinky, Perky, Goosey and Hammy respectively.

'He was here two weeks ago, and I got him a boat to Panama. If you need one, there's a Hamburg Line ship leaving in two days,' said Fernando. 'Now, is there anything else I can get you? Girls, boys, coke, blow, sheep, goats, guinea pigs?'

Assuring him that we were Zen Buddhist bikers with no need of any of the above, especially the guinea pigs, we wandered home, fell into bed and were seduced into sleep by the sound of the sea.

The passport office was housed in an old colonial mansion in the leafy part of town.

In lofty rooms where once the descendants of conquistadors had lounged the idle hours of a dying empire away, earnest women of a certain age now tapped at computers below posters saying: 'Colombia: Land of Flowers ... and much more!'

'Which reminds me,' said Andres as we waited for our passports to be cleared, 'never ask for Coke in Colombia. Always Coca-Cola. Talking of which, let me tell you how crazy the people of this country are. We have over a hundred different types of fruit, and we drink something which takes the rust off nails.'

At 10 a.m., we found ourselves back at the office of Judith, who was wearing a T-shirt saying 'Private Street Number Fifty: Apply generously wherever needed'. She was also, yet again, talking into several phones simultaneously. When she finally put the last one down, the good news was that she had found a cargo boat to take our bikes.

The bad news was that it was not leaving for six days, and would take a further three to get to Panama.

But then, adventures have a habit of not going to plan. Ask Scott of the Antarctic.

It was strangely apposite, though, that the country we had feared the most, yet come to love the best, was the most reluctant to let us go. And yet again, the people of Colombia had been phenomenally helpful: within two days of arriving, we had got the bikes on a boat to Panama, and could either follow them in a plane or a sailboat.

I tried to imagine two Colombian bikers with poor English arriving in Belfast and trying to do the same thing, and thought what a nightmare it would be. Unless they happened to chance upon Carson McMullan of All-Route Shipping, of course.

Judith, her assistant and the two of us climbed into Andres's car with a sheaf of documents, and within an hour, we had been to the customs office and the public notary, where we were attended on by a lawyer, three legal secretaries and a beggar who just wandered in off the street and asked me for some money. Since he cost less than the lawyers, I was happy to oblige, particularly since I looked around the room, counted a team of seven now working for us, and realised that we had, yet again, accidentally turned into Ewan and Charley.

By now it was lunchtime, and we repaired to a nearby hostelry and ate spicy bean stew with most of a pig floating in it.

'Mmm, mmm, chomp, slurp, guzzle. God, I love beans,' said Clifford, polishing his off in thirty-four seconds flat. I feared the worst later.

In the meantime, though, Andres drove us back to the hotel to pick up the bikes and ride them to the yard where the shipping crates would be built around them. Clifford climbed aboard, pressed the starter button, and nothing happened.

'Bloody hell. And somebody's nicked my lucky teddy bear,' he said, pointing to the space on the handlebars where the bear had been wedged since Puerto Montt. We started the Aprilia with a push, rode both bikes through the burning afternoon to the yard, and left them there. Tony had been the one to suffer through South America. Only time would tell if it was now April's turn, but we would burn that bridge when we came to it.

Clifford went for a wander around town, I sat down to write and we agreed to meet in the square at half seven. He sauntered up at five to eight, just as I was fending off the 317th hawker in a row.

'Bloody hell, Pancho, you're never on time,' I snapped.

'I'm not that late, am I?' he said.

We apologised over a beer, but we were probably both on edge. Not only over the starter motor, but the fact that the crash and the boat hiccup had now left us over two weeks behind schedule, which meant a fortnight's more accommodation to pay for, and no clue yet how much the shipping and Andres's bill would come to.

Since the paper had kept half the sponsorship money, that had left no contingency fund for disasters and emergencies. And on adventures, there are always plenty of both.

However, what I've found is that worrying about money doesn't create any money, it just makes you worried, so in the circumstances, I did the only sensible thing and ordered more beer.

'You know,' said Andres over coffee at our hotel the next morning, 'this was an old hippie haunt in the Sixties. I used to come here and get stoned on pot and LSD with the gringos. One day I was convinced the sea had turned into mountains, and I tried to climb them. When the rest stopped me from drowning myself, I sat down and talked non-stop for twelve hours. I gave up acid the next day and found the Lord instead.'

The word from the yard, meanwhile, was that the boys were spending more time scratching their heads than building the crates, but when we arrived, we found they had simply been working on the principle that one minute head-scratching is worth five minutes running around like a headless chicken, and the crates were almost finished to perfection.

That sorted, we returned to Judith's office for our now daily visit, armed with a heart-shaped box of Ferrero Rocher which Clifford had picked up on the way.

'Well, the good news is the boat is definitely leaving on Tuesday,' she said.

The bad news was that because of their fuel tanks, the bikes were classified as dangerous goods which might spontaneously combust at any moment. Indeed, as you well know, there's nothing worse than driving down the street behind a motorbike when it suddenly explodes, leaving a helmet sitting atop a small pile of charred buckles and smoking leather.

Because of this, they required a special licence which would take three days to prepare, meaning that they would miss the boat and go on the next one, sometime around Christmas the year after.

Judith sat down, got on her four phones again, and simultaneously started tapping away at a desktop and laptop for good measure. Her voice, which was loud and husky to start with, got louder and hoarser. After half an hour, she put down the phone.

'They are seeing what they can do. They will call back at one,' she said.

Time passed. We sat on the floor, drank coffee and looked at photos of her husband, son, parents, in-laws and assorted cousins. More time passed. I began to think it would be quicker to go out, buy two machetes and start hacking a road through the Darien Gap.

It was ironic, I thought, that motorcycle adventures were all about escaping from offices, yet here we were spending most of our time in one. Still, at least all of us were doing something we had never done before, since Andres and Judith had confessed that no one had ever asked them to ship motorbikes to Panama before. At lunchtime, Judith's son Paolo arrived from kindergarten, and her manner switched instantly from fiery and combative to soft and quiet.

'Hello, my little pumpkin, coochiecoochiecoo, how is my

little chickadee, my little love angel, the apple of my heart?' she said. I'm translating loosely, but you get the picture.

Paolo then spent the next two hours running around drawing on every available piece of paper while his mother made, by my estimation, four billion phone calls. Even at home, shipping motorbikes required a lot of time, energy, calls and documents, but in South America, I was being reminded for the first time since San Antonio, all of that is multiplied by infinity. Squared.

Still, when the news came, late in the afternoon, it was good: we didn't need the dangerous goods certificate after all, so the bikes were safe from random immolation.

After the good news, of course, came the bad, in the form of the bill. Based on the private yacht option, we had budgeted $600 for us and the bikes. Instead, we found ourselves gazing in horror at a commercial fee of $1,000, not to mention the $400 for us to fly or sail to Panama.

Add to that the $100 a day we were paying Andres, and the cost of at least two weeks' extra bed, board and food, and it looked like we were going to be busking to grizzly bears by the time we got to Alaska.

And, as we all know, grizzlies are notoriously tight with money, using the feeble excuse that they have no pockets for change.

Conscious of our newly straitened circumstances, we set out for dinner that night at the cheapest restaurant in the poorest part of town. Sadly, we had picked Cartagena's only geographically dyslexic taxi driver, who drove around aimlessly for the next half an hour looking at street signs with an expression of slightly more than interest, but slightly less than recognition. After we had driven through the same square for the fourth time, we got out and walked, just as aimlessly, but more cheaply.

Finally, more by luck than judgement, we found the place we were looking for, sat down and ordered dinner.

'Dinner?' said the owner. 'But we only do lunch.'

'That would explain why it was empty,' I said as we wandered off through streets full of exquisite but inedible architecture until we found ourselves at the same place where we had eaten the night before. Since it, too, was empty, we were welcomed in like long-lost friends, so we resigned ourselves to fate and sat down with that most delicious of feelings.

Not so much looking forward to dinner, but knowing exactly what the bill would be.

Outside the customs office at the docks, as we waited for our carnets to be stamped the next morning, natives sold delicious mashed corn, wrapped in its own leaves and served with salty goat's cheese.

'Haven't I seen you somewhere before?' I said to a man with cheekbones like razors as he passed me a steaming cup of black, sweet coffee.

'I was the forty-eighth Indian from the left in *The Mission*,' he said. 'They brought forty bus loads of us from the interior to appear as extras, and I liked it so much, I stayed.'

'Great film, that,' said Andres as we drove away. 'I got nine months' work as a driver out of it.'

'Here,' said Clifford suddenly as we drove past a travel agent, 'I've been thinking. Since we're here for a few days, would you mind if I flew down to Cali to spend the weekend with Sonia? I'll stick it on my credit card, like.'

'Not a bit, Pancho. Go for it.'

He nipped in, and came out five minutes later with a smile on his face.

'Two hundred quid, but what the hell. Love has no price,' he grinned.

A whole weekend without Pancho. Good heavens. I would miss him. Maybe not the fact that he was completely manic, and at any given moment was either talking, cackling at his own jokes, farting, burping or clearing his nose loudly, but him as a person, with one of the most sincere hearts on the planet.

And at least he was manic in a positive way: with Clifford, everything was fucking incredible, fucking gorgeous or fucking amazing.

'I know I'm a bit intense,' he had said when we talked about it. 'It's just me. I do try to relax, honestly.'

Anyway, I was sure he found me impossible to live with, since like most writers who make people laugh for a living, I was a grumpy bastard most of the time, not to mention a moody, stubborn, obsessive, passive-aggressive manic depressive, although in a charming kind of way, of course.

Anyway, in the meantime, it was Friday night, and time for a beer. It was a funny thing, but at home I virtually always drank wine, whereas on the trip, a cold beer had always seemed more appropriate after a long, hot, dusty day on a motorbike.

Wine, of course, affects you in a different way to beer. For a start, it makes you feel tiddly in a sophisticated but slightly edgy kind of way. After one glass, you feel that everything is possible, the way you did when you were young. After two glasses, of course, nothing is.

Beer, on the other hand, makes you feel all warm and fuzzy and content with the world, a feeling which increases exponentially up to a peak of two or three, after which you should then stop, since you have reached the stage where life is wonderful, but not the stage where you throw up over the cat, leaving it warm and fuzzy and not at all content with the world.

Here endeth this evening's sermon, courtesy of me and Homer Simpson.

When Francis Drake sacked Cartagena in 1586, it claimed unfair dismissal.

When that didn't work, the citizens set to building a seven-mile defensive wall, and inside it the castle of San Felipe, the most impregnable fortress the world had ever seen. Today, it may seem less impregnable, in that you only have to hand over $5 to get in, but you then have to run the gauntlet of traders selling everything from statues of Don Blas to giant conch shells. However, I had the perfect excuse: on a motorbike, there is no room for either.

Inside the fortress is an interminable network of rooms, traps, escape routes, dead ends and tunnels constructed so that you could hear the slightest enemy whisper hundreds of yards away, in the same way that the floorboards of the Imperial Palace in Kyoto were built to creak at the footsteps of intruders.

Today, the system is still eerily effective: if you listen carefully enough upon leaving the fortress, you can hear the distant echo of yourself arriving an hour earlier, thus imbuing you with the ghost of yourself as a slightly younger person. If you do this several times a day, at the end of the month you will have taken years off yourself. There is no charge for this advice, on the basis that I just made it up.

As for the city which the fortress guards, the best way to see it is to simply go for a dander, so I did, starting in the Plaza de los Cochos, in which slaves were once sold.

Their descendants are still there, standing in the shady archways all around and selling freshly made juices and fried balls of maize, cheese or egg.

Unable to decide, I had all three, and chewed my way across to the Museum of Modern Art. It was aptly named, since half of what was inside was art, and the rest was simply modern.

I was having a pee in the toilets when a beautiful mulatto woman sauntered in and handed me a piece of paper with her phone number on it. I took it politely off her with my free hand.

'If you want a friend in the night,' she said sweetly.

'Thanks, but I have a friend in the night at home,' I said. 'And a cat.'

'Oh well. Do you want to buy some emeralds, then?'

'No thanks. My wife doesn't like them. Not to mention saving me a fortune by being allergic to perfumes.'

She gave up at this point, and suitably chaste and unbejewelled, I walked around the corner to the Monastery of San Pedro Claver, the seventeenth-century monk who spent his life ministering to African slaves at a time when his compatriots treated them like pack animals. The first person in the New World to be beatified, he spent his nights in a spare cell which looked disturbingly like our hotel room.

When the Spanish could spare a few minutes from looting Inca gold, building fortresses and importing slaves, they liked nothing better than putting to death heretics, witches and anyone who looked at them the wrong way. These unfortunate souls were denounced from the ornate Palace of the Inquisition up the street, then dragged to the Plaza de Bolívar and subjected to a pleasant afternoon of disembowelling, flaying and roasting, with a half-price special offer on Saturdays for Protestants.

Slightly more fortunate were the worshippers in the nearby church of Santa Toribio de Mangrovejo, who were busy at their prayers one Sunday when one of Edward Vernon's cannonballs flew through the window and missed them all.

And most fortunate of all was Rafael Nuñez, the former president, poet and lawyer who wrote part of the constitution and all of the national anthem. He lived just outside the city walls in an airy wooden mansion which was now a museum.

I padded across its dark floors, admiring the trappings of a rich life: the Paris dinner set, the monogrammed cigar case, the silver-topped cane, the Victrola gramophone, the painting of his wife with a long-suffering expression which gave some indication as to why they slept in separate rooms.

Which was not a situation Pancho was likely to be faced with this evening, I thought as I wandered up to the Plaza de Bolívar, which had once echoed to the screams of Inquisition victims.

Today, the only sounds were the tinkling bells of the ice-cream vendor and the cries of the women selling fruit from baskets on their heads, their melodious, haunting calls floating up through the still, warm air until they were indistinguishable from the liquid, fluting song of the orioles nesting in the almond trees.

A great wind arose in the night, howling and gibbering through the courtyard.

And in the morning, Cate texted me to say that her much loved aunt and godmother had died.

I got into a taxi immediately and went to a *cabina telefónica* to call her. As we talked, I imagined her standing in the kitchen of our house, dealing with a great loss alone, and felt a dull ache in my heart that I could not be there with her. I had missed her every single day of the trip, but it was at moments like these, in the silence after we said goodbye and hung up, that I felt the distant emptiness of her footsteps into the living room, the space beside her as she sat on the sofa having a glass of wine, eating supper or watching an old movie.

All the things we always did together, denied by my absence.

I sighed deeply and wandered along Bocagrande beach, alive with Sunday afternoon families, until I was hailed in Spanish by two likely looking girls.

'Sir, how tall you are! What big muscles! Would you like a back massage?'

'How much?' I said.

'Only four thousand pesos.'

Two dollars, I thought. Twice what Clifford had paid the day before, but fair enough. I sat on a beach chair, and one of them got to work, while the other whipped off my shoes and got started on an uninvited pedicure and manicure.

'Right, how much in total?' I said when they had finished.

'One hundred and fifty thousand.'

'You must be joking. You said four thousand for the massage, so I'll give you ten thousand for the lot.'

'No, I said forty dollars.'

'Like hell you did. Do you think I'm deaf?' I said, surprised by how much my Spanish was improving. 'My mate got a back massage for two thousand on Marbella beach yesterday.'

'Two thousand! Impossible. That wouldn't put food in our mouths,' etc. etc. etc.

They sat there and looked sulky, and I sat there and twiddled my thumbs, since I had nothing else to do and it was only their time I was wasting. An hour went by. Every ten minutes they would reduce the price by ten thousand, and I would laugh. After a while, several heavies appeared and stood about trying to look menacing.

Eventually, the price came down to forty-five thousand, and I gave them forty, or about twenty dollars, and walked away, only to find my way barred by one of the heavies.

'You haven't paid enough,' he said.

'I have paid more than enough. Get out of my way,' I said, and walked on, expecting to be hit on the back of the head by a pair of manicuring scissors. However, all was well. It had been the only example of bad faith in Colombia, and since we had expected to be kidnapped and shot the moment we set foot in the country, that wasn't bad going.

'The same thing happened to me the first week at Bocagrande. It's the only place in the country you'll get ripped off,' said Fromm, a German arts student I met at the beach bar across the road that evening. He had come to Colombia for a holiday two months before, and never left. Lucy, the reason, was sitting beside him, small, dark and charming, with her friend Wilma.

'As in the Flintstones,' said Wilma as the sun sank into the ocean, a sliver of moon rose, and we were joined by the town drunk, who declared that we were beautiful, the moon was beautiful and Colombia was beautiful.

He wandered off, and was replaced by the local vet, who handed me a small bundle of trembling fur. It was a Chihuahua pup, only a few weeks old and smaller than the palm of my hand. It looked up at me plaintively, then buried its head in the crook of my thumb.

'Don't worry, chum,' I said. 'Colombia is perfectly safe, as long as you don't get your nails done at Bocagrande.'

It was good advice, for within a minute he stopped quivering and nodded off. The vet lifted him carefully from my hand and went home, and after a while the town drunk came strolling back the other way, announced that the whole world was beautiful, and fell asleep on the beach.

Next morning, I was sitting on the same beach minding my own business when the sunglasses salesman turned up.

'Genuine Ray-Bans, *señor*, only $20.'

I pointed to the pair sitting on my nose.

'I've got a pair already, *amigo*.'

He peered at them suspiciously.

'How much did you pay for them?'

'A hundred dollars.'

'A hundred? But these are only $20!'

'I know, but mine are real.'

'OK then, $10.'

'No.'

'$5?'

'No. No. A thousand times no. And no massages, manicures or pedicures either.'

He wandered off in search of another gringo, only to be replaced by the T-shirt salesman.

'Pablo Escobar shirt, *señor*?' he said, holding up a bright yellow T-shirt bearing an image of the notorious, and now thankfully dead, Medellín drug baron.

'No thanks.'

'Cuban cigars? Emeralds? Flip-flops three sizes too small? Gerbils? Performing dolphins? One-legged contortionists?'

I was just about to ask him if the dolphins were by any chance heading for Panama when Andres turned up to go to the airport and collect Pancho after his weekend of lurve. The latter appeared through the arrivals door, looking not quite his usual jaunty self.

'Food poisoning. Spent all of yesterday in bed,' he muttered.

As for Andres, the news was that the bikes would be searched for drugs today, and shipped tomorrow. We would get the Bill of Lading the day after, and would then be free to leave. Half an hour later, we emerged from the travel agent with two flight tickets to Panama City.

What a splendidly exotic thing to possess, I thought, admiring them respectfully. Particularly since the original plan, to go by sailboat, would have left us in Colón, the town on the north coast of Panama of which British journalist James Anthony Froude said in 1886: 'In all the world there is not, perhaps, now concentrated in a single spot so much swindling and villainy, so much foul disease, such a hideous dung-heap of moral and physical abomination.'

It was, apparently, much worse today, but still just as aptly named.

In the meantime, Clifford went off to the beach for a therapeutic nap and dip, and returned an hour later.

'Some bastard nicked my sunglasses while I was swimming,' he said. 'We'll have to go into town and get another pair. And have another look for Colombia stickers.'

Instead of a taxi, we took a *chiva*, one of the psychedelic communal minibuses which hurtle around Cartagena with their destination on the front. Ours had a huge pair of seductively coy eyes painted on the windscreen, and inside, rainbow-striped curtains, multi-coloured tassels, disco lights, a fur-trimmed rear view mirror, a horn like a squadron of psychotic budgerigars and a sound system pumping out vallenato, the native musical beat which in the nineteenth century was adapted to incorporate a shipment of accordions stolen by bandits from a German mule train on its way to Richacha.

Neither the Germans nor the mules would recognise it now.

We found no stickers, but Clifford bought a pair of genuine fake Ray-Bans from a street trader for $5, and we sat down for a beer and some barbecued chicken.

'So listen, apart from the throwing up, how was your weekend?' I said.

'Brilliant. Great crack, got my clothes washed and hardly spent a penny.'

'Aye, sounds like the perfect Scottish weekend break,' I laughed, making a mental note to get the Glasgow Tourist Board to start organising day trips to Cali immediately.

I spent the next morning sitting in the sun outside our little room, planning the next few weeks through Central America.

If we ever got there, that was: at two, Andres arrived to take us to Judith's office, where she had told him the final payment details were ready, not to mention news of when the vital Bill of Lading would be released so we could leave the country.

At five, we were still waiting.

In the meantime, Judith, wearing a T-shirt which said somewhat superfluously in silver glitter 'LOOK AT ME', swanned about the office, ordered everyone around and made several dozen noisy phone calls to no apparent effect. I was beginning to realise, as I sat on her floor for the fifth endless afternoon in a row, that behind all the apparent energy and drive was just an attention-seeking drama queen who turned every problem into five acts of Shakespeare.

I wouldn't have minded quite so much if we hadn't been paying Andres $100 a day to watch the performance with us.

We left with a promise that the Bill of Lading would be ready by ten the following morning.

'Andres,' I said grimly as we got up to leave, 'please tell Judith to phone you tomorrow when, and only when, she has the piece of paper in her hand.'

'And tell her we want on one sheet of paper, not twenty, the name, address and phone number of the agent in Panama, the name of the ship, and exactly when and where it docks,' said Clifford.

Andres started to tell her, but after half a sentence she got bored, picked up one of her several phones and started another loud conversation. Thanking our lucky stars we weren't married to her, we fled.

'Listen,' said Clifford, 'since we're paying Andres for the afternoon anyway, let's get him to do something really useful and find us some Colombia stickers.'

In the end, he did even better: from a stall at the back of the market, two sheets with every flag of the world, which solved our sticker problems all the way to Alaska.

I stuck all the relevant ones on Tony's top box immediately,

Clifford announced he would save each of his until we had crossed the appropriate borders, and to celebrate, we went out for beer and a burger at the little restaurant on the corner. The background music was, serendipitously, Bob Marley's 'Everything's Gonna be All Right'.

'God, that brings me back. The first time I heard that was at a party thirty years ago,' said Clifford. 'I was supposed to be flying to France the next morning to go skiing with some mates, but I ended up going to a party with this chick. I woke up at six, still stoned out of my head and wearing a pinstripe suit and white gutties. We drove all the way to Glasgow Airport at 100mph in her wee Fiat 131, hit roadworks and got there at ten to eight for a flight at eight. They wouldn't let me on, so I got another flight to London, then on to France, and spent the week wandering around in the snow wearing the pinstripe suit and gutties.'

'What, you hadn't brought any ski gear?'

'I hadn't even brought any luggage.'

I looked at him, surprised we had got as far as Belfast City Airport, never mind Cartagena.

At dawn, Ronan Kelly from U105 phoned to say congratulations.

'On what?' I said, baffled.

'You won the features journalist of the year award last week. You mean nobody told you?' he said.

'Haven't heard a peep, Ronan.'

After we had recorded the weekly show, I got a taxi to a phone cabin in town and rang Cate to tell her the good news.

'This calls for a celebration,' said Clifford when I returned, then disappeared mysteriously.

For the first time in the whole trip, or possibly ever, I spent the rest of the day enjoying the simple, glorious pleasure of doing nothing much.

Just watching the dappled light play on the window of our bare little room at the Hotel Bellavista.

Or saying hello to Wilma as in the Flintstones, our next door neighbour, as she came and went on her yellow bicycle with the permanent slow puncture in the back wheel.

Or listening to the burble of talk and laughter between the old black fruit seller and her daughter in the courtyard, as they sang to each other the songs their ancestors had sung while they picked cotton and fruit all over this continent, and the one beyond.

And to the snick of the gardener's shears as he trimmed back the lemon tree, and the clunk clunk of the handyman's hammer as he repaired that door jamb which had been creaking all winter.

I thought, too, about the past year: a year in which there had been days when I was so stuck and overworked and down that I had gone to the office, worked all day and driven home without speaking to a single soul.

And yet today something worthwhile had come out of those dreadful months.

I was quietly glad of that, this sunny afternoon in Cartagena, although not as glad as I was of what I had come home to on the worst of those days, closing the front door behind me, hanging up my coat and looking down the hall or up the stairs to see my wife, a sight worth a thousand awards.

At seven, Clifford reappeared as mysteriously as he had disappeared.

'We're going out. Get your bow tie on,' he said with a mischievous grin.

In the little restaurant on the corner, the table was set with flowers, champagne chilling in an ice-bucket and a candle in the shape of a number one. Symbolically, it was one of those candles that you cannot blow out, no matter how hard you try.

'Pancho, you are a genius,' I said, as Wilma arrived from the hotel and Yena, the restaurant owner, sent the champagne cork soaring towards the Caribbean moon.

Then, the next morning, Andres appeared with a grin, waving the long-awaited Bill of Lading, the key which would free us at last from the gilded cage of Cartagena.

We packed and said a sad farewell to our little room.

And a sad farewell, too, to an old friend: my battered copy of Herbert Lanks's *By Pan-American Highway through South America*, since he had veered off to Venezuela at this point, after wondering briefly when the bit of the highway through the Darien Gap to Panama would be completed. Possibly never, Herbert, possibly never, I thought as we walked through the airport doors and got out our passports and tickets.

'Is it Filbert?' I said.

'Nope,' said Clifford.

'Here, didn't I see you two on TV?' said the check-in woman, then charged us $84 for the privilege of leaving her country.

In the narcotics room, armed soldiers took our bags apart and searched every crook and granny, as an enthusiastic dog bounded around and sniffed everything in sight. As you would, if you were a Labrador with a cocaine habit. Finally, we were sent through to departures, where I was busy trying on duty-free sunglasses when I was approached by a man called Don from San Diego.

'Wow, you're pretty tall,' he said. People are always telling me this, as if all these years I've thought I was a leprechaun. Still, at least he noticed my height before he noticed the damage to my arm, which meant that rest, sun and sea had done it some good in Cartagena.

'You wanna watch that arm in the tropics,' he said. 'I got an itsy-bitsy little scratch in the Philippines once, my whole arm swelled up, the doc almost hadda take it off.'

He had, it transpired, just returned from having all his teeth out in Cartagena.

'Far cheaper than in the States, I tell ya. Best thing I ever did. Ya see, the decay and the poison in the fillings leak into your blood and make their way to your brain.'

'Don't worry, there's nothing in my brain to poison,' I said, realising that Don was simply the inevitable evolutionary result of a nation obsessed with germs.

Still, at least he gave me directions to Rocket Motorcycles, the Triumph dealer in San Diego. Shaking hands with him and walking away before I caught a paranoia about hygiene, I went back to where Clifford was sitting reading the horoscope in the local paper, his Spanish having improved immeasurably since the start of the trip, when his method had involved simply attaching an *o* to the end of English words, then speaking like Manuel from *Fawlty Towers*. Strangely, it had been surprisingly successful.

'It says here travel is on the cards, so we may be actually leaving Colombia at last,' he said, just as the check-in woman came striding over.

'*Señor* Hill, I'm afraid the narcotics dog has found a problem with your bag. Please come with me immediately,' she said.

Good grief, I thought. I knew I should never have tried to hide those Junior Disprin in my powder puff. I'm for it now. Back at the drugs desk, my bag was painstakingly unpacked, and every inch searched, but what the dog had detected was a mystery.

He was taken away and told off for crying wolf, I was led back to the departures lounge, and half an hour later, our flight to Panama City took off, freeing at last the Colombia Two.

Colón, which James Anthony Froude described in 1886 as 'a hideous dung-heap of moral and physical abomination'. Today, it is much worse.

14

A short history of Panama

1513
Spanish explorer Balboa, first European to see Pacific, reports success to jealous superior Pedrarias the Cruel, and is beheaded for his trouble. Motto: always ask yourself why boss deserves evil nickname before you open your mouth.

1513–1881
Country becomes major overland trade route between North and South America.

1881
French have brainwave, after several glasses of wine, that canal would make country major sea trade route as well. French start canal, but make major coq-up.

1903
Using method which is to become standard US foreign policy, President Roosevelt bribes, tricks and bullies Panama into letting US build and control canal instead.

1968
Amid growing resentment of US influence over country,

President Trujillo demands that US hand over control of canal by 2000.

1981

Trujillo dies in mysterious plane crash, and after fraudulent elections is replaced by CIA-funded drug baron Manuel Noriega.

1989

Noriega falls out of favour with US. George Bush orders invasion. Stealth bombers and helicopter gunships level poorest part of Panama City, leaving 15,000 homeless.

1999

US pulls out of Panama, leaving country with lots of McDonalds, but no money for cheeseburgers.

In Colombia, the airport taxi had been a ramshackle Toyota with a blown exhaust.

In Panama, it was a white Mercedes with DVD system which whisked us in air-conditioned silence through canyons of glass and steel in which were reflected the glittering neon signs for Donna Karan, Wendy's, Starbucks and a cornucopia of hotels and casinos. Coming from the walled city of Cartagena, we felt like two medieval serfs transported to Vegas. We found a hotel, and fell into bed.

The next morning, studying the shipping documents over breakfast, Clifford suddenly choked on his eggs.

'Bloody hell. The stupid bitch has sent the bikes to Cólon instead of Panama City,' he spluttered.

'Cólon? The most dangerous, crime-ridden, disease-infested swamp in Panama? That Cólon?' I said, aghast.

'Aye, that's the one.'

He handed me the Bill of Lading. He was right.

This left us with two options:

a) Fly back to Cartagena, strangle Judith with her 'LOOK AT ME' T-shirt, and spend the rest of our lives in a Colombian jail.

b) Get a bus to Cólon, and take our chances.

While the first would have been much more satisfying, the second was more practical. We phoned the docks in Colón, to find the good news that the bikes had actually arrived.

'But of course it is not that simple. You will need four billion forms before they can be released,' said the man on the other end.

Of course we would. How could we have expected anything else?

He gave us the name of Anibal Esposa, a shipping agent in Panama City who could help, and we took a taxi to her office and handed her all the documents we possessed, including the TV licence and the cat vaccination certificates, just to be on the safe side.

She picked up the phone, and we entered yet again into that dream world of sitting around with our lives in other people's hands, not having a clue what was happening, or what was going to happen. Anibal, as quiet and efficient as Judith had been loud and chaotic, finally put down the phone.

'You only need one form, but you do need to go to Colón,' she said. 'Here is the address and phone number of the best shipping agent there. Her name is Gladys.'

Half an hour later, we were on the bus to Colón to see Gladys, passing on the way railway tracks which made me wonder if there was a train still running to Colón. After two hours, the bus driver prised us out of our cramped seats and dumped us in a dusty square at the end of the world. Around it were standing several men who looked like they would happily slit our throats if they could only afford a knife between them.

In truth, Colón was not always like this. Founded in 1852 as the Caribbean terminal of the transisthmian railway, it reached its peak as a fashionable cruise destination in the 1950s, when the glittering chandeliers and ornate double staircase of the New Washington Hotel were graced by the likes of Bob Hope and Juan Perón.

Today, though, apart from the duty-free shopping zone

around the port, it was a shadow of its former self, although you would have been hard pushed to find a shadow in the baking midday sun.

We discovered Gladys, looking exactly like a Gladys, in an office which was basically the front room of a house smelling of fried fish.

'Ah, the men with the motorbikes,' she said, looking up at us over stern glasses. 'Today is Friday, so counting the weekend, they will be released on Tuesday morning.'

Tuesday? Good grief, I thought. That would mean a total of two weeks farting about in offices since we had first arrived in Cartagena.

We looked down at the helmets which we had optimistically brought in the hope of being able to ride them back to Panama this afternoon, and our hearts sank. Especially Clifford's, since he had already been told by work that he had to be back by the end of May, which gave us only seven weeks to get from Panama to Deadhorse.

'I think this blows my chances of making it to Alaska, mate,' he said gloomily as we got into Gladys's lime-green Hyundai and drove to the customs office in France Field, the duty-free zone which was a gem of capitalist fervour in the dust of Colón's decay. By five we at least had the release form in our hands, and were climbing on the bus back to Panama.

Only for a woman to scream 'Cockroach!' and lead a mass exodus from the vehicle with a ferocious example of the species clinging gamely to her back.

Half an hour later, we climbed back on the fumigated bus and returned, smelling faintly of disinfectant and disappointment, to the glittering lights of Panama City.

Standing in the Plaza Catedral, you could almost feel the history seeping into your bones.

From behind the peeling and boarded facade of the Hotel Central, you could, for example, virtually hear the cheering crowds who gathered there in 1903 to celebrate independence by pouring champagne over the head of General Huertas, the defecting garrison commander, for an hour.

Across the square was the vast white space of the cathedral, empty except for the whisper of God, and just up the street was the presidential palace, where Jimmy Carter's security advisers accidentally killed all the resident herons by spraying the building with disinfectant before he arrived to sign the canal treaty.

Just as unlucky was the glorious seafront officers' club, which was left a gutted shell by the 1989 US invasion.

This area of San Felipe was already being renovated in patches, and would soon be as prettified as Cartagena, but for the moment it was as real as the locals who were sitting on their ornate balconies, idly wondering how long it would be before they were evicted by the planners.

'Favourite spot of the trip so far. No doubt,' said Clifford happily as we strolled around the corner from the National Theatre and bumped into a young woman coming the other way. She turned out, naturally enough, to be Maria Nelly Rivas, the Nicaraguan Minister of Tourism, in town for a conference with her husband Matthew, an architect from Yorkshire.

'Give me a call when you get to Nicaragua,' she said. 'I'll be glad to help.'

She got into a limo, and we got into an ancient Datsun taxi and headed in the direction of Panama's most famous sight, the eponymous canal.

Hacked out of fifty unforgiving miles of rock and swamp in 1903, the canal was US territory for almost a century, the country's financial blessing and political curse, until it was finally handed back to the Panamanians on 31 December 1999. The story of its birth is told in a museum in the old town, full of hefty tools and photographs of engineers gazing out earnestly from a break in their manly endeavours.

In the broiling sun, we hiked up the long hill of Cerro Ancón to see it first from afar, encountering on the way snakes, iguanas, deer and a guinea pig, to whom we apologised for eating his cousin Jimmy in Ecuador. At one stage, we rounded a corner to come knee to beak with a flock of vultures, who looked up optimistically in the hope that one of us would keel over for lunch.

'Not today, chaps,' we said, toiling on to the top to find splendid views of not only the entire city and the canal entrance but Chile and Alaska, if you looked hard enough and had brought some imagination with you, since it doesn't take up much space, after all.

We were so high up, in fact, that below us a little Cessna descended to the nearby airfield for a landing which looked like there was a nervous student at the controls, with a white-knuckled instructor sitting beside him.

Suddenly, as we walked down the hill, yet again passing the disappointed vultures, it grew dark. This meant one of two things:

a) I had gone blind, as my mother warned me so often all those years ago.

b) Night had fallen.

Thankfully, it turned out to be the latter, which meant that the canal would have to be postponed until tomorrow.

'Here, I've just had a brilliant idea,' said Clifford. 'Let's go and see if there's a Saturday night show on at the National Theatre.'

Indeed, it did turn out to be a brilliant idea, apart from the fact that there wasn't. Disconsolate, we wandered up the street, found a little square with a little restaurant, and consoled ourselves with beer and steak, and then some more beer, just to be sure our disconsolateness was completely cured.

Behind us, two Americans were comparing the relative advantages of gilt-edged bonds and bond-edged gilts, in front of us, a man in a ragged shirt searched in a bin for food, above him, a man with no shirt at all stood on a balcony cuddling his baby daughter to sleep, and above that again, the moonlight danced alone on a church spire covered entirely in abalone shells.

Wandering through the streets afterwards past *cantinas* with a dangerous air seeping out through the swing doors, we were approached by a dark and bony man. He turned out to be Jacques, a Haitian priest who said he was fluent in seven languages.

'French, English, Spanish, Portugese, Creole and Latin,' he listed, proving that he was better at languages than maths.

Fleeing religious persecution to the States, he had spent three years in Guantanamo Bay before stealing a US Marines landing craft with thirty-nine others and escaping to Panama.

'Can we take a train to Colón?' I said, since he seemed to be an expert in alternative travel arrangements.

'No, not any more. But the boat from pier 6 at the fish market gets there in thirty minutes.'

'That's impossible,' said Clifford. 'It takes nine hours through the canal.'

'Ah, but it does not use the canal, it uses the river,' he said mysteriously, disappearing into the night and leaving us wondering why, if there was a river to the north coast, they had bothered building the canal.

Next morning, on the way to the canal, we asked the driver about the fast boat to Colón.

'Never heard of it,' he said. 'The train does still run, though. Leaves at dawn, costs $22. Buses leave all the time, cost $2.50. No contest.'

He had a point, I thought as we drove through Balboa, the former US residential area which still had the sleepy, ordered air of a small American town about it.

At the Miraflores Docks visitors' centre, too, all was clean, efficient and organised.

We handed over $16 and were ushered into an air-conditioned cinema for a film on the history of the canal, from when it was built for $400 million by 75,000 workers doing ten-hour shifts for a decade to finish a challenge so monumental it made riding a motorbike from Chile to Alaska seem like a Sunday afternoon outing.

Not that the building has ever really stopped: they were still at it, with a $1.5 billion widening scheme to let through American cruise ships whose waistlines were expanding as fast as their passengers. From a viewing platform upstairs, we watched in wonder as 50 million gallons poured from one chamber to another, 700-tonne gates swung open and four muscular locomotives hauled a vast container ship forward. Charged by weight, it would pay $130,000 for the privilege, although there were cheaper ways: in 1928, legendary cheapskate Richard Halliburton swam the length of the canal, paying 36 cents in tolls.

'I just hope the skipper didn't get all his traveller's cheques in $20 lots like you did,' I said to Pancho as the ship popped out the other end. 'There's only one thing puzzling me, though. If the Pacific and the Atlantic are all part of the one global body of water, how come they're at different levels?'

'It's the bit in the middle that's at the different level. It's called the land, you dickhead,' he said diplomatically as we drove off past a sign for the Shamrock Irish Bar advertising that most traditional of Celtic customs, the Friday night Mongolian barbecue.

At Pier Six, there was no sign of the mysterious supersonic boat to Colón, just a fat bloke in a peeling craft chopping up a dozen sharks into heads for cat food, bodies for steaks and fins for the lucrative Chinese soup market. Beside him lay a coil of line vicious with hooks.

'You'd think those sharks would learn eventually,' I said, 'rather than thinking: "Oh, look, all my mates are getting a free tow across the bay. I'll just grab that chunk of meat they missed."'

'About time we changed some traveller's cheques,' said Clifford, looking in his wallet.

What he had said, since it had no connection with sharks, was a non sequitur. It is not to be confused with a non secateur, which is when you mention garden shears for no apparent reason.

'You know,' said Luis, the teller at the bank we went to, 'I was only eighteen when the Americans invaded, and I saw it all from the roof of our flat: the helicopter gunships, the bombs, the shooting from the ground below. Incredible. Then my sister was working in New York on September 11. She was missing for two weeks before we found her in hospital.'

We tiptoed out gently, since these things usually come in threes, and got the bus to Colón. On the way out of town, we passed the Bridge of the Americas, the gateway west over the canal.

'It'll be a great feeling when we ride over that tomorrow,' I said.

'Ah, we'll cross that bridge when we come to it,' said Clifford.

Two hours later, we were back in the worst place either of us had ever been, which was saying something: a town on which not a cent had been spent since the Fifties, in which the buildings were derelict, the streets rubble, teenagers roamed around with Uzis, where armed robbery in broad daylight no longer even merited a mention in the local paper, and where visitors were routinely mugged within a minute of arriving. Fortunately, we found a taxi within fifty-nine seconds of stepping off the bus, and within five minutes were walking into the grimy lobby of the Hotel Internacional to be met by a stunned silence from the locals.

We were, I imagined, this year's tourists.

The receptionist demanded $30 in advance, and gave us the key to a room for which the word dive would have been a hyperbole. I switched on the air-conditioner, and the air filled with poisonous fumes. Coughing our way back to reception, we demanded a better room, only to be told that we were already in the best one.

Just out of interest, we took a taxi to the grand New Washington Hotel, where presidents once strolled among the palms and Bob Hope sang to the troops. Only to find that rooms there were a mere $44.

Cursing the fact that we'd paid up front for our hotel, we returned in a taxi.

'Whatever you do, don't go out here at night. Or during the day,' said the driver, dumping us at the door of our temporary prison and driving off at speed. We took him at his word, and had dinner in the hotel restaurant.

'What's your name?' we asked the matronly waitress as she brought us a plastic menu to match the tablecloth.

'Gladys,' she said.

'Of course.'

We had fish, as bony and vaguely satisfying as seducing a catwalk model.

'I actually feel more at home here than in the New Washington,' said Clifford. 'I've had the bright lights, the fast cars and bikes and the faster women, but I think the rest of my life will be softer, more gentle than that.'

He paused, and took a sip of his beer.

'You know, I think the happiest time of my life was when I was nineteen. As part of a business deal, my dad bought a gardener's lodge on a big estate, and my brother and I lived there and worked three acres of market garden. Working the earth. I think that's what I'll go back to.'

After dinner, he went to bed to read for a while and I took a beer up to the flat roof. Below, the city raged, and above the sky joined in, conjuring up an electrical storm which split the heavens, pouring rain from the gaps into the streets below and washing, for a few blessed minutes, a hundred years of dirt, shame and depravity out of the worst place on earth.

Suddenly, the phone in my pocket beeped. It was a text from Helen, the lovable but insomniac assistant editor at the paper, to tell me that the editor had retired unexpectedly. I looked at the message, stunned at the news.

As it sank in, there was a crash and a flash across the rooftops. I took it to be gunfire, but it was a midnight firework display to mark the start of Holy Week.

I watched, the rain streaming down my face, then looked at the message again, and began to laugh, at the strange wonder of life.

I dreamed of India, and woke at dawn.

At breakfast, we met a loud American who had spent the night in the hotel with a Panamanian girlfriend half his age and waist size.

'Her mother doesn't approve of us sleeping together,' he said by way of explanation. 'Say, what the hell are you guys doing in a shit-heap like Colón?'

We told him.

'Damn, I'd have brought you and the bikes on my yacht for 800 bucks. Not quite legally, of course,' he winked.

We checked out, and at eight on the dot, as requested, we were sitting on Gladys's doorstep. Only to be told the bikes were still not ready, for no obvious reason.

'Maybe this afternoon,' Gladys shrugged.

Knowing by now that that meant tomorrow, or possibly Christmas, we sighed deeply and hailed a cab whose roof sign bore the word Taliban on the front and a Nike logo on the back in an intriguing and possibly unique pairing of Western capitalism and Islamic fundamentalism.

We drove to the New Washington Hotel, booked in, and waited. We were getting very good at it by now.

After a while, I began to wonder if we would ever leave Colón, or if we would have to move in permanently, buy two Uzis and make a living by robbing the local teenagers. That would surprise the little buggers.

In the afternoon, with still no word from Gladys, we drank coffee on the terrace and watched cargo ships slide to and fro across the bay.

'We're going to sit here for ever,' said Clifford. 'We'll grow long beards and cobwebs while behind us the hotel crumbles to dust.'

'And we'll become a tourist attraction,' I said. 'People will come from far and wide to see us, saying: "They came here years ago, but no one can remember why."'

At three, we phoned Gladys to find that she knew nothing about anything. At four, I tracked down a man called Irving in the shipping office. It turned out that part of the cargo had been subject to quarantine, possibly a cage full of guinea pigs on their way to a Peruvian restaurant in Panama City, and the man responsible for filling in the forms properly hadn't.

Making a mental note to find him and set his own guinea pigs on him, we resigned ourselves wearily to the inevitable: another night in Colón. We returned to the terrace, and had a beer.

The sun sank in a thunderous sky, and the moon rose to take its place.

Frogs burbled in the undergrowth, and the lights of ships came on one by one across the bay until we lost count at thirty.

I looked beyond them to where, far across the ocean, my wife lay sleeping, the rise and fall of her breathing a gentle wind that kept my soul aloft. In the tropical night, the warm breeze whispered in the coconut palms above our heads and wafted across the top of my empty bottle with a sound, as low and mournful as a Canadian train whistle, which matched exactly the almost palpable sense of love and longing I felt at that moment in my heart.

The next morning, we rose early and sat around like Spitfire pilots waiting for the order to scramble. To help things along, I ordered eggs for breakfast, and it seemed to work, for soon afterwards the phone rang with the news that the bikes were ready, willing and able to be liberated from the docks.

We checked out, and within half an hour were in Gladys's office, handing her $450 we could ill afford in handling charges, which, since we hadn't actually handled anything yet, seemed a little unfair.

An hour later, we were actually at the docks prising the machines out of the crates, then screwing on windscreens, number plates and panniers which the Colombian drugs police had dismantled in their fruitless search for my Junior Disprin.

Clifford was using an impressive looking toolkit, and I was using the screwdriver on my Swiss Army knife. So far so good, I thought as we stood back, admired our handiwork, and thought how good it was to see our little darlings again.

Then April refused to start.

Sighing deeply in what had become our standard form of expression in Latin America, we got a gang together, push-started her and rode to the nearest bike shop.

'We have no mechanic. We just sell bikes, but I will phone someone for you,' said the owner.

The mechanic arrived an hour later, and as he set to dismantling April, I oiled the chains and checked Tony's tyre pressure, only to find practically nothing in the rear one. Ho hum, I thought. It never rains but a sheep falls on your head, as my grandfather was so fond of saying after a few pints.

'How much are those new bikes in your window?' I asked the shop owner as we watched the mechanic strip off all of April's bodywork to get at the battery.

'Nice Liffan cruiser, made in China, very reliable, only $1,800,' he said.

'Might be cheaper to just buy two of those and start afresh,' I said to Clifford.

'Too true,' he muttered gloomily.

After an hour, the mechanic finally hauled out the battery, took one look and announced that the acid had evaporated in the heat. He went off with it, presumably to the nearest distilled water lake, and we sat in the sun waiting for him, contemplatively licking coconut lollies from a passing ice-cream salesman with a trolley and a little bell.

'You know, Pancho,' I said, 'this trip will either kill us or make men of us. I mean, we'll either go home, sit in an armchair in front of the fire and never move again as long as we live, or we'll realise, like Biggles, that there is no problem that cannot be overcome with courage, tenacity and patience.'

'Or foreseen. I wouldn't have thought of that battery problem in a month of Sundays,' he said.

Soon the mechanic returned, reconnected the battery, tried the switch, and April started like she'd never been stopped.

'Genius,' said Clifford. 'Sheer bloody genius.'

I looked at my watch. It was half past four, and there was no point of even thinking of setting off for anywhere.

We paid the mechanic $25, rode to a garage and pumped up Tony's back tyre, and fifteen minutes later were presenting ourselves to the surprised doorman at the New Washington Hotel, to whom we had bid a tearful farewell only that morning.

'You know,' I said as we sank into comfortable chairs on the terrace and watched the sun go down, 'I know I try to be a Zen Buddhist and live in the eternal now, but I will be so, so glad to get to a country which is safe, easy, where they speak English and where everything is not a constant challenge.'

'You're getting soft in your old age,' said Clifford, taking a long sip of his beer, 'but I know exactly what you mean.'

'Clove rock or lemon bon-bons, señor?'
'I'll take the lot, and throw in some gobstoppers while you're at it.'

15

I was awakened at six by Clifford in the shower, singing 'Gotta Get out of this Place' at the top of his voice.

It felt strange at first, getting back on the bikes, setting off and watching Tony's mileometer, which had lain dormant for so long, yawn, stretch and start counting the miles again. Half excited and half nervous, for the first few of those miles I became convinced that the bike would self-destruct or fall over without warning, or that the tyres would spontaneously explode, flinging me into the jungle to be impaled on the beak of a surprised parrot.

However, the only exciting thing that happened was that we were soaked by a tropical downpour, then dried by the equally tropical sun. And then, suddenly, it became glorious again: not only the feeling of fleeing Colón, but of being out on the bikes in the fresh air, and heading up the road again. Even if we were riding south for forty-three miles before heading in the right direction again.

Before long we were in Panama City and riding across the Bridge of the Americas, the soaring arch which is the gateway to the rest of Central America and all points north. How lucky I felt to be alive at that moment, with the Panama Canal, busy with ships, stretching away to the right, and the Pacific glittering on the left until it slipped out of sight behind the trees.

'See you in San Diego,' I said to the last glimpse of it.

Along the road, we got used again to the sight of people waving from cars, the same question on all their faces: two big bikes, loaded up and heading north – wonder where they're headed for?

Alaska. If only they knew.

At our first rest stop, a boy of about eight was selling pirated DVDs on the kerb until the local drunk, staggering out of the *cantina* from his liquid breakfast, sent them flying. We helped the boy tidy them up, refused his kind offer of a copy of *Pride and Prejudice*, assured him that it wasn't because we suffered from either, and went on our way,

An hour later, we were at the El Nispero zoo, one of whose delights, according to the guidebook, was the *Gallina Inglesa*, or English chicken. It looked, you will be pleased to hear, pretty much like an English chicken. You know, standing around looking imperiously for an Irish chicken to invade.

By teatime, having done quite enough for a first day back in the saddle, we stopped at a little roadside hotel, and within five minutes were in the pool. We were only 200 miles up the road from the dirt, depravity and decay of Colón, but already it felt like a million.

At teatime, the television news had more native protests in Ecuador, floods in Colombia, a machete murder in Colón and riots at the bus station in Panama City.

'Looks like we've left a trail of devastation wherever we've gone,' I said to Clifford as we wandered down the road to a restaurant, only to find everyone staring glumly into their soup.

The reason soon became obvious: because it was Easter, all alcohol was officially banned in Panama until Saturday afternoon, two whole days away. Good grief, I thought as we sat down to spaghetti bolognese washed down with a thrilling glass of water, it's going to be like a Free Presbyterian Groundhog Day.

There was only one thing for it. Get out of Panama as fast as possible.

The next morning, after the nervousness of the previous day, was glorious: a climb into wooded hills on a smooth and empty road. It was so perfect that I had to pinch myself several times to remind myself that I was actually riding a motorbike through Central America on a Friday morning. Heavens, I was so relaxed that I even started singing inside my helmet for the first time since before the accident. Selected hits from Simon and Garfunkel, since you ask.

Not only that, but I thought of a line of dialogue for my next novel which had been troubling me for some time. Here it is, at no extra charge.

'Is anyone living in there?' said the policeman.

'Yes, but only just,' he said.

Remember, you read it here first.

All around us as we rode were green hills and shining rivers, and I could already see myself turning into the sort of old duffer who sits in the corner of gentlemen's clubs saying things like: 'Well, of course the Lake District is all very well, but it's not a patch on the Chirique Highlands of western Panama. Not to mention the central Colombian coffee plantations. You see, when I was a younger man ... '

However, this would probably never happen, since the chances of me ever being able to afford to join a gentlemen's club were about as slim as my increasingly anorexic wallet. I made a note to send out begging letters to the tourist boards from California to Alaska asking if they could help out with accommodation, and late in the morning, we stopped at a *cantina* for fresh pineapple juice.

It was, naturally, owned by a woman called Gladys. On the wall hung a life-size representation of Santa, below which a TV broadcast a lugubrious Good Friday service to the nation. Somewhere above us, Jesus could be heard muttering: 'And just remind me what was so good about it, exactly?'

Across the road, three horses, one white, one brown and one

black, galloped across a meadow in the sun.

At that moment, it seemed a much more apt expression of the joy of life than the ancient rituals of death and suffering, or even the fat jolly chap on the wall, courtesy of Dutch reformists and the marketing department of Coca-Cola.

A short history of Costa Rica

1506
Spanish arrive. Natives, unaware that they should just roll over and die, launch thirty-year guerrilla campaign.

1540
Spanish defeat natives, discover that country has no gold, and ignore it for several centuries, creating such poverty that in 1719 governor famously complains that he has to till his own land.

1821
Independence. Country discovers coffee, and wealth percolates through land with seductive aroma of freshly roasted dollars.

1980
After almost two centuries of prosperity and stability, including the establishment of a welfare system, UN launches investigation into claims that Costa Ricans are not Latin American but Swedish.

1989
Coffee and banana price-slump leads to $5 billion foreign debt, interest payments for which gobble up 30 per cent of annual government budget. Country remains stubbornly prosperous and stable. Swedish rumours escalate but remain unresolved to this day.

At the border, all the formalities seemed to be handled by a diminutive fourteen-year-old called Humberton, who led us to the Panama passport office. They told us firmly that we didn't need an exit stamp, and, naturally enough, the Costa Ricans 200 yards up the road insisted that we did. This game of diplomatic tennis, with us as the ball, went on for some time, undoubtedly amusing everyone except us.

'Keep smiling,' said Clifford as we stood for the fourth time beside the Panama passport window, looking at a sign saying, in English, 'We Don't Accept Tramitors'.

Quite right. I wouldn't either. Whatever they are.

Finally, after the usual 4,836 forms, not to mention $28 in customs duties, plus $5 and a can of Sprite for Humberton, we were free to enjoy Costa Rica.

And enjoy it we did, through an afternoon of the sort of weather I had thought only existed in Ireland, where it is both sunny and raining at the same time. For the last hour we had the tropical forest to our left, a river to our right, the cloud-piled sky above us and a rainbow in front. It was, it seemed, the perfect end to a perfect day.

Until we got to the jungle village of Buenos Aires, checked into a simple *cabina* with cold and cold running water, and discovered to our horror that the Easter beer ban applied to Costa Rica as well. Never mind the accident and the shipping delays and costs: this was the biggest disaster of the trip so far.

Even worse, it looked like we were going to get no supper either, for a quick search of the village revealed that the inhabitants were a deeply religious lot who had rolled up the pavements and gone home to pray for the weekend. At last we found a fruit and veg shop that was just closing. Since the owner had already locked the top half of the security grill, we were forced to limbo dance our way in, emerging with a tomato, a tin of tuna and some stale bread. Even better, down the street we found the only Satanist in town, who sold us two cans of warm beer wrapped in brown paper.

Splendid. I mean, don't get me wrong. I don't mind religion, but religion and no beer is a different matter.

Now, if you'll excuse me, I have a goat to slaughter, since the village seems to be running short of virgins this evening.

'Up and at 'em, Atom Ant!' declared Clifford at 6 a.m., leaping out of bed and jumping into the shower.

'God, I love being in the country,' he said as he towelled himself dry. 'I don't know how people can live in cities.'

He looked around our bare room, with its concrete floor, threadbare curtains and dubious bedclothes.

'This is real travelling for me. I can't stand being in places where you have to tip someone to carry your bag for you.'

'Pancho, you've never given anyone a tip for carrying our bags the whole trip,' I said.

'I have the reputation of the entire Scottish nation to uphold,' he said, then went outside with his binoculars to watch two parrots snogging at the top of a coconut tree. Oh well, nothing like a cold shower and no breakfast to make a man out of you, I thought, leaping out of bed myself and subjecting myself to the frozen deluge.

Still, we found coffee and scrambled eggs at a truckers' *cantina* up the road, with the sound of the trucks competing with the TV in the corner, which even at seven in the morning was blasting out soaps.

In the stillness of early morning, we climbed through green mountains until we felt on top of the world, both literally and figuratively.

Soon, however, we descended to valleys of river and jungle, and as if to make up for the cool of the morning, the afternoon was like being baked at gas mark 6 in a fan-assisted oven. It was, as my mother would say, great drying weather.

Still, unbearable thought the heat was, it would come in very handy when we got to Alaska, I thought, storing away as much of it as I could in the spare nooks and crannies of the panniers at our next rest stop.

It was Easter Saturday, and for miles in the opposite direction sat cars, either broken down in the heat or full of families proceeding towards the coast at approximately 2.2mph. They would, if they were lucky, arrive at teatime, sit on the beach for an hour, have dinner, go to bed and then repeat the process in the other direction the following day. Some families, too poor or sensible to roast in a car all day, contented themselves with sitting in rivers here and there with the water up to their noses.

As for us, our destination was nowhere in particular, and that's exactly where we ended up, stopping at four for no other reason than that we had ridden 225 miles in holiday traffic, which in that heat was quite enough, even for men of steel.

And bikes, come to that: unloading Tony, I looked at the broken stumps of the indicator and rear view mirror, the twisted handlebars, the welded and gaffer-taped generator cover and the lacerated tank, and thought what a remarkable tribute to a long line of fine British motorcycle manufacturing he was. In spite of being fed a diet of dodgy fuel, then flung down the road at 60mph by a careless owner whose only mitigation was that at least he had had the good grace to fling himself down the same road in sympathy, he had kept on going, through baking heat and torrential rain, dirt and dust, thick mud and thin air alike. Even the panniers and top box, which had hit the road so hard in the crash that they had been flung off their locked mountings, had slotted back on afterwards without a murmur of protest.

As for the nut on top of the tank, meanwhile, he was doing his best, in the tradition of dancing like no one is watching and loving like you've never been hurt, of riding like he'd never fallen off.

However, when I mentioned this to Clifford over supper, he voiced the opinion that I was riding slower than an arthritic slug and had, in fact, been passed by a group of cyclists that morning.

'Well, those guys looked pretty fit to me,' I said, hurt.

It was all right for him: he was a former Isle of Man TT champion. I was just a bloke who rode motorbikes across continents and fell off occasionally. However, his criticism of my astonishing riding ability wasn't the biggest tragedy of the evening.

No, it was the fact that on the night beer became legal again throughout Costa Rica, we had picked the only restaurant in the country without a drinks licence.

As I was loading up Tony just after dawn the next day, a woman from Alberta walked past wearing a T-shirt which said: 'If a man speaks in the desert when no woman can hear, is he still wrong?'

'Nice T-shirt,' I laughed.

'Nice bike,' she said. 'I did my test on my brother's old BSA. Do English bikes still have the gears on the wrong side and upside down?'

'No, they fixed that with a little encouragement from the Japanese,' I said as Pancho appeared, ready to set off.

If the mountains of Costa Rica had been coffee country, the grassland was cowboy country, and here and there, noble *caballeros* on matching horses were rounding up cattle to go to Easter Sunday Mass, although one or two recalcitrant specimens could be seen hightailing it for the horizon in a cloud of heathen dust.

For the last twenty miles before the border with Nicaragua, the road was a biker's dream, a sweep of curves through the blessed dapple of trees. Heavens, I even kept up with Pancho. Well, once. Oh, all right then, it was just for the five yards after the filling station, if you want to be so picky about it.

Anyway the blessing of trees was the last blessing for a few hours, for we were about to encounter another border crossing.

A short history of Nicaragua

1522
Spanish arrive, find no gold and enslave entire population. Nothing happens for 300 years.

1821
Independence.

1855
Country invaded by US mercenaries led by Tennessee adventurer William Walker, who reintroduces slavery and declares English official language.

1860
Walker captured by British and executed for acting like an Englishman, but not speaking like one.

1903
President José Santos proposes Nicaragua as site for new canal. US chooses Panama. Santos invites Germany and Japan around for coffee and scones to discuss rival canal. US invades Nicaragua, installing corrupt bully General Somoza as president.

1956
Somoza shot by romantic poet called Pérez. National Guard shoots Pérez fifty times. Pérez dies, inevitably but romantically. Somoza's sons take over and start campaign of torturing dissidents.

1979
Sandinista rebels overthrow Somozas in civil war which leaves 50,000 dead, country in ruins and population broke but happy. Sandinistas set about rebuilding country, improving literacy, health, education and role of women hugely.

1984
First free elections since 1928 see left-wing Daniel Ortega elected president. Ronald Reagan celebrates with US trade embargo. Oliver North scandal later reveals that CIA sold illegal weapons to Iran to raise $20 million for toppling legally elected Nicaraguan government.

1984–1998
Country goes to dogs. Dogs go to Costa Rica.

1998
Country devastated by hurricane. Two main banks collapse.
Faced with poverty, unemployment, recession and instability,
Nicaraguans comfort themselves with thought that at least
things can't get any worse.

2000
Country hit by another hurricane, then earthquake.
Nicaraguans give up thinking.

Here is probably a good time for some useful advice for secret
policemen around the world.

If you want to get someone to confess to something, forget
the white noise, the rubber truncheons, the electrodes and the
good cop, bad cop routine.

Just get them to cross a Central American border in the
midday sun. After an hour, they'll sign their name to anything,
including sinking the *Titanic*, starting the Holocaust, bombing
Hiroshima and inventing *Big Brother*.

I will spare you the grim details, since it pains me to
remember them: the endless traipsing to and fro in the baking
heat clutching a pile of documents whose production would
have kept a Norwegian paper baron in profit for a year. Suffice
it to say that we arrived early in the morning, and it was
lunchtime before we were set free.

Still, it could have been worse. I could have worked there: as
the woman at the final desk was stamping her millionth form
that day, she said wearily: 'You're going to Alaska? Do you
want to take me with you?'

'It's very cold,' I said. 'Do you have a warm shirt at all?'

It would, I thought as we rode off, only to be stopped after
fifty yards and asked for a spurious $2 entrance tax, be a lot
easier if all the countries in Central America got together and
created one huge border post, preferably in Milton Keynes.
You could then go there, spend two days filling in forms, and
emerge with a single piece of paper which would allow you to
travel unhindered from Panama to Tijuana and vice versa.

I mean, how hard could it be? The countries of Europe had done it, and they didn't even speak the same language. Except the English and the French, who thought they ought to. Even better, I knew just the person to run it: Humberton.

Anyway, we had our reward soon enough: at first a storm of swallows who turned the sky black as each of them dipped to greet us, missing us again and again by miraculous inches. And then the vast and glittering expanse of Lago de Nicaragua, after the Great Lakes the largest body of fresh water in the Americas.

As if that wasn't enough to be going on with, the far shore was lined by a row of volcanoes, all improbably topped with snow. Snow! Even the idea seemed impossible, as we toiled across the valley in the heat, with only the beat of swallows' wings to cool us.

We took a rutted side road to the elegant lakeside colonial city of Granada, but I somehow managed not to find it, riding around the suburbs for a frustrating hour until we came to a lakeside *cantina* with disco music. As elegant colonial experiences go, it wasn't the best.

Clifford went for a swim, and I made a note to go to navigation classes when I got home, if I could find them.

'It's like the Ganges down there,' he said when he came back. 'You can barely see the lake for the people in it.'

We set off again, painstakingly threading our way along the extravagantly potholed highway, only to be stopped by two policemen who tore our luggage apart, obviously hoping that we would give them a bribe. Instead we stood around smiling and looking stupid, which we found surprisingly easy, until they gave up and let us go.

We rode off into the evening light, passing several strange human effigies hanging from trees by their necks, presumably bikers who had tried to get through Nicaragua without paying a bribe. Only tomorrow would tell if we would join them, or continue safely towards Honduras.

In the meantime, we found a happy family hotel by the roadside in which to spend the night. There were happy kids splashing about in the pool, happy mums lying on loungers looking like Bianca Jagger and, best of all, happy dads sitting around drinking beer.

Thank you, Lord, I whispered. I knew I was turning into Homer Simpson, but I didn't care.

That night, I dreamed that I was walking around my old university halls of residence when I met a man who was riding to Tierra del Fuego on a motorbike. Mind you, if he was doing it via the Malone Road in Belfast, he had an even worse sense of direction than I had.

'God, I wish I could do something like that,' I said to him, then realised, even in the dream, that I was, and laughed myself awake.

An hour later, we set off towards Managua on a road running across high, desolate moors, a bit like Yorkshire except for roadside shacks for which the expression dirt-poor would have been wild hyperbole. Outside one, a man was painting a single strand of barbed wire with red lead to make it last for a few more years, although what exactly it was meant to be guarding remained a mystery. Perhaps only the same sense of pride evident in the fact that every single man, woman and child to be seen was dressed in immaculate clothes, as if to say: 'I may be poor, but I am clean.'

Outside another hovel, a boy stood optimistically dangling two dead iguanas for sale. As we entered the outskirts of Managua, we passed another example of that strange Third World tradition of similar crafts huddling together as if for comfort, in this case an entire row of shops selling bird cages. Mind you, it is not a tradition confined to the Third World: witness Savile Row.

Built on eleven seismic faults and regularly destroyed by earthquakes, fires and civil wars, the Nicaraguan capital was to ancient colonial charm what George Best was to sobriety. Not only that, but it was hotter than hell and had a record for armed robbery only beaten by Colón.

After half a second's careful consideration, we decided to drive straight through it. This proved, for once, easier done than said, since the city had been levelled so many times that it seemed to consist of a single road past people gazing thoughtfully at piles of rubble from the last disaster.

Still, the good news, since we were broke again, was that one of the buildings left standing was a bank, inside which I discovered that the Nicaraguan love of paperwork was not confined to its borders. I emerged an hour older, not much wiser and slightly richer.

'You didn't happen to see a set of Triumph motorbike keys knocking around anywhere, did you, Pancho?' I said, hunting in vain in my trouser pocket.

'They were in the ignition, where you usually leave them,' he said, dangling them tantalisingly in the sunlight.

In the afternoon we rose through the mountains, away from the inferno of the city into the blessed cool, and by nightfall were only a few miles from the border with Honduras.

Clifford was happy because, late in the day, we had passed a sign outside a hacienda saying Rancho Pancho, and I was happy because tomorrow, since the stretch of the Pan-American through Honduras is only sixty miles long, we would attempt a world first: crossing two Central American borders in one day.

A short history of Honduras

1502
Spanish arrive and hold first Mass in Latin America.

1536
Native chieftain Lempira holds first mass rebellion in Latin America. Spanish invite him to peace talks and shoot him. Most of population enslaved and sent down mines. Lucky few die of smallpox.

1823
Independence. Civil war. Chaos.

1867
First stable government in decades celebrates by planning national railway. British banks lend government £6 million for railway at such crippling interest rates that debt rises to £30 million and is only finally paid off in 1953. Railway never built.

1876
More chaos. Government asks US to help out. US takes over lucrative mining, coffee and banana industries, effectively controlling economy.

1969
Country distracted briefly from chaos by riot at Honduras v El Salvador soccer match. El Salvador invades, resulting in eleven-year war. Honduran government takes advantage of chaos to scarper with millions. US takes advantage of chaos to use Honduras as base for attacks on legally elected Nicaraguan government. US and Korean companies take advantage of chaos to set up huge garment factories paying poverty wages.

1998
Hurricane leaves trail of devastation which president claims has set country back fifty years. Hondurans wonder how he can tell.

An even shorter history of Honduras

Man-made chaos, interspersed with natural disasters.

A short history of our time in Honduras

Three hours at border with Nicaragua getting in, including the exciting new wheeze of having to provide photocopies of every document we possessed. Naturally, we couldn't do this on the photocopier sitting in the corner of the customs office, but had to trudge half a mile up the road in searing heat to the photocopy shop, the owner of which bore a suspicious family resemblance to the customs officer. Coincidence, naturally.

Two hours riding through country across high sierra, passing cowboys, cows and a dead horse being towed along the road by a pick-up.

At least I assume he was dead, since he was lying on his side.

Either that, or he was taking the sleeper service to Panama.

Or perhaps he had signed up for the Honduran Horse Club's complete roadside breakdown recovery service.

Three hours at border with El Salvador getting out, not helped by passport office, customs office and photocopy shop being several miles apart.

The End.

A short history of El Salvador

1524
Spanish arrive, find highly organised and civilised Mayan culture, kill almost everyone and establish system of virtual slavery under rich landowners.

1822
Independence, followed automatically by civil war and chaos.

1820–1929
Coffee boom makes landowners even richer. Peasants stay poor, although now enjoying a much better cup of coffee every morning.

1919
Wall Street crash. Coffee prices collapse. Faced with even greater poverty, peasants rebel, provoking landowner backlash which leaves 30,000 dead.

1932–1980
Landowners install military government to maintain status quo.

1980s
Reagan administration gives government $1.5 billion.
Government uses money to step up corruption, assassination
and terror against opponents, resulting in civil war.

1992
Ceasefire and peace. Well, apart from unchecked gang
warfare, kidnappings, hurricanes and earthquakes.

After the mind-numbing, energy-sapping and time-draining
experience of two border crossings in one day, we rode an hour
to San Miguel in El Salvador, and collapsed into the nearest
hotel. After half an hour of lying on our beds comatose, with
documents and photocopies flashing before our eyes, we felt
well enough to walk down the street looking for supper.

It turned out that we were in the middle of the red light
district, with every building a brothel with darkened windows
and a man sitting outside with a pump-action shotgun and an
expression on his face which suggested that when he was a boy
he had not exactly dreamed of doing this when he grew up.
Fortunately, at the end of the row of brothels we found a local
restaurant serving pints of margarita and plates piled high
with chicken and beans.

On stage, a singer was busy mangling 'Imagine' by John
Lennon to the extent that the lyrics sounded like: 'Imagine
there's no liver, imagine there's no beer.' Since I had had quite
enough of imagining there was no beer over Easter, I stopped
listening at this point and ordered a large bottle.

Exhausted by the day, we fell into bed immediately after
supper, and slept like logs.

I was sweeping up the leaves the next morning when Clifford
picked up the Gideon's New Testament which was lying on the
bedside table.

'That'll do nicely. I've been looking for something to read other than those four million guidebooks you've brought with you,' he said, shoving it in his bag.

'Pancho, I can't believe you're nicking a Bible.'

'I'm not nicking it. They get them free,' he said, loading the bag on the bike, starting up and riding off.

I followed him, sure that we would be blasted at the gate by the guard with the shotgun, or at the very least dragged off to prison in the Vatican and forced to say four dozen Hail Marys and How's Your Fathers before breakfast.

Talking of breakfast, we hadn't had any, since the hotel restaurant was unaccountably closed. Two miles up the road, we found a truckers' café where the owner brought us eggs, beans and black coffee thick with sugar, because that's the way everyone took it.

After the palpable and heartbreaking poverty of Nicaragua and Honduras, El Salvador was as prosperous and tidy as Holland. Heavens, I even saw a driver using his indicator at lunchtime, although it may have been a mistake, since he switched it off immediately again, probably for fear of being thrown out of the Latin American Drivers' Association.

Early in the afternoon, we arrived unexpectedly at the border with Guatemala, which we had not expected to cross until the next day. I looked at Pancho, and he looked at me.

'Will we go for it?' I heard myself say.

'Aye, why not?' he said and, filled with a mixture of Buddhist calm and Kierkegaardean fear and trembling, we plunged yet again into the Dante's Inferno that is a Central American border crossing.

A short history of Guatemala

1500 BC–900 AD
Mayans create vast empire of cities, palaces, pyramids and roads.

1523

Spanish arrive, creating usual death and suffering, followed by 300 years of rigidly hierarchical colonial rule, from pure-blood Spanish landowners down to indigenous slaves.

1821

Independence, replacing Spanish tyranny with home-grown variety. New government confiscates land and sells it to large corporations. From 1901, country virtually ruled by US-owned United Fruit Company, backed by landowners.

1958

Liberal president Jacobo Arbenz gives land back to Guatemalans. CIA, whose director is member of United Fruit Company board, accuses him of being a communist and persuades US to invade, installing military government specialising in corruption, incompetence, patronage and death squads which murder opposition politicians, union leaders, reformers, students, priests, journalists and lawyers.

1999

Self-confessed murderer Alfonso Portillo elected president and promises justice and human rights, but delivers corruption, poverty, discrimination and almost complete breakdown in law and order. Otherwise, all is well.

'Here, didn't I see you two on Colombian TV?' said the man in front of us in the queue for the passport office. He turned out to be Minor – 'as in Major' – just returning to Guatemala from holidays in Cartagena.

As Clifford was queuing for the last document and I was minding the bikes, a small boy of about twelve came up to me, introduced himself as José, and looked up at me with very large hazel eyes.

'Where are you going, *señor*?' he said.

I told him.

'You are heroes, for doing such a thing,' he said.

I looked back at him, and saw in his eyes myself as a boy of the same age, wondering what adventures I would have when I grew up. At least for one small fellow, we were boy's own heroes, I thought as José walked away, passing Clifford coming back with his final document held triumphant.

'Is it Frodo?' I said hopefully.

'Nope.'

Two hours later, in the divine cool of early evening, we fell through sweet glades of pine to a little inn by the river. It had a metal sculpture of Don Quixote and his faithful sidekick on the wall, which seemed as good an omen as any to rest our heads there that night.

What a very fine country Guatemala was: a green and pleasant land of pine forests, alpine meadows and women washing bright clothes in splashing streams.

Even Guatemala City, as we rode through it the next day, had a pleasant and organised air about it, unlike the usual chaos of Latin American capitals. Even if every other car did have a pump-action shotgun poking out through the window.

We followed a truckload of pigs through the streets, emerging triumphantly at the other side and stopping at a filling station to celebrate with Magnum bars and a top-up of 95-octane fuel. Ninety-five octane! If our luck held like this through Mexico, I could dump the plastic bottles of octane booster which since Peru had been making one of the panniers smell like a Russian oil refinery.

Several times, as the bikes sat in shimmering heat at one border post or other, I had feared that the inside of that pannier would reach such a heat that the booster would spontaneously combust, leaving Tony a charred wreck and the trip in ruins.

We set off again, and were soon bouncing over the cobbles of the magnificent colonial city of Antigua, a multifarious joy of pastel facades, wooden pillars and shady courtyards. As we got off the bikes to admire it properly, a BMW owner from California called Lee walked over and asked us what we were about.

'God, I'd love to do that trip,' he said, as we were joined by Dan and Tom, two Australian backpackers who also had bikes at home. Before long, we were surrounded by young men, who went away promising themselves that they would go home, sell the house and follow in our tyre tracks.

Leaving a legacy of adventure and probably divorce behind us, we sped off through countryside which seemed to be one huge market garden, with men and women in straw hats and extravagant costumes tending to giant cabbages and the like.

Once, we passed the only two-storey thatched house I had ever seen. Shortly after, we stopped at a traditional Mayan inn, with Abba, that well-known Guatemalan quartet, on the CD player, and had coffee and pie, that old favourite of Route 66 days.

We rode on, passing a forest glade in which a shepherdess sat weaving a rainbow from a hand loom on her knee as she tended her flock.

We rose into cloud forests, and took the winding road down towards Lake Atitlán, of which Aldous Huxley had said in *Beyond the Mexique Bay* in 1934: 'Lake Como, it seems to me, touches the limits of the permissibly picturesque, but Atitlán is Como with the additional embellishments of several immense volcanoes. It is really too much of a good thing. After a few days of this impossible landscape, one finds oneself thinking nostalgically of the Home Counties.'

Honestly, that Aldous. What a wag.

For half an hour, however, the cloud was so thick that we could barely see our hands in front of us, and I began to think that, as in Ecuador, this was going to be the finest view I had never seen. Then, everything cleared as we rounded a corner to be greeted by a vista so stunning that both of us stopped the bikes and laughed out loud at the impossible beauty of it.

Minutes later, we were riding down the main street of the lakeside village of Panajechel, only to see walking towards us Iveagh, a pharmacist from Cavan whom we had met briefly at the Panama–Costa Rica border. He greeted us heartily, in the way of Cavan men, and practically ordered us to join him for beer in the nearest pub as soon as was practically possible.

We checked into a hotel with a hot tub in the garden fed by volcanic springs, and did as we were told. You don't argue with a man from Cavan, after all, especially where beer is concerned.

Late in the evening, we wandered at length back to the hotel. Clifford hied himself hence to the hot tub, and I stretched out on the bed to re-read Graham Greene's *The Power and the Glory* and Malcolm Lewis's *Under the Volcano*, as a gentle introduction to Mexico.

I shouldn't have. By the time I fell asleep, I was convinced that the country was filled with drunken priests and stoned consuls staggering to their deaths in a whisky- and mescalin-induced haze, watched with fatalistic apathy by a ragged-trousered populace worn to the bones of their souls after centuries of persecution by Mayans, Aztecs, Spanish, French, Americans and the World Bank.

A populace governed by presidents like General Santa Ana, who in the nineteenth century applied himself diligently to the task of selling off more than half the country.

He was only distracted briefly by a jaunt to the Alamo to quell demands for independence by Texas, which was then part of Mexico. In spite of killing Jim Bowie, Davy Crockett and 150 others, leaving their wives to get by on Alamony payments, Santa Ana still managed to get himself captured and lose Texas anyway.

A hundred years later, things were little better, with unemployment at 25 per cent, inflation wishing it was only 25 per cent and the country over $100 billion in debt.

I fell asleep, thinking that maybe my overdraft wasn't so bad after all.

Next morning, the morning market in Sololá was a symphony of noise and colour. Mayan men and women, outdoing each other in the extravagance of their clothes, walked down the cobbled streets of the village into the square before dawn, with their wares, wrapped in impossibly large bundles, carried on their heads.

And not one iota of this spectacular display was for tourists, since as usual, we were the only gringos in sight.

The children, meanwhile, were so heart-mendingly beautiful that I decided there and then to suggest to Cate that if we had kids, they should be Guatemalan ones.

Suitably enthralled, we sped off in the morning sun towards the Mexican border. But first, a twisting climb through the highlands into the clouds, with a frustrating row of trucks in front. We picked them off one by one, with Clifford doing the mirror work, since I had been devoid of mine since the crash.

And then again, the glorious freedom of a motorbike with the open road in front.

That is, until we rounded a corner and ran into a trail of leaked diesel, the most dangerous substance known to bikers apart from no beer. Clifford's front wheel hit it, slid, and he came within a whisker of falling off in front of an oncoming bus, recovering only by sheer instinct and skill.

We skirted it carefully for the next fifteen miles until it disappeared as mysteriously as it had appeared.

'I swore I was down then,' said Clifford when we stopped to refuel. 'God knows how I saved it.'

We rode on towards the Mexican border, through a river valley cut into such an exact *V* that it could have been done with a machete.

A really big one, naturally.

Worth every bit of the paper it's written on: Clifford with the priceless Mexico customs document.

16

A short history of Mexico

1519
Spanish arrive to discover, to their astonishment, Aztec capital of Tenochtitlán, hub of greatest civilisation on earth. Aztec emperor Montezuma greets them warmly with gifts of gold. Spanish respond warmly by kidnapping him, massacring Aztecs, razing city and fleeing across lake causeway with gold.

1600
Smallpox reduces native population from 25 million to one and a half million. Survivors put to work mining gold and silver, all of which is exported to Spain.

1820–1851
Independence. Chaos, with over fifty different governments, one of which has bright idea of declaring war on US. US invades and forces Mexico to sell Arizona, California and New Mexico for $15 million, depriving Mexicans forever of skinny lattes. Rest of country now owned by 3 per cent of population of Spanish descent.

1863

French invade and install Maximilian and wife, Carlota, as emperor and empress.

1867

Maximilian executed. Carlota flees to Belgium and goes mad, which is the effect Belgium has on people.

1911

Revolution led by Villa and Zapata. More chaos. Eleven presidents in ten years, including one who lasts for all of forty-five minutes.

1934

Modern Mexico emerges from ashes, dusts itself off and nationalises oil companies. Oil boom results in huge borrowing spree.

1982

Oil bust. Huge borrowing spree results in huge foreign debts, inflation, chaos, bankruptcy, corruption and drug wars, enlivened by occasional earthquakes.

2000

New president promises peace and prosperity. *Sí, mañana*, say Mexicans.

By three we were almost at the border, and stopped for a drink at a roadside *cantina* before we plunged into the usual inferno of chaos. Leafing idly through the guidebook, I almost choked on my coffee when I noticed that due to terrorism in the Chiapas area, journalists were not allowed in. Not only that, but you needed your birth certificate to bring a vehicle into the country, presumably in case you were a unicycle-smuggling android.

When we got to the passport office on the Mexican side, I wrote Manager in the space where it said Occupation, and just prayed to the Lord and the Seven Sainted Sisters of Constantinople that no one would ask for my birth certificate, which was 8,000 miles away in the study. Fortunately, no one did, and I emerged an hour later and $29 poorer, but with the windscreen sticker which allowed me fifteen days to make it to the US border.

However, disaster was just about to strike.

Clifford went in for his turn, and came out after half an hour.

'They won't let me cross the border. No way, no how,' he said grimly.

My heart sank.

'Why not?'

'Well, you know the way I had to leave without the original bike registration document because it hadn't arrived from Swansea?'

'Aye, I know that, but you have a letter saying that you're legally entitled to use the bike. It's worked at every border so far.'

'Well, not at this one. I've tried begging, I've tried pleading, I've tried being calm and reasonable, I've tried bursting into tears and I've tried pointing out that we're raising money for orphans. Nothing's worked.'

'Did you try hinting at a bribe?'

'I did. I asked if there was any special payment that could be made for temporary transit, and he said no. He's not shifting. It's original documents, or nothing. I'm stuffed.'

He went across the road, found a Canadian Spanish speaker called Mike who had been waiting seven hours for a bus, and went back in to try again. An hour later, they came out with the good news, of sorts, that the customs official would accept a faxed copy of the document. I looked at my watch. It was one in the morning at home. I hauled out my BT charge card, and from a phone box we called Clifford's mate Yannick.

Incredibly, he was still up, and promised to go to Clifford's office first thing in the morning, see if the DVLA had finally sent the original documents, and fax them.

In the meantime, since we could neither go back to Guatemala or on to Mexico, we rode the bikes across the road to a ramshackle building with a peeling Hotel sign on the front.

'Welcome to limbo. Or possibly purgatory,' said Clifford as the proprietor showed us into a bare cell with a single bulb, a concrete floor and a resident ant colony, and we settled down for the longest night of our lives.

Dawn broke to reveal the worst possible news from Yannick. The registration document for Clifford's bike had never arrived in the licensing office in Swansea. Like us, it was lost in limbo. Even worse, today was, naturally, a Saturday, so the chances of anyone doing anything about it before Monday were nil. Even then, it would take Swansea weeks, or even months, to chase up and replace the document.

Since we didn't have weeks or months, the trip was over for Clifford, after all we had gone through together. I couldn't believe it. We sat in the sun outside our two-bit hotel, sick at heart and wondering what to do.

'What if Yannick scans a document from another vehicle, changes the details to April's and faxes a copy of that?' I said.

'No way. If we get caught at that lark, it'll mean jail for both of us, and I don't fancy spending years in a Mexican jail, thanks very much,' he said.

We sat on, racking our brains for a solution.

'Listen,' he said at last, 'it's Saturday morning. There'll be a new customs official on today. I'll tear a spare page out of the carnet document, which looks official and has my name and all the bike details on it, and see if I can pretend that's the registration document.'

'That's never going to work, Pancho. These guys aren't stupid.'

'I know, but I can't think of anything else.'

He went back to our room, returned with the page from the carnet, and walked across the road to the customs office. I had never seen him looking so drawn and weary. His endless optimism, it seemed, had finally run into a brick wall. It was so ironic, I thought, after all the tough border crossings we had been through, that the very last one before the Big Easy of the United States would prove impassable.

I sat there for an hour as the sun and the heat rose, until the door of the office finally opened and he came walking back across the road, his face impassive. It was only when he was halfway across that he could contain himself no longer. His face burst into a huge grin, and from behind his back he produced the elusive sticker and held it aloft.

Of all the stickers he had craved on the trip, this was the one that mattered.

'Miracle. Get on the bikes,' he said. 'We have to get out of here before he changes his mind or calls the boss.'

We ran back to the room, threw everything in our bags in seconds, started the bikes and leapt on them. I followed Clifford out onto the road and rode past the customs post, my heart pounding. All it would take was one phone call, and we would be hauled back inside, and jailed for attempted fraud.

We raced down the road. For the first five miles, I kept glancing over my shoulder, sure that I would see flashing lights and hear the growing wail of sirens. There was nothing. I glanced nervously ahead, convinced that a customs official disguised as a tree would leap out from the hedgerow, demand our documents and then have us strung up by the dongles.

But there was nothing. Nothing except the open road stretching all the way to the US of A.

As I rode along under the endless blue sky, past farmers working in the fields, their wives hanging out washing and their children playing in gardens bright with bougainvillaea, I was overcome with such a sense of relief and wellbeing that for the rest of my life, if anyone asked me what happiness was, I would say it was this day.

We climbed through pine forests and dappled glades, each with a resident shepherdess or woodcarver, and by nightfall found a motel by a river.

It turned out, in fact, to be a love hotel, with a steady stream of couples arriving nervous and leaving happy. I suppose we should have suspected something when we saw how many mirrors there were in the room. Not to mention the rotating food hatch in the outside wall, like a secular, or possibly sexular, version of the ones found in the walls of closed nunneries.

And then, the evening brought good news, and bad, from home. The good was that *Way to Go*, my last book, had been reprinted again because of US demand, and that my brother Trevor would be joining us on a rented Harley for a week up the west coast of the States.

And the bad news was that Cate would not, as we had originally hoped. She was, as we had increasingly feared, too snowed under by work to get away. I had thought many times, during the long, hard slog up South America, of what I would feel when I saw her in Los Angeles. It would, I had imagined, be the same as the feeling I had every time I saw her after an absence: as if all the love in the world had been squeezed into a heart too small to contain it.

So now I would not see her in California after all, but we would meet again, before sooner became later, and I would have her for the rest of my days.

In the border crossing of life, that was worth all the stickers in the world.

In the *zócalo* of San Cristóbal the next morning, the men began gathering at first light, crouching over mugs of hot, bitter chocolate to ward off the mountain chill as their womenfolk laid out for sale dresses and shawls whose infinitely complex patterns had not changed for a thousand years. Oh, and New York Yankees baseball caps, Coca-Cola key rings and portable televisions. But we'll ignore those just for the moment.

Down the side streets leading away from the square, the old colonial buildings were painted vivid lilacs, oranges and burnt ochres, and in the food stalls of the market, upturned wooden crates were piled high with chillies, every fruit and vegetable imaginable, freshwater fish, crabs, prawns and tamarind pods like sleeping mice. Marimba music throbbed from pirate cassette stalls, and tiny children, their almond eyes and high cheekbones more Oriental than Latin American, scampered everywhere.

In a white tin dish, a Tzeltal man shaved a pig's head with an old razor, while beside him his wife, wearing the soft autumnal colours of the hill village of Tenejapa, clutched in one hand their child and in the other an enormous bouquet of Madonna lilies, in a scene straight from a Diego Rivera mural.

On the steps of the fantastically Churrigueresque church of Santo Domingo, other men drank to ward off the evil spirits in their stomachs. Once they had drunk *pulque*, the mild distillation of the maguey cactus which is so rich in vitamins and minerals that it was given to children, until the twin efforts of evangelists and soft-drink salesmen forced them to switch to Coca-Cola. In front of the town hall, several of the same evangelists were holding a revival meeting, watched by a mixture of hill villagers who had been thrown out of their families because of their conversion, and baffled Zinacantecans in their pink tunics and flat straw hats.

It was time to leave, and we took the mountain road north, at first winding through pine-clad hills, then coming more and more upon flamboyant plants with no sense of scale, and finally plunging into a dense world of green punctuated here and there by whimsical splashes of yellow mimosa.

At Agua Azul, we ate ham sandwiches below the mighty falls while women and their daughters sold us pineapples and bananas from bowls balanced on their heads. It is the women who do all the work in these hill villages, while the men lounge around looking moody and mean, as if they are working up their courage for a jungle expedition. But then, in any traditional hunter-gatherer society, the men, for all their posturing, only bring in 15 per cent of the food, while the women quietly gather the rest.

We rode on, past one-room wooden houses outside which entire families sat, watching the occasional car go by. Behind them, in clearings hacked out of the jungle, their weekly washing danced in every colour of the rainbow from clothes lines and bushes.

It was another hour before we reached our destination: Palenque, the lost city of the Mayans and the symbol of their greatest hour. In the seventh century after Christ, under the influence of Lord Pacal and his sons, it was the finest achievement of Mayan architects, a vast complex of which even today archaeologists have only uncovered a fifth.

The first of them was Count Frederic von Waldeck, who in the 1830s established himself in one of the five temples at the northern end of the site, and spent two years wandering around scratching his chin and dreaming up theories that the Mayans were distant cousins of the Phoenicians in dress and the Egyptians in architecture. In the end, it turned out that his theories were as spurious as his aristocratic title, but his heart was in the right place: after leaving Palenque, he was killed in Paris at the age of 109, felled by a carriage after he looked the other way to admire a beautiful woman.

Clifford would have appreciated that, I thought as we climbed a series of terraces to be greeted by the sight of dozens of pyramid temples rising from the rain forest.

They looked as if they had been carefully lowered there by aliens, with two doing the work, four leaning on spades and one saying: 'Down a bit, left a bit, steady, steady, STOP! Oh dear, oh dear. Quick, slap a bit of stucco on it before the guv'nor gets back.'

And then we climbed to the highest of all, to see before us the rectangular opening uncovered by Alberto Luis Lhuillier in 1949, revealing a flight of rubble-covered steps leading down into the darkness. It took him four years to excavate the stairway, and at the bottom, in a sealed crypt under a massive sarcophagus, he discovered, buried beneath 1,000 pieces of jade, the body of Lord Pacal lying where it had lain since 683 AD, watched down the slumbering years by the carvings on the walls of his ancestors and the nine gods of the night. And, in the flickering light of Lhuillier's candle, the skeletons of the six guards who had been killed with their eighty-year-old lord so that their souls could protect him on his long journey through the underworld.

We emerged blinking into the light and rode west, out of the jungle and into meadows filled with cherry-blossom trees. They were stunning, but not as stunning as the Mexican toll road charges, which over the course of the day were to add up to a staggering $100. Even worse, they charged the same for a bike as for a car, which considering that it only has half the wheels, is most unfair. And as if that wasn't bad enough, the swines tried to short-change us at two of the toll stations, unaware that Clifford was Scottish and was having none of it.

'My Spanish may be crap, but my counting's great,' he said as we rode off yet again.

By the end of a very long day, we had ridden 340 miles. To put that into context, it was like going from Belfast to Dublin, back to Belfast, back to Dublin then almost halfway back to Belfast again, although why you'd want to do all that, unless you were particularly absent-minded and had forgotten something important like your children each time, is quite beyond me.

After the toll price shock of the day, we sat down that evening, had a three-beer conference and decided, by a vote of two to nil with no abstentions, to use instead the A-road north, which turned out to be almost as fast and much more interesting, not to mention not costing us a packet. We were, in fact, spoilt for choice: since the Pan-American splits into four north of Mexico City, we simply chose the one up the middle, which shoots straight into Texas, brakes sharply, then takes a hard left for California.

In any case, in spite of the costs and the corruption, I was still glad to be in Mexico.

Not just because we were now less than 2,000 miles from San Diego.

Not even because it was a miracle we had got across the border at all.

No, a much more important reason than that: it was the country in which Gordon Banks made that save from Pelé in the 1970 World Cup.

That night I lay in bed and read, having by now consigned Green and Lowry to the bottom of a pannier, a description of Oaxaca, where we would be the next day.

'The people eat rose petals in water, the flowers of the bean plant in chilli sauce, of the pumpkin plant in pies, of the cacao tree in *tejate*, carnations in preserves and gardenias in *horchata*,' it said, and went on:

> The colours of the Indian fabrics are also obtained from nature: sixteen shades of red from the cochineal insect, blue by fermentation from indigo, black from the huisache, yellow from rock moss and purple from the sea snail that is caught, milked and returned to the sea. Hernán Cortés moved here from Mexico City, Nietzsche wished to move here, John Lennon loved the high peaks nearby and Porfirio Diaz, who was governor of the state, would ask his wife Carmelita every day in his Paris exile what was the news from Oaxaca and how could one live without its light and sky, without its fiestas and markets and without its food. The French surrealist Andre Pieyre de Mandiargues dreamed, after having loved the women, that a small female angel appeared before him, wrapped in shining armour over a field of Madonna lilies. There are festivals fortnightly, and twenty earthquakes a day, but only every couple of weeks is one strong enough to be felt.

A city where they ate flowers, milked snails and had festivals and earthquakes on alternate weeks.

It was too good to miss, which was why the next morning, Clifford having gone off to hunt down some more octane booster and find an internet café, I found myself standing outside Oaxaca's market. Beside the entrance, a battered old man with a battered old Remington typewriter sat at a battered old card table. He was the *escritor público*, who for a small fee would type out everything from tax forms to love letters, then discreetly forget the contents of both.

Wishing him good day, I squeezed down narrow alleyways, my shoulders brushed by fabrics of every colour and my nose filled with the smells of pineapples, cacao beans, herbs, beans, limes, peppers, tomatoes and chillies. A woman sitting on the ground was selling from one basket the spines of cacti, used to settle the stomach, lose weight and cure diabetes, and from another basket grasshoppers which had been starved for two days to empty their bowels, then fried with lemon and garlic.

However, it was not grasshoppers I was after, but a hammock, since I had bought one two years before, then held a hammock-warming party at which one of the guests, taking me a little too literally, had burnt a hole in it. I found a hammock stall nearby, and entered into the most civilised of transactions: hammocks were laid out for my inspection, then held up for careful measurement, colours were compared, prices were discussed, chins were scratched, agreements were reached, and eventually I handed over about $30 and was presented with my carefully wrapped purchase.

Throwing it over my shoulder, I walked around the market until my senses were full to the brim, then walked up the hill to Santo Domingo, which Aldous Huxley described as one of the most extravagantly gorgeous churches in the world. Begun in 1572, work continued on it for another 236 years, then was only complete for 25, until the army converted it into stables in 1869, destroying the fourteen side altars and stealing the gold from the altar and the wall behind. Restored today, it is a riotous tribute to Churrigueresque architecture.

It was all too much, and I stepped out through a side door to be greeted by the refreshingly simple sight of two lovers sitting under a bougainvillaea tree.

And then I looked at my watch, and realised it was time for afternoon tea with the honorary consul, whose name I had been given by friends of friends.

The honorary consul was a remarkable man. Wolfgang Wilczek Westphal had been born in Berlin of a Prussian family of bishops and Junkers whose records dated back to 1316. He came out to Mexico, fell in love with the light, the colours and a beautiful girl from a hill village, in that order, sold up his architectural practice in Germany and flew back to Mexico, where he started a ranch, married the girl and learnt her strange, sing-song language of Zapotec, much to the annoyance of her mother, who could no longer complain about him. Sadly, neither the ranch nor the marriage lasted, but the indefatigable Wolfgang had been shortly afterwards approached by the German Embassy in Mexico City, and then, quaintly, by the Court of St James in London, asking him to be the honorary British consul as well.

I arrived early, and waited for him in the courtyard of the Hostel de Alcaria. The tablecloth was white, the napkins teal, the walls mustard and the portals indigo. Scarlet poinsettias danced in the breeze, and a fountain tinkled at my back. It was no use. I was going to die of terminal hedonism, I thought as the honorary consul arrived thirty seconds late.

'I do apologise. I had to make some arrangements for a minor royal visit, marry a German couple and save three British backpackers from jail by the skin of their teeth. They were caught smoking pot in the square,' he said, ordering hot chocolate for both of us. 'Of course, they were as guilty as hell. Even now I don't know how I got them off. A lot of talking, a lot of phone calls to some good friends, a little baksheesh.'

'And were they grateful?'

His grey Prussian moustache trembled, and he leaned across the table.

'No! Not a bit of it! And let me tell you something: Mexican jails make Midnight Express look like kindergarten. Unless you have relatives to bring you food, you get nothing to eat but rotten bananas and scraps.'

'Tell me, what exactly does being an honorary consul mean?' I said.

'It means I get all of the honour and none of the money,' he said, polishing off his chocolate, wiping his moustache, looking at his watch, bidding me farewell and striding out briskly into the street to test yet again the impossible alchemy of Prussian discipline, British diplomacy and Mexican languor in the crucible of the afternoon sun.

I drained my own chocolate, then wandered around the streets aimlessly until, more by accident than design, I found myself sitting in the square having a beer, eating a bowl of grass-hoppers and listening to the state band playing Beethoven's Pastoral Symphony. I was just beginning to wonder why I was eating grasshoppers, since they tasted like twigs and it would, by my reckoning, take 1,057 of them to make one decent meal, when the son of the unluckiest man in the world sat down beside me.

He was English, married to a German woman, and in Oaxaca on business. Before the war, his father had been a multimillionaire factory owner, with all his savings invested in Malayan rubber and Egyptian cotton. Then the Japanese invaded Malaya, the Germans invaded Egypt, the Luftwaffe bombed his factory in London and the RAF destroyed his factory in Hamburg. Within a matter of weeks, he had gone from being fabulously wealthy to penniless, with no way of regaining his fortune.

What a day it had been, I thought as I wandered back to the hotel. I had seen people ask for money outside a church filled with gold, and ask for food outside a market filled with the endless fruits of the earth. I had bought a hammock, had tea with the honorary consul, eaten grasshoppers and met the son of the unluckiest man in the world.

'Do much today, Don?' said Clifford as I arrived back in our room to find him editing his book of Pan-American beauties.

'Oh, nothing much. Just pottering,' I said.

By late the next afternoon, we were on the outskirts of Mexico City. At least I think we were, because no one exactly knows where the city begins or ends.

Before us, under an army blanket of unremitting smog, lay the world's largest urban nightmare, an endless heap of life over which crawled thousands of green beetles, the Volkswagens which Mexicans use as taxis, and which they call belly buttons, because everybody has one.

No one knows how big the city is – estimates range from 22 to 30 million – but everyone knows how polluted it is. On an average day, there are 600 tons of gunge in the air above the city, caused by 2.5 million cars, 20,000 buses, 35,000 taxis and 30,000 factories, and trapped by the extinct volcanoes which surround it. On eight days out of ten, the city exceeds 100 points, the maximum ozone level permitted by international health standards, and in March 1992 it reached a world-record 398 points.

Popular mythology has it that living there is the equivalent of smoking forty cigarettes a day.

We took a deep breath and plunged in, riding at first through shanty towns apparently made entirely of cardboard boxes, and then into a more permanent scene in which God had taken all the concrete in the world, painted it all the colours of the world, shaken it up and dumped it in a heap.

It began to rain. As we rode to our hotel in the downpour, the traffic bobbed and weaved around us like in every other Latin American country, but in honk-free silence. It was like being in Colombia, but underwater. At one stage we were passed by an ambulance, its siren gurgling plaintively as it crawled along. I didn't give much for the chances of the patient inside. In this city, you have to book your heart attacks in advance, and leave for the maternity hospital the minute you discover you're pregnant.

The hotel was an oasis of calm around a fountainy courtyard. Flowers rose silently from pots and exploded in mid-air, and in an ancient cabinet by the restaurant wall sat dozens of silver napkin rings, each one engraved with the name of a regular diner. In the candlelit bar, eighty different tequilas sat on oak shelves. We ordered two, and the waiter brought each on an oval silver tray, bearing two slices of lime, a tiny salt cellar, a shot glass of tomato juice and another of tequila.

Sprinkle, suck, slug and gulp, and you had in quick succession the tang of the salt, the smack of the lime, the punch of the tequila and the comfort of the juice. It was, I imagined, like being hit by your lover, then caressed.

We sat back, glowing gently.

'Muchas gracias,' I said to the waiter, who was hovering nearby.

'De nada, señor,' he replied in the soft voice typical of Mexicans. They are such gentle, gracious people that you can see why they've been persecuted for centuries. Even when the Spanish came to ruin them in 1519, they welcomed them with gold and jewels. They are to the Spanish as the Canadians are to the US Americans: all of the warmth with none of the occasional arrogance.

The waiter brought glorious soups, of spice and cheese, meats and chicken, and wine as sharp and grassy as a lawnmower blade. Later, two men in dark suits brought to our room tiny bananas, strawberries swaddled in chocolate, two tiny glasses. They went away laughing uproariously and as I picked up one of the glasses it slipped from my fingers, miraculously tinkling unbroken across the marble floor with a sound which mocked the plish and plash in the courtyard outside.

I picked it up, thought of my wife for the thousandth time that day, and in that moment felt as alone as a whisky priest.

In the morning, we breakfasted on figs and rode out to the great volcano Popocatépetl, to which in 1519 Hernán Cortés came marching out of the east, bearded and proud.

Behind him on the Mexican shore he had left the ashes of his ships, so that there could be no going back. With him he brought 550 men, a few dozen horses, some dogs, a cannon, and the egocentric surety of belonging to what was then the greatest colonial empire in the world.

Imagine then, if you will, his astonishment at scaling the rim of this volcano to see below, sprawling across a vast man-made island in the middle of a huge lake traversed by wide causeways, the fantastic Aztec capital of Tenochtitlán. Bernal Diaz, Cortés's scribe, wrote at the time: 'When we saw all those cities and villages built in the water … and that straight and level causeway leading to the city, we were astounded. These great buildings rising from the water, all made of stone, seemed like an enchanted vision from the tales of Amadia. Indeed, some of our soldiers asked whether it was not all a dream.'

Unfortunately for the Aztecs, Montezuma thought Cortés was a dream as well: the bearded, pale-skinned god Quetzalcóatl, long prophesied to return from the east, where he had vanished many years before. Fearfully welcomed and given gold in tribute, Cortés and his men responded by making Montezuma a prisoner in his own palace, killing the Aztec priests and finally destroying the entire city.

Ironically, there is more left today of the Mayan civilisation which preceded the Aztecs, in the shape of the pyramids of the sun and the moon at Teotihuacan, built two centuries before Christ by a people whose knowledge of time, astronomy and mathematics was far in advance of anything in Europe. When they and the city around them were finally abandoned, it was, ironically, partially because the vast forests destroyed in their building had left the land incapable of supporting the people who lived there.

By the time the Aztecs and the Spanish arrived, the pyramids had long been abandoned, and when they were first excavated at the start of the twentieth century by a lunatic named Leopoldo Batres, it was with the aid of copious quantities of dynamite.

Even so, today the scale of the pyramids is astonishing. We rode up to them through roadworks guarded by a man waving a flag, since hiring him all day was cheaper than buying a sign. When I was a child, my parents had a stereoscopic Viewmaster which you held up to the window to look at transparencies, mounted on cardboard discs, of the world's greatest sights. Looking at these pyramids on rainy Saturday mornings in Tyrone in the Sixties, they had seemed completely outside my conception.

And they still did today, even sitting on top of them after climbing the 248 steps in the midday sun to the spot where over the centuries tens of thousands of sacrificial victims were given the intriguing choice between having their hearts cut out or being skinned alive.

How can a civilisation which built these things have vanished so completely, you think as you climb down and walk away, haunted by the voices of the obsidian and silver peddlers who, as you approach them and walk past, chorus: 'Three hundred pesos, señor, 200, 100, almost nothing,' like a sort of financial Doppler effect.

The answer, I suppose, I had seen as we rode into the city, passing old women crawling on arthritic hands and knees in the pouring rain up the long steps in front of the Cathedral of the Virgin of Guadalupe, in an immensely painful act which they somehow imagined would bring them salvation. But even as they climbed, their cathedral was locked and barred, slowly fracturing and sinking into the soft mud of the lake on which Tenochtitlán had once stood; sinking as surely as Cortés's men sank when they tried to return to their camp across the causeways. Refusing to let go of their golden booty, over half of them drowned.

Civilisations and conquerors, religions and empires come and go, and perhaps all that is left is to do good to the other fellow.

In this case, the other fellow was the man selling silver bracelets at the foot of the pyramids. I bought one from him after he said that the money would help him to go to college and escape from poverty. It cost me £1. A small price to pay for salvation, and not too much to carry over a causeway.

Today, all that is left of the lake the Aztecs built are the floating gardens of Xochimilco, where every weekend Mexicans come to play, to breathe and to pay seven times the cost of a silver bracelet to climb aboard brightly decorated punts and be punted around the miles of waterways. In between drinking, laughing, eating and good-naturedly fending off attacks by floating mariachi bands, poncho peddlers and ancient native women stooped over mounds of tortillas warmed by potentially lethal charcoal braziers, while all the while, small dogs and large cows roam the banks under the rambling bougainvillaea and eucalyptus.

Stuffed to the brim with tortillas, we stayed there until the lilac twilight crept around, then waddled back to the bikes and trundled back to our hotel. That night, the moon was out hunting stars, and all night long, the church bell tolled the hours in the plaza below the window. It sounded so much like the doorbell at home that I kept waking, wondering who was calling at this time of night, then realising that if I wanted to find out I'd have to get up and fly back to Belfast. It hardly seemed worth the effort, so I finally fell asleep, and woke up to go walking through rain which swept along the streets and flung itself like a curse in the faces of churchgoers.

As the clock in the square struck half past nine, I was walking through the door of the Palacio de Bellas Artes, a lusty serenade to art deco and the home of the Ballet Folklorico de Mexico, who every Sabbath morn present a history of their country's myth and magic in song and dance.

And it being a Sunday, there is included a morality play, which went something like this.

Groom approaches wedding on donkey, spots beautiful Indian girl and stops for spot of canoodling.

Groom continues to wedding for much dancing with women wearing bananas on heads and with eyelashes so luxuriant that every time they blink, a gust sweeps through the auditorium and ruffles the petticoats of the grandmothers dozing in the back stalls.

Suddenly rival to groom appears wearing snazzy green silk

shirt bought in January sales at knock-down price. Rival dances with bride.

Groom, enraged by this in spite of the fact that he canoodled with beautiful Indian girl on way to wedding, snatches machete and slays rival, making right mess of snazzy green shirt.

Dancing resumes, involving women wearing bananas etc.

It was a love story of sorts, but it was not the one I was after. No, that was to be found at the house in which Frida Kahlo was born in 1907, suffered polio as a child and to which she was brought back, crippled for life by a bus accident when she was a teenager.

When Kahlo was thirteen and beginning a lifetime of painting which ended with her premature death in a wheelchair at forty-seven, she fell obsessively and irretrievably in love with Diego Rivera, the fat, ugly and brilliant doyen of Mexican muralists whose vast and hypnotic works dominate public buildings all over the country. It was the most troubled of relationships: because of her injuries, Kahlo was unable to bear the child of Rivera for which she craved, and at one time she was having a brief but intense fling with the disenfranchised Trotsky while Rivera was sleeping with her sister Cristina.

It is the strangest of places, her house: bathed with light, painted in the strong, life-affirming colours of Marrakesh blue, cinnabar and powdery white, and filled with fine examples of Mexican folk art, it has, nevertheless, an air of disease and death which you can actually smell.

But then, it is hardly surprising. For, in truth, Kahlo did not have the certainty in her work which marks greatness. She did not have the certainty of a life free from pain, or the certainty of knowing that when she died, the children of the man she loved would live on. No, the only certainty she had was her deep, abiding passion for Rivera. You can see it in the intense, painfully proud expression of the single portrait of her in the house, in the family room.

I stood and looked at it for a long time as the evening light drew near, and then I realised that I was thinking of something else altogether. I was thinking that it had just occurred to me for the first time where she got her remarkable single eyebrow from. So continuous that it renders the plural superfluous, it looks like one of those shapes that children produce when they are asked to draw a bird in flight. Her father, that's where she got it from. All you had to do was look at his portrait in the same room. Frida's eyebrow was, quite simply, her dad's moustache turned upside down.

We left at dawn the next morning, conscious that we had dallied too long in the city, for both our sanity and our lungs.

For me, the next few days, as we rode the long miles through Mexico for the US border, were in many ways the most heroic of the trip. Men of steel, we rose at dawn and sped north, with flies in our teeth, a song in our hearts and the wind in our hair. Well, except for Clifford, who had lots of wind but no hair.

By now, we were only days away from the border with the home of the brave and the land of the freeways which, unlike in Mexico, lived up to their name. The land of big rock-candy mountains, sugar-lump trees and ice-cream soda fountains. I could hardly wait.

But I would have to. The more impatient we got, and the faster we wanted to go to make it to the border, the more crucial it was that we slowed down and took it slow and easy.

I knew only too well from Colombia, when I had been thinking of Cali rather than the corner in front of me, of the potentially fatal consequences of thinking too far ahead down the road. So we curbed our impatience, and made up the miles by starting early, and finishing late.

At sunrise, we would pass trucks loaded with peasants on their way to a day's work in the fields, as their fathers and grandfathers had done, and at sunset, we would pass them coming home. Nothing stopped us as we ate up the miles day after endless day, overtaking startled pensioners and flattened iguanas at will.

Nothing, that is, until April refused to start at a filling station.

'Bloody battery again,' muttered Clifford, hauling it out and setting off to find a mechanic with some acid.

'Don't know why you can't get yourself a nice reliable Triumph,' I called cheerily after him.

He seemed to take it well, apart from the spanner which missed my head by an inch.

Sadly, there was no acid to be found in the whole village, so we rounded up a team of willing volunteers for a push start, and for the rest of the day, April was kept running every time we stopped briefly for a drink.

That night, we found a hotel with a hill outside, and Clifford went looking for a charger, only to return with the news that there was not one to be found in the whole of Mexico. He flung himself on the bed in disgust, and made the mistake of switching on CNN news on the television. On the screen, two presenters took turns telling us that shopkeepers were rioting in Nepal.

Below them, for those who had trouble concentrating to the end of a whole spoken sentence, the same story was summarised in subtitles. Below that again, a continuous stream of words across the bottom of the screen told us that Belgium had defeated Russia at tennis, Michael Schumacher had won a Grand Prix and Tiger Woods had done a bungee jump. The irrelevant broadcast to the uninterested, it was a world away from the reality we had experienced every minute of the day for the past two months.

Next morning, we started April with a push down the hill, and that afternoon, we were having coffee in a plaza, listening to the *cantina* owner's tape deck, when it suddenly struck me how similar Mexican rap was to Ulster politics: the same words repeated over and over again, ad nauseum. I suddenly had this disturbing and deeply meaningful vision of Ian Paisley wearing basketball boots with the laces undone, baggy trousers and a baseball cap on backwards, muttering darkly into a microphone: 'No I say no, no no I say no, I say no, Ulster says no I say no I say no surrender, yeah.'

It was obviously time to move on. I drained my coffee, we got back on the bikes, and by evening we were climbing into the mountains, stopping for the night at a handful of log cabins on the edge of a canyon.

It was so deep that out of curiosity I rose before dawn the next morning to see if I could see the bottom, standing on the edge as the first glimmerings of light began to ghost over the edge of the world. Below, there was an impenetrable darkness in which mist was ghosting into Xanadus of the imagination, cities which twisted and vanished even as they were born. As their walls and turrets burned up in the gathering light, their inhabitants came whirring up out of the dark, metamorphosing into hummingbirds as they rose. At my feet, they sipped from the yellow flowers which grew along the lip of the canyon, their wings invisible.

As I watched, enthralled, there came a sound behind me which almost made me fall off the edge. I turned, to find an ancient Tarahumara woman swaddled in an indeterminate number of bright clothes. Above the chaos of faded colour, her face was like a piece of sun-dried driftwood you would find on a beach and take home to wax and polish for no other reason than the beauty of its shape.

'I am sorry, sir, I did not mean to startle you,' she said in slow Spanish. 'I come up here sometimes, for the beauty of the morning. And because I do not sleep well, since my husband died.'

'I am sorry to hear that. When did he die?'

'It was forty-four years ago. I am a little lonely these days because my daughter has not been to see me for a while. She has moved away.'

'Where to?'

'To the next valley. They're getting more rain than we are these days. Maybe they are more Catholic.'

She sighed, and began to walk back up the path into the

woods. I walked with her, for no other reason than that it seemed the right thing to do. Her home was a tiny log cabin with smoke curling up through a hole in the roof. In front of it lay a kitten the colour of dust, and three dogs so small they should have just clubbed together and become one. I stopped, breathing hard, since at this altitude oxygen molecules are only one a penny, and she beckoned me in.

Inside, a black pot of beans bubbled over a fire on the dirt floor, in the centre of which stood a rough table and chairs. On the wall hung a ramshackle linoprint of Christ, his eyes cast up to heaven as if someone had just said something incredibly obvious to him. Perched on the frame of the print was a hotel from a Monopoly set. The only light was through the hole in the roof and the open door, and apart from the occasional mewing of the kitten, there was not a sound in the world.

'I have been living here since before aeroplanes began. When I saw the first aeroplane, I had already been living here half my life,' she said. 'How many days is it to where you live?'

I tried to work it out, and settled on a couple of weeks, since I had stopped thinking in terms of aeroplanes.

'Two weeks? That is a long way. What is your home called?'

'Ireland.'

Her eyes grew vague. 'I have heard there is a place across the sea,' she said as the kitten strolled in, stretched all four legs in turn and sniffed the beans in the pot, but they were not ready yet. Annoyed, it chased the smallest dog out the door. The old woman turned to me, and took my hand.

'May things go well with you, sir. You are far from home,' she said.

'And with you,' I said, squeezing her hand and walking away down the path.

Back in our log cabin, I found Clifford stirring.

'Get up, Pancho, you lazy bastard,' I said. 'We have to be in Alaska by teatime.'

We fell from the mountains to the desert again. Once, we

passed a milk lorry in which the sunlight exploded first off the serried ranks of silver churns, then off the golden heads of the father and two sons in the front. In the burning heat of the desert, their pale skin and blond hair was such a shock that you wanted to stop and check the colour balance on your vision.

They were, in fact, Mennonites, members of the sect which was founded in the sixteenth century by Dutchman Menno Simons, and which had been going off in a huff ever since. In 1776 they had been granted a home in the Ukraine by Catherine the Great. A century later, ordered to join the army, 100,000 of them went off in a huff to Canada. When the Canadians insisted that they send their children to state schools, they went off in a huff to Mexico, where they lived in a community with more banks per acre than anywhere else in the country.

We passed it up the road, and stopped. In the dairy, women in long dresses, their heads bowed, stood stirring pools of milk, the liquid light lapping on the underside of their chins. The single ones wore white headscarves and the married ones black, which didn't indicate that Mennonite husbands were a whole bundle of fun. In another room, a woman made quilts while her son played with a laptop. It was a strange vision, of both purity and uncertainty. Were they happy, or sad? It was impossible to tell, for they are among the most silent people on earth.

We crept away, and rode north.

By nightfall, we were in Chihuahua, home of the dogs which are so ugly they should only be used as guide dogs for the blind. A friend of mine had one once which looked like a tumour covered in threadbare grey Dralon. Thankfully, we were unlikely to see one, since they are both nocturnal and wild, roaming the desert in packs looking for a coyote supper. When they do find one, the coyote usually just rolls over and dies from the embarrassment of being cornered by a bunch of Dralon swatches.

We were riding aimlessly down a dusty street when we

found a hotel such a shocking shade of pink that it would have been better named Blancmange Boulevard. At the check-in desk, the clerk handed me a form asking 'How did you learn of our hotel?'

'From arriving outside it one minute ago,' I wrote carefully.

In the bathroom, the delights included a small bottle of viscous yellow liquid bearing the legend The Original Ma Evans Herbal Shampoo, above which was a line drawing of a matriarch resembling the great-grandmother of the bride of Frankenstein. I switched on the air conditioner and, to the accompaniment of a noise like a thousand asthmatic bees roused from their slumbers, the room slowly filled with cold dust. I was going to like Chihuahua, I thought, as Clifford went out looking yet again for a battery charger.

He returned empty-handed, and we went walking through the streets until we found a restaurant which fulfilled all three of our criteria: it was cheap, there were people inside, and they were alive.

At the next table, a birthday celebration was underway, and on a small stage, a mariachi band was playing Johnny Mathis's 'When a Child is Born'.

'Bit early for Christmas, isn't it?' I said to the waitress.

'No, late from last Christmas. This is Mexico,' she said.

'God, she's lovely,' said Clifford, picking up his camera. 'I think I feel another photo coming on for the book of Pan-American beauties.'

That night, as we were settling down to sleep, there came a knock at the hotel room door. It was Isidro, the boy from the garage down the road where Clifford had asked in vain for a charger. He had cycled ten miles home after work, borrowed his father's, and cycled back with it in the dark.

'I will collect it in the morning,' he said. 'Just leave it at reception.'

It was just another of the countless acts of spontaneous goodwill we had been offered every day of the journey.

As Clifford set to work taking out the battery and connecting the charger, I was looking idly at the map when I suddenly realised that we were now a mere 300 miles from the border. He finished working and we switched off the lights, but I lay awake, too excited to sleep, like a child on Christmas Eve.

Clifford woke at dawn, reconnected April's freshly charged battery, pressed the starter button, and was met with a silence broken only by the mocking call of the jays in the tree above. Still, until we found a new battery, it was nothing a push start wouldn't cure, and it hardly mattered, compared to the fact that we only had a few more hours left in Latin America.

No more wondering what the Spanish for battery charger was, and no more octane booster, the last of which was added to a final tankful of fuel, and the bottle ceremoniously dumped in the nearest bin.

No more giant potholes lurking under flooded roads, no more mountains of mud, no more three-hour border crossings in the searing heat, and no more native protests, unless the Californian Gay Vegetarians Against the Bomb were on the rampage again.

Not to mention luxuries such as toilets with paper and sinks with plugs.

For once, I didn't mind push-starting April, and soon after, we were first in the queue for the house of Pancho Villa. Or Pancho's villa, if you like. In fact, we were the queue.

If the earnest Emiliano Zapata was the Ernie Wise of the Mexican Revolution in 1911, Villa was the Eric Morecambe. A cattle rustler turned brilliantly innovative bandit, he refused to take anything seriously, travelled with a film crew in tow and allegedly arranged his battles to ensure they took place in the best light for filming, then finally retired to this fifty-room mansion around which his widow, Luc Coral, showed visitors until her death in 1981.

These days it was run by the tourist office, which with no obvious sign of irony had put up signs all over the place banning revolutionary activities like eating, smoking, drinking, shooting, letting your children run around or sitting on the furniture. Inside, the bed was in the sad state of repair you would expect from a man who had twenty-five different children by several women, but not quite as sad a state as the Dodge limousine he was driving when he was gunned down during a family vendetta in 1923, and which sat out in the courtyard, with the meter on the dashboard showing that the battery was still charged. They sure built them in those days.

Villa, suspecting that he might be killed, had already built a magnificent mausoleum in Chihuahua where he wanted to be buried, but since he was killed 200 miles away in Parral, he was buried there instead. Two years later, someone dug him up and cut off his head. Today, his head is lost, his body is in Mexico City and his mausoleum is empty. There was a photograph of it in the Chihuahua tourist brochure, accompanied by the inspired caption: 'Mausoleum where Pancho Villa is not buried'.

We emerged, blinking into the sunlight. The thermometer on the wall read 104, and I looked at my watch. It was ten in the morning, and time to break for the border.

Then, as if in a last-ditch bid to stop us making it, in the last 100 miles we were met by a plague of giant caterpillars scurrying across the road. By swerving carefully, we managed to get away with only squashing 568,432 of them. Then a cloud of primrose yellow butterflies appeared on the scene to do their bit, bouncing off the windshields with gay abandon. There would be a few tears around the butterfly campfire tonight, I feared. Or whatever it is that butterflies do of an evening.

The miles sped away, and before long we were tearing off our once-precious Mexican stickers and sitting in the queue for American passport control, edging ever closer to the Stars and Stripes fluttering in the breeze at the other end.

'Sorry, you'll have to speak up.' Geoff's revolutionary South American earplugs were eventually replaced by Clifford at vast expense.

17

'After two weeks of Central American border crossings, you don't know how glad I am to see you guys,' I said to the border guard.

'I bet you are,' he said as he inspected our passports, then handed them back.

'What? No three-hour wait? No demands to walk five miles back into Mexico and get copies in triplicate of my dog licence?' I said.

'Nope. None of those. Welcome to the USA,' he grinned.

Thank God, I thought. I don't even have a dog.

As Clifford handed his passport over, I had a sudden thought.

'Is it Frankenstein?' I said.

'Nope,' he said.

'Frank, then.'

'Nope,' he said, and rode off. I started Tony and followed him down Main Street, USA, a smile on my face as wide as Fifth Avenue, and exactly the same feeling in my heart, I imagined, as in that of every dusty refugee who has entered this promised land to forge in the crucible of his ambition the shining future of his very own brave new world. I'll tell you how deeply moved I was. Even the sight of a Wal-Mart brought a tear to my eye.

At the first set of lights, I shouted over to Clifford: 'Hey Pancho, it's seven o'clock and I'm running on empty. Do you fancy calling it a day?'

'Aye. We'll just find a motel near a gas station close to the freeway,' he said, then proceeded to ride past several buildings with the word Motel in large letters on the front, several others declaring that they were owned by companies called Shell, Texaco, Esso and so on, and head off down the freeway into the empty desert. Five miles down the road, I finally caught up with him.

'Pancho, what's the plan, man? I'm running on fumes,' I said.

'So am I. I'm just looking for a motel and a gas station.'

'But we've just ridden past a dozen of both.'

'Well, don't fucking blame me. I've never been here before,' he said, roaring off in a cloud of smoke.

However, all was well. We found a gas station up the road, even if it did only swing to 91 octane.

We filled up anyway, apologised to each other, rode back into town, found a cheap motel, went out for burgers and beer and fell into our beds, warm and comfortable in the bosom of what would, at least for tonight, pass for Western civilisation.

The next morning, I remembered one thing I didn't like about America.

Food so bland and processed that it should have come with signs saying Try Our New Sawdust And Cotton Wool Combo! Money Back Guarantee If You Find Any Taste In Our Coffee! Wash It All Down With Beer That's Like Making Love In A Canoe! The reason I remembered was because I had bacon, eggs, coffee and juice in a local fast-food joint, and felt increasingly queasy all morning as we sped through Texas past wooden arches saying Cactus Jack's Ranch, Lazy J Ranch and Hard-Working B, Although Takes the Occasional Sunday Off Ranch.

Behind them stretched dusty trails all the way to ranch houses in which lived men who wrestled ornery steers, smoked Marlboro and drank bourbon straight from the bottle. Probably slept with their sisters, too, I'll be bound, and if you saw their sisters, you wouldn't blame them.

Halfway through the morning, we were stopped by a border patrol, presumably to check that we weren't a couple of run-away Mexicans trying that old Chile to Alaska on motorbikes stunt to get across the border.

And then it began to rain.

All in all, it was turning into one of those days. First that breakfast, then I'd pulled a hamstring push-starting April, and now rain, which I had thought was banned by law in Texas, along with breaking wind in a lift and shooting buffalo from the second floor of a building.

And then, as if to prove that Murphy was wrong when he said bad things only come in threes, I started to feel as if I had the flu, just for a change from feeling queasy. I rode along grimly in the pouring rain, feeling miserable and thinking that it was a day when I would have been better tucked up in bed with a hot whiskey and matching wife.

And then, in the middle of a large town, April's fan suddenly packed in and she started to spew forth torrents of hot water in a very passable impersonation of Vesuvius. Closer inspection revealed that the battery was finally banjaxed, and the fan had come loose and punctured the radiator.

'Funny, you fit a radiator guard to protect it from the front, then it gets attacked from behind,' said Clifford, gazing across the road to where a large sign said O'Reilly's Auto Parts.

He walked across, and five minutes later came back carrying a brand-new battery.

'You're never going to believe this, but they had a battery for a 1978 Aprilia Pegaso. Aprilias aren't even sold in the States,' he said.

He installed it, fixed the fan into place with wire and gaffer tape, poured a large measure of Radweld into the radiator and pressed the starter button. April coughed into life of her own volition for the first time in days, and he celebrated by going off for a test spin, returning to announce that all was well.

As for me, I was so knackered and ill that I found us a motel down the street and went to bed, even though it was only four in the afternoon. My main fear, to be honest, was that I had come down with some sort of nervous exhaustion from the constant strain of all the highs and lows of both planning the trip and carrying it out.

I slept straight through until eight the following morning, but even so, felt so woozy when I got up that I shouldn't even have been operating a pencil sharpener, never mind a large, powerful motorbike. However, I had no choice. The bikes were booked in for their service in San Diego, and Trevor had already confirmed his flights.

'Are you sure you're OK?' said Clifford as I climbed wearily on the bike.

'Yes,' I lied, and we set off into the rain, stopping after a couple of hours for a warming coffee at the Dryden Trading Post, whose chief delights, according to the sign leaning against the rusting Model T Ford sitting outside, were Beer, Corn, Ice, Saddles and Cigarettes.

In the afternoon, the rain was replaced by a fierce wind which threatened alternately to throw us under oncoming trucks or into the ditch, and I was, although I had thought it impossible, an even wearier man than I had been in the morning when I stepped off the bike that evening, had something to eat and fell again into bed.

Thankfully, I woke feeling half alive, which to a statistician may be the same thing as half dead, but to me felt a whole lot better.

Sadly, I then managed to forget the four basic rules of relative motorcycle temperature.

If you think you're going to be warm, you will be cool.

2

If you think you're going to be cool, you will be cold.
If you think you're going to be cold, you will be freezing.
If you think you're going to be freezing, stay at home.

As a result, I rode along for the first hour through the desert dawn with no fleece under my jacket, and no gloves on. Of course, being a bloke, rather than do the sensible thing and stop to put them on, I rode grimly onwards, convincing myself that it would warm up at any minute. It didn't, and my hands had just moved from blue to an interesting shade of purple when we passed a sign saying 'Prison Zone: Do not pick up hitchhikers'. It should really have added, just to be on the safe side, 'Especially ones wearing stripey clothes and a black mask and dragging a ball and chain'.

About half an hour later, at about the time I started shivering uncontrollably, I realised it was time to stop. As I was pulling on my gloves with trembling hands, two old-timers on Harleys pulled up to see if we were all right, the way only bikers do for each other. You can't really imagine a Toyota owner pulling over to see if he can help out when he sees a Corolla stopped by the roadside, for example.

They turned out to be Brien and his mate Rock Mountain, a man whose face lived up to his name. A full-blood Apache whose grandfather had fought with Geronimo, he had run away from the reservation when he was fourteen to find his father in Chicago.

'I saw everyone else sitting around the reservation getting drunk every day, and thought there had to be something better than that,' he said.

He had found his dad two years later, but by then had got himself started in the construction business, eventually running his own company so successfully that he'd bought his own Lear jet.

'Had to sell it to pay off my third wife, though,' he laughed.

Retired at fifty-four, he had just celebrated his sixty-ninth birthday by riding his Harley to Alaska.

'I had a few meetings with Mother Earth on those gravel

roads up there – as I see you've had,' he said, nodding towards the scars on Tony.

They roared off at a speed we could not match, but we ran into them an hour later at a Harley dealership, where Rock was getting a new back tyre fitted. We wandered about for a good hour, trying desperately to resist the temptation to get out our credit cards and finish the trip on two brand-new Road King Classics. You know, those ones with the nice whitewall tyres.

Shame on us. Clutching only a postcard and a T-shirt, and with our tails between our legs for even thinking such a thing, we slunk out to our trusty steeds, climbed aboard, and rode out west.

In the afternoon, we stopped at what looked like the only gas station in the desert.

'That's weird. This place only has 93 octane. I would have thought everywhere in the States would have had 95,' I said.

Clifford went inside, and came out with a bottle of octane booster, a sight I had thought not to see again. As we were filling up, there came from up the road several Harleys and their owners, presumably on their way to the Harley dealers to bolt on a few more chrome accessories.

There is, I thought as I went inside to pay for the fuel, something beautiful to the point of lyricism about the snore of a big V-twin, then the sight of a Harley sweeping past on the open road, with only the sand and the sky beyond to complete the perfect image of freedom.

'Warning – severe dust storms, may cause zero visibility,' said the signs we passed next morning. If they did, though, how you were supposed to see the signs warning of them remained a mystery.

Half an hour later, we rode along the edge of a river valley in which a large crowd had gathered to watch a rodeo, although in the minute we took to pass the scene, the cowboy in the arena did nothing but sit on a stationary horse. It was obviously a new type of Zen rodeo, in which they stood in a meditative state for several hours until the horse fell out from under the rider with the sound of one hoof clapping, then they went off to drink sake at the little karaoke bar on the corner until they achieved the enlightenment which comes from being at one with the nothingness at the centre of the liver.

I love it when you find a sane and rational explanation for things, I thought as I sped west. It brings out the accountant in me.

Almost our only companions on the freeway this morning were the big trucks whose very names – Mack, Kenworth, Peterbilt and the like – conjured up manly endeavour and the spirit of America's open roads. Even if all they were really just a bunch of fat blokes hauling widgets from Wisconsin.

Talking of fat, as we were refuelling Tony and April at the next small-town gas station, a monstrous pick-up pulled in beside us, plastered with stickers like 'People without guns get shot' and 'I'm a Patriot – You got a problem with that?'. Out of it stepped, or rather flowed, a woman wearing no shoes, a pair of grey shorts which must have used up all of China's annual cotton production for the previous year, and a T-shirt which she had slipped coyly off one gargantuan shoulder to reveal a butterfly which had long since perished through cholesterol by osmosis. She was followed by a boyfriend who made her look anorexic.

Resisting a strong temptation to walk over and say cheerily: 'Hey, have you folks ever thought of not eating for, say, a year or two?', I watched them fill up the tank with 4,000 gallons, which would get them at least to the end of the block, then waddle off to pay.

Something had gone dreadfully wrong, I feared, with the youthful sense of endless possibilities that I loved about America.

I can achieve anything I want had become I can do anything I want. I can eat anything I want, shoot anyone I want, sue anyone I want, drive anything I want, or elect an idiot for a president twice in a row if I want. The problem with all of this was that it missed one of the essential truths of a mature democracy: that with rights come responsibilities. The responsibility, for example, after spilling hot coffee in your lap, to take the blame rather than sue McDonald's.

We went in to pay for our fuel and have a late breakfast of oats, orange juice and coffee. Across from us, the Titanic Two were tucking into twin mounds of eggs, bacon, sausage, hash browns, biscuits and gravy, washed down by a gallon of milkshake each. She was reading a paper whose front cover declared 'Our Boys Kick Ass in Iraq'.

Actually, I thought, it's unfair to criticise some midwestern Americans as obese people who drive obese cars and whose only exercise is shooting each other. Sometimes they go abroad and shoot other people too.

We finished our coffee, and rode on.

All around us were giant cacti pointing at the sky with prickly accusation as we rode on, Pancho some distance ahead and me cocooned in what had become over the past two months my little office, with its row of dials telling me that we had done 272 miles that day, and 9,767 since the trip started, that we were travelling at 60mph, that the engine was turning over at a shade under 4,000 revolutions per minute, that it was running nice and cool, that I had half a tank of fuel left and that it was 2.15 in the afternoon.

All of which meant it was time for a break, to be immediately surrounded by a bunch of Harley riders on their way back from a rally in Laughlin, Nevada.

'Seventy-five thousand Hogs, man. You should have heard them,' said an ex-Marine called Jed with a goatee beard and several dubious tattoos. Like most bikers, he looked like he'd sell his granny for gas and ask for change, but was actually so soft and gentle that he probably still wrote to Santa every Christmas.

'Now that's a hell of a thing. I was brought up in Alaska,' he said when I told him where we were going. 'You might just get there after the snow melts and before the blackflies arrive.'

'They're the ones the size of grizzlies, aren't they?' I said.

'No, that's the mosquitoes. The blackflies are a hell of a lot bigger.'

It looked like the sooner we got to Alaska the better, I thought, climbing back on the bike and following Pancho west. After a while I found myself singing The Eurythmics' 'Love is a Stranger', but then I realised I was making up a new song which went:

> Love is a stranger, who takes you to the fair
> Takes you all the way, then leaves you standing there
> So that you wonder where home is
> And then you wonder where love is
> Wonder where love is
> Wonder where love is
> You look for it everywhere
> And then realise you're standing there
> Standing on your shadow in the midday sun
> Standing right on it before you know it's there
> And then night comes and that shadow is gone
> But the next day dawns and another comes along
> And you know it's not love, but it'll do for a while
> And you know some day you'll go that extra mile
> But then winter comes, and all the shadows start to go
> And you reach for the bottle, 'cos it's the only way you know
> To stop the tumblers falling, falling in your heart
> As they try to find the combination, the alchemist's art
> Of finding out where love is
> Finding out where love is
> Finding out where love is.

There. Latvia's future in the Eurovision Song Contest secured, I rode on into the setting sun.

Trevor in a rare vertical shot. Still, at least he fell off at safer speeds than his brother.

18

A short history of California

1542
Spanish arrive, but having no credit cards and unable to decide between a double decaff espresso and a frappomochacino with a twist, leave.

1769
Spanish missionaries, carefully chosen for disinterest in coffee and money, arrive on a mission to build missions.

1841
First pioneers arrive overland in covered wagons. Covered mostly in Apache arrows, that is.

1849
Gold rush, followed in close second place by silver rush. Population of San Francisco grows from 500 to 50,000 in five years.

1869

Transcontinental railroad reduces journey west from a month to five days, creating further population boom, except among Apaches.

1911

Film industry moves from east coast, establishing image of state as land of dreams, which in 1930s Depression attracts thousands of dustbowl farmers, followed closely by John Steinbeck, with notebook.

1950

Every family has two giant cars and matching fridge.

1960s

Endless summers of love. San Francisco populated by barefoot flower children, high on life and other substances. Ronald Reagan elected governor. Colonic irrigation and aura analysis for poodles made available free from public funds. Thinking banned. Intellectuals flee to east coast. Rest stay behind to make movies.

1992

Rodney King riots. O.J. Simpson trial. Movies still in colour, but everything else black and white.

2003

Arnold Schwarzenegger elected governor. Waistlines and IQs greater than 34 banned. California still the promised land, however, at least until the San Andreas fault implodes.

I could tell we were in California when an organic carrot hit me on the head. It fell off a passing truck, bounced off my helmet, and was probably picked up later by a grateful rabbit.

At noon, with Tony leaking oil from his damaged engine and air from a rear tyre, and with April held together with wire and gaffer tape, we limped in hope and glory into San Diego.

And then we found a motel on the beach, and plunged into the cold yet welcoming heart of the Pacific Ocean, in the same way that Paddy Minne and I had once been embraced by the Black Sea after the endless sands of Persia. In fact, the ocean wasn't the only thing that was cold: the moment we had ridden down from the desert into San Diego, the temperature had dropped to the point where we spent the rest of the day walking around in fleeces.

'This is more like bracing Skegness than sunny California,' said Clifford as we sauntered along the boardwalk in a stiff breeze, stepping aside now and again to avoid being mown down by septuagenarian power walkers.

'It's Trevor I'm worried about,' I said. 'I told him it would be like Easy Rider, and all he'd need would be a T-shirt, shades and a pair of jeans. He'll die of hypothermia.'

The next morning, the stroke of nine found me pulling up outside Rocket Motorcycles, a place I had often thought during the trip I would never get to see. Mark McCaffrey, the owner, stuck his head around the door, came out and shook me warmly by the hand.

'Good to see you, my man. You're the first adventurer we've had since Ted Simon,' he said, referring to the legendary author of *Jupiter's Travels*.

'Funny, he had an accident in Colombia too. Must be compulsory. Anyway, Alex here will take good care of you.'

Alex got to work inspecting the damage, and I pottered about happily, sitting on Bonnevilles and Thruxtons and leafing through books like *Triumph Twins Restoration* by Roy Bacon, on the cover of which a chap and his girl were proceeding down a leafy English lane towards a thatched pub for a Melton Mowbray pork pie and a pint of Old Sparrowfart.

'You know, Mark,' I said, 'something's been puzzling me ever since we got to the States and discovered that the highest octane fuel is 93. If this is a US spec bike, how come Triumph UK told me it needs 95 octane?'

'It doesn't. It'll run on 91, or even 87 at a pinch.'

'Bloody hell. You mean I've been hunting around every filling station in South America for octane booster for no reason?'

'Looks like it,' he laughed. 'If I was you, I'd head right back down and get your money back from all of them.'

'No way, José. North is the only way I'm heading.'

Ho hum. Oh well, having sorted that out, I got a lift over to the aerospace museum in Balboa Park, where I spent a blissful morning wandering past assorted Albatrosses and Spitfires, admiring everything from Richthofen's machine gun to Lindbergh's goggles, and watching old Movietone newsreels of the war against the Japanese in the Pacific. With a wonderful irony, they were all shown on Sony televisions.

However, among the most apposite exhibits was the aircraft in which in 1981 Ted Gildred recreated the flight his father Theodore had made from San Diego to Ecuador fifty years before. 'The senior Gildred had hoped to make the journey in ten days, but was hampered by fog, rain, jungles without landing fields, mountain peaks and delays in getting permission to cross the Panama Canal Zone,' said the inscription.

It all sounded scarily familiar, I thought as I walked next door to the car and motorbike museum, where I found, to my astonishment, a Rudge Ulster of exactly the type my father, not to mention Clifford's, would have raced in the Fifties. I stood and looked at it, and, overcome with emotion after hours of looking at old aeroplanes and the heroic chaps who flew them, then standing in front of the sort of motorcycle raced by my dear old dad in the days when he was a hero too, almost burst into tears of what I can only describe as empathetic nostalgia.

Pulling myself together before I was thrown out of the League of Chaps, I went outside and phoned Rocket Motorcycles to find that the damage to Tony was even greater than I'd suspected.

'The front axle is bent, the brake rotors are bent and the forks are out of alignment both horizontally and vertically. Alex is busy cannibalising a brand-new Tiger in the shop to replace them,' said Mark. 'To be honest, I'm surprised you got this far.

I wouldn't have ridden that bike to the shops and back, never mind all the way from Colombia. In fact, normally when a bike comes in with this much damage, it would take us two or three weeks to sort it out.'

'Two or three weeks?' I gulped.

'Normally. But we can have you back on the road by tomorrow lunchtime.'

'Mark, you are a wonderful, warm, caring human being, and that colour suits you,' I said, and meant it.

As for Tony, it seemed he was an even more remarkable machine than I had thought. I got a cab back to the motel to find Clifford arriving on a freshly serviced April, and my brother Trevor appearing soon after, not on the Harley he had promised, but on a shiny BMW. He had, I was glad to see, completely ignored me and brought a jacket.

'For God's sake, Trevor,' said a disgusted Pancho, 'you can't ride up the California coast on that thing. Why didn't you get a Harley?'

'It is all Geoff's fault,' said Trevor lamely. 'He wrote in *Way to Go* that a Harley sounded like two flatulent hippos making love underwater, and I couldn't get the image out of my head.'

'Flatulent hippos,' said Clifford. 'I like it.'

'You would,' I said. 'Now go and buy some bloody toothpaste, since you've been scrounging mine for the past month.'

'It hasn't run out already, has it?' he said, walking off to find a drugstore.

I arrived at Rocket Motorcycles next morning to find not only that Alex had done an incredible job putting Tony back together, but that Triumph had refused to accept a single cent for what must have been $3,000 worth of work and parts.

'And you get a free T-shirt!' laughed Mark, handing me a Rocket one.

I shook hands with them all several times over, invited them to come and stay in Belfast whenever they wanted, and rode off on a rejuvenated Tony, marvelling yet again at the kindness of people.

Back at the motel, Trevor and Clifford were packed and ready to go on their own new and refurbished machines. It felt like a combination of Christmas and The Magnificent Seven. Give or take a few.

Best of all, Clifford, fed up with me moaning all the way from Chile about having to keep the noise levels down inside the helmet by shoving toilet paper in my ears, had gone to the local hardware shop and splashed out $2.99 on a pair of genuine earplugs you could mould to fit the shape of your ears.

From a Scotsman, that meant a lot.

I led the way north in blissful silence, until by late afternoon we were in Santa Monica and pulling up outside the Hotel Casa del Mar, an opulent Jazz Age pile by the beach. You see, after the budget-breaking fortnight shipping the bikes from Colombia, I had written those begging letters to the tourist boards of California, Oregon, Washington, British Columbia and the Yukon, and they had responded with open hearts and matching wallets, providing free accommodation all the way to Alaska.

The Casa del Mar, for example, was an establishment for which the word opulent falls far short of the truth. As I was checking in at the reception desk, all too aware that I was wearing a jacket and trousers which had been patched with shredded bag by a Colombian tailor, the man next me to said: 'Is everything set for my meeting with Al this evening?'

'Everything is in order, Mr Shriver. Mr Pacino is expecting you,' said the receptionist.

I should hope so too. From my memory of Al's films, he tends to shoot people when things aren't just the way he likes them.

We had dinner at a restaurant on the pier called The Bubba Gump Shrimp Company, after the Tom Hanks movie. After two beers, I had this startling revelation: life is not like a box of chocolates, Forrest. In a box of chocolates, you know exactly what you're going to get. Just look at the card under the lid, you dickhead.

There. Having sorted that out, I walked back to the hotel, greeted the night porter cheerily, and fell asleep on a pillow for which several Hungarian geese had given their all.

After days of cloud and cold winds, I pulled back the curtains the following morning to reveal sand, sea and the Ferris wheel on Santa Monica pier basking under a warm blue sky. It was the herald of several days of hedonistic pleasure from California's golden shores.

We rode north up the Pacific Coast Highway, past signs from films, books and songs: Ventura, Hollywood and Sunset Boulevard, and had breakfast on a sunny patio in Malibu. As I sipped freshly squeezed orange juice, I began to long for that life of careless ease: of hanging out at the beach, playing volleyball and going out for a beer with my buddies. What I was really longing for, of course, was the endless, glorious summer of my youth, when after university I had come out to California to play volleyball for a team in Los Angeles.

For Clifford, too, this was an emotional part of the world: he had cycled up the coast three years before for what turned out to be a last family holiday with his long-term partner, Emma, and their son, Benjamin, before they had split up. It had broken his heart, and it was only now beginning to heal.

'I keep seeing places where we all had breakfast together, or beaches where I took Benjie for a swim, and bursting into tears,' he said at breakfast. 'I have to go through this, though. I feel it's the last painful part of letting go, so that I can move on.'

I listened to the sadness and hope in his voice, and felt, yet again, immeasurably lucky to have Cate.

At lunchtime, we were filling up with fuel when a middle-aged man rode in on an astonishing custom-built motorbike. He turned out to be called Reuben, and it turned out to be a Titan worth $38,000 which he had won in a raffle at a bike show.

'Lucky old me. I hadn't had a motorcycle for ten years, and

then I get this for $10,' he said, as a couple on a BMW rode in, followed by a man on a Harley. Before long, yet again, we were having our very own bike convention. Even better, as we were standing on the harbour in the hamlet of Morro watching whales breaching in the bay, there rolled by a gleaming cavalcade of classic, vintage and hot-rod cars on their way to a weekend rally up the coast.

Standing there in the late afternoon sun watching the stunning offspring of America's long love affair with the car stream past in the late afternoon sun, we felt, at that moment, held in a perfect dream of California.

As we rode up the coast next morning with the ocean on the left and the sun slowly seducing the mist off the wooded hills on the right, feeling that we were in paradise, it was not hard to see why William Randolph Hearst had decided to build a little hilltop holiday home here.

Hearst, the man on whom Orson Welles based Citizen Kane, was the only son of remarkable parents. His father, George, walked all the way from Missouri to California in his late thirties, made a fortune in silver mining and real estate, bought fifty miles of the California coast, and married Phoebe, a nineteen-year-old schoolteacher.

William Randolph, their only son, was born with not so much a silver spoon in his mouth as the whole cutlery drawer. He then grew up as a typical spoilt only child, believing that he could do anything he wanted. The difference was that he could. After building a movie, radio and publishing empire based on the four principles which have kept tabloid journalism where it belongs to this day – emphasise the sensational, elaborate the facts, manufacture the news and print lots of games – he turned his attention to a little building project. The site he chose was the hilltop overlooking the sea where he had spent many happy childhood days camping with his father, and the inspiration was an eighteen-month cultural tour of Europe his mother had taken him on when he was ten.

The result was Hearst Castle, the world's greatest tribute to boundless ambition and wealth, loosely based on your average Mediterranean billionaire's village and filled with 22,000 pieces of art, furniture and statuary collected by Hearst. Here, every head of state, every major Hollywood star and everyone who was anyone, or wanted to be, would be invited to stay in sumptuous rooms with matching views, swim in two vast heated mineral-water pools, lounge in sitting rooms so huge they had an internal phone at each end, and dine at a table so long that passing the salt took a week.

It was, as one guest wryly remarked, a great place to spend the Depression.

More a museum with sofas than a home, it is the ultimate 'My, hasn't he done well for himself' architectural statement, and we can only thank heavens, I thought as I rode away, that e-Bay wasn't around when Hearst was alive, or the castle would have covered all of California.

We rode on, through the rugged piney hills of Big Sur, and by nightfall were in the Hotel Sainte Claire in San Jose, whose residents at one time or another had included a list of Hollywood stars as long as the drive at Hearst Castle.

Not to mention Bobo the monkey, who lived on the fifth floor and spent his time unscrewing the light bulbs and flushing them down the toilet.

If Hearst Castle had been an exercise in extrovert ego, Winchester House in San Jose was one of introverted neurosis. Its owner, Sarah Winchester, was the wife of William, the head of the repeating rifle company which will be known to all John Wayne fans.

When her baby daughter and husband died in close succession, Sarah became convinced that she was being punished by the spirits of everyone who had been killed by the Gun that Won the West. Unfortunately for her, but fortunately for the San Jose carpentry industry, a local mystic convinced her that only constant building would appease them. She hired every workman in sight, and set them to work, twenty-four hours a day, 365 days a year, for the next thirty-eight years until her death.

We spent two hours next morning wandering around the endlessly rambling house that was the result, past doors which opened into walls to confuse the spirits, up convoluted staircases with two-inch steps because of her arthritis, by chimneys that ended short of ceilings so that ghosts couldn't get down them and through rooms with thirteen windows because she was obsessed by the number.

After the 1906 earthquake, she had forty of the 160 rooms boarded up for the rest of her life because she thought the quake was a sign that the spirits were angry with her. Such a lonely life she lived that when President Roosevelt arrived at the front door for a surprise visit one day, the butler was so stunned to see a guest that he told him to use the servants' entrance like everyone else. Roosevelt turned on his heel and walked away, never to return.

It was a strange, dark, gloomy place, the walls heavy with sadness, and I was glad to escape into the morning sun, climb on the bike, and ride up into the wooded hills for lunch at Alice's Restaurant. That's right, the one Arlo Guthrie sang about, where you can get anything you want, except for Alice.

We rode in and parked the bikes: Trevor's shiny BMW and a dusty and trailworn Tony and April. They sat proudly among dozens of gleaming Harleys, Ducatis and Hondas, whose owners strolled over, looked at the mud on April and the scratches on Tony, and asked us where we'd come from.

'Wow. Chile to Alaska. Wow,' they said. 'Every biker in the world would love to do that trip. You are lucky boys.'

'We know,' we said, since we sometimes forgot how lucky we were.

We spent three glorious hours there, sitting at a scrubbed wooden table having coffee and soup in the sun while men in battered leathers came, talked about motorbikes, admired other motorbikes, and left on motorbikes. On the stereo, Steely Dan was telling Rikki not to lose that number, Jackson Browne was running on empty and Van Morrison was insisting that his girl was as sweet as Tupelo honey.

After the gloom of the morning, it was the most joyous of afternoons, and it was about to get even better, with a ride down through the pines and across Golden Gate Bridge. One of the great experiences of an adult life, it was a perfect moment in what was, both in the experiencing and in the hindsight, a perfect day.

We rode on through the setting sun to the woodsmoke-and-pine spa town of Calistoga, stopped the bikes and took off our helmets, men who had been joined by a common bond that day.

Calistoga may have looked like a simple one-street town, but it was home to the sort of sophisticated people who played air violin as teenagers, and who now drove vintage Porsches and took the waters at Doc Wilkinson's Hot Springs every weekend. The Doc came to the area in 1952, and discovered the curative properties of the local mineral water and volcanic ash. He mixed the two together into a miracle gloop, and his name had been mud in the town ever since.

Which was why the next morning we found ourselves being lightly cooked in a mud bath, briefly boiled in a hot tub, gently steamed for a few minutes, wrapped in swaddling clothes, then rubbed all over with aromatic oils.

Not surprisingly, we found ourselves nodding off as we rode north, and had to stop for reviving home-made fudge in the Knotsville General Store, which did a sideline in T-shirts saying 'Knotsville – Pop 25' and 'Knotsville Women's Sewing Circle and Terrorist Group'.

'We did those as a joke just before 9/11, but they haven't been selling too well since. Now, chocolate fudge or peanut butter?' said the woman behind the counter.

'Both,' we three said as one man.

Around us as we rode on, the landscape changed from rolling vineyards and orchards to the giant redwoods of northern California, dwarfing us in their icy shade and turning the sky into an azure ribbon far above our heads.

We found a lodge by an icy river, parked the bikes, and watched as the moon finally struggled its way above the tallest of them. And then we barbecued steak by our little cabin, drank beer and felt like men.

The place where we were staying, River's Run, had been bought six years before by part-time vicar Keri Barnett and her lover, Joan. It was just a collection of simple wooden cabins at the bottom of a gorge, and the vertiginous, winding gravel track down was as bad as any Ecuadorean diversion, but they had made it work: families would come here to swim in the river, play with the dogs, toast marshmallows at the campfire and recreate their real or imagined childhoods.

'We get a lot of bikers, too. Big, soft guys covered in tattoos,' said Keri. 'They don't take any crap, though. Once, a guy on a new Harley arrived and complained about how hard the track down to here was, and they all turned around and said simultaneously: "If you can't ride it, sell it."'

Saying a silent prayer of thanks that I'd kept my mouth shut about how close I'd been to falling off on the way down, I finished my beer and we all went to bed, to be lulled to sleep by the flutter of hummingbirds' wings and the rustle of racoons snogging in the trees.

We rose at seven, put our fleeces and jackets on to ride up out of the morning chill of the canyon, and did not take them off for the rest of the day, as the mercury fell on the long road north.

Halfway through the afternoon, we saw a sign saying Wild Elk, and set off down a six-mile track to see them. After half a mile of potholes and gravel, though, Trevor got stuck in a ditch, and I decided that I had had enough of dirt tracks to last me a lifetime. Helping Clifford push the BMW free, I told them to say hello to the elks for me, and went back to the car park by the road, to sit on the grass, make some notes and admire the ladybirds which crawled over me for the next hour.

Even better, about a minute after I sat down, a dozen wild elk appeared in the adjacent meadow.

On my left as I lay there in the warm sun sat Tony, that fine motorcycle who had never let me down, the gouges along his left side evidence of what he had been through. In front of me stretched my boots, battered by the crash, baked by sun, covered in mud and drenched by rain, and trousers patched by a tailor in Cali. And on my right sat the tankbag, with the map of our route in the transparent pocket on top which had been a handy conversation point for South American traffic policemen, diverting them from their original intention of asking us for a bribe.

I looked at it, with the Pan-American Highway marked in red from southern Chile all the way up Peru, Ecuador, Colombia, Panama, Costa Rica, Nicaragua, Honduras, El Salvador, Guatemala, Mexico and the USA to where I sat at this moment in the sunshine of northern California, with the blue sky above, the sweet pines all around, a ladybird wandering over my knee and elk contemplatively chewing grass in the meadow there.

Even on a map, which normally makes journeys look easier, what we had done seemed impossible, and it was not even over yet.

After two hours, Clifford and Trevor returned, announced that Trevor had almost drowned crossing two rivers and that the elk over there looked much like the elk over here, and we set off again, sweeping down by the ocean and up by the pines, to yet again spend the night in a cabin by a river.

A short history of Oregon

Pre-1840
Nothing much happens.

1840–1870
After Lewis and Clark discover fine climate, fertile soil, mighty forests and rivers full of fish, 250,000 pioneers back east pile into covered wagons, trek overland for three months, settle down and start farming.

1870–present
Nothing much happens, again.

We crossed the state line into Oregon, and rode into a land of forests and lakes which would make a man want to rush out, buy a checked shirt and an axe, and go out to smite in twain the mighty redwood. Or, indeed, buy a rod and go fishing.

Which is what Dirk van Zante, a Californian marine biologist we met at breakfast, did as a boy. As a man, he came back and built a simple riverside lodge with all the raw essentials for rural life: open fires, hot tubs on balconies overlooking the river and gourmet cooking.

'Well, I was working on the principle that us guys are pathetic,' he said. 'We want to take our wives somewhere nice, then we want to go fly fishing, so we built the place to satisfy both. The wife walks in and says: "Wow, Egyptian cotton towels", and the husband says: "Wow, great river."'

In the afternoon, we stopped at a sign saying Sand Dunes Frontier out of interest, and five minutes later found ourselves in a dune buggy being terrified witless by a good-natured sadist called Wayne.

'I found this job was good therapy for me after I got out of prison,' he said as he unstrapped us afterwards. I think he was joking.

'You should really have a pilot's licence, Wayne, since we spent most of our time airborne,' I said.

'I thought it would be more scary,' said Clifford.

'I don't see how it could have been,' I said, as Trevor got on his BMW, and immediately fell over.

He had now done this so often that we were thinking of phoning up the Guinness Book of Records and seeing if they had a category for stationary motorbike accidents. Mind you, they were a lot less painful than the sort his brother engaged in. I walked over to help him pick it up.

'Do you want a hand?' said Clifford.

'He ain't heavy, he's my brother,' I said.

'Yes, yes, very good,' said Trevor.

By now it was time for afternoon tea, and we had an appointment with Lee Gray, the Wild Gourmet of Lincoln City. Lee was a bored and burnt-out chef in Beverly Hills who gave away almost everything he owned and came to Oregon with his dog, his backpack and his guitar to live in a cave over the winter. There, he discovered that he could live off the seaweed, sea slugs, sand shrimps and plants that grew wild along the seashore, and now he made a living selling them to the sort of restaurants where he once worked eighteen-hour days.

We wandered along the rugged shore with him, gaily munching seaweed, fiddlehead ferns, whin blossom and assorted flowers. People out walking their dogs gave us strange looks, then saw who we were with, said a cheery hello to Lee and went on their way.

Promising to call him on his twenty-four-hour kelpline if we found a new type of edible seaweed, we set off for McMinnville and the Evergreen Aviation Museum, founded by Michael King Smith, the talented son of aviation tycoon Delford Smith. A brilliant scholar, Michael learned to fly at sixteen, was already performing aerobatics in a Spitfire when he was twenty, and was on his way to a dazzling career in the US Air Force when he was killed in a car crash at twenty-nine.

His legacy was a museum in which, dwarfing all the other exhibits, was the Spruce Goose, Howard Hughes's 1947 version of Hearst Castle with wings. The world's largest wooden aircraft, it's still bigger than a Jumbo, and if aeroplanes have feelings, it must be rightly pissed off that Hughes flew it once for a mere mile then put it in storage, along with his sanity.

Rather wonderfully, in the same way that the space race created the non-stick frying pan, the technology behind the Goose was used to build the Hughes Sportster, marketed in the Fifties as the world's finest rowing boat.

That night, we found ourselves in Portland, with the rare luxury of a room each in the White Eagle, a former Polish hostel which was now a hotel complete with its own brewery and the ghost of a prostitute called Sam.

It may have seemed perfect, but it was not the best bit of the day. No, that was a moment I had been looking forward to for weeks: taking the ton of books, maps and notebooks on Latin America I no longer needed from the panniers, which had been strained well beyond their alleged 6kg limit, and packing them into a bag which Trevor would take home the next day.

At dawn, we said a sad farewell to him as he set off to ride 1,000 miles south to Los Angeles in two days to return the BMW, then fly back to grim reality after his week in the sun. He rode down to the corner, almost fell off, gave a cheery wave, and disappeared.

Clifford went off to do some maintenance on April, and I went in search of America's only vacuum cleaner museum. Ted, the salesman at Stark's Vacuum Cleaner Store (est. 1932), could not have been more honest about the museum, which was housed in a corner of the store.

'It's underwhelming, but interesting in a weird kinda way,' he said.

He wasn't wrong. Here, you will find every weapon in the long war against dust, from Victorian hand-pumped machines, when one had the servants to do that sort of thing before one killed them all off in the First World War, to the gleaming gold 1950s Haley Comet. Born in an age when Americans were looking forward to the two-day working week, this bore the legend: 'The age of space, the Rocket Race, Push Button leisure day, Be first to clean your jet set home the Haley Comet Way.'

'That one over there's the Filter Queen,' said Ted, pointing to a Heath Robinsonish contraption. 'Mostly it just blew carbon dust from the motor all over your carpet. Their hairdryers did the same thing. Strange they're still in business.'

Not far away was Powell's, the world's largest independent bookshop, with a million volumes lining the shelves. I spent an hour wandering among them to see if the book I was writing was among them, thus saving me the bother of finishing it, but failed, and had to comfort myself with coffee and a bun in the café over the local paper.

On the lonely hearts page, it had a Chance Meeting section, full of sad little ads saying things like: 'We met at the furniture store while you were buying a pink velour sofa. You gave me a look which suggested you'd like me to shag you senseless right there and then on an E-Z-Boy recliner, but I did nothing about it. Interested in a decaf at Starbucks some lunchtime?'

It's too late, you dickhead! You should have asked her out at the time! You rarely regret doing things, but you always regret not doing them! Life is not a box of chocolates! Ask Forrest!

There. Having used my entire day's supply of exclamation marks in one sitting, I got a cab back to the White Eagle and continued to investigate their fascinating selection of beers.

'I see you're in the room haunted by Sam the hooker,' said the barman. 'That's where she was killed by a jealous lover.'

'Thanks for letting me know,' I said gratefully.

In the evening, we had dinner with Chris Chester from the tourist board, a jolly Japanese-American divorcee in her fifties who at twenty-one had run away from home in Idaho to travel the world on a cargo boat. She later ended up with a food processing company which used a $1.5 million Microsoft scanner with four cameras to scan and reject substandard runner beans in a Madridosecond. The shortest time span in the known universe, this is the period between when the lights change to green in Madrid and the driver behind honks his horn.

I thought back to the days when, during student summer holidays, I had spent endless nights in a canning factory in Essex, sorting runner beans by hand in a freezing hut in the middle of a field. The job consisted of standing on a platform in front of a vibrating perforated metal belt on which a fascinating array of runner beans passed by, and sorting the beans by hand so that the small ones fell through the holes. Because the belt was connected to the platform, of course, everything vibrated, and me with it. At one in the morning, a bell would ring and I would troop off, still vibrating, to a canteen to buy a cup of coffee. I would then vibrate half of it onto the floor, drink the other half and go back to work.

I had never eaten runner beans since.

Perhaps, I thought as we shook hands with Chris and hailed a cab, Bill Gates wasn't so bad after all.

Back at the hotel, I discovered a text from Trevor to say that he had covered a remarkable 650 miles and was south of San Francisco. Even more remarkably, he hadn't fallen off once. Mind you, that was probably because he hadn't stopped.

As I woke the next morning, I noticed the strangest thing. The window, which I had firmly locked before I went to bed, was lying wide open. Then I remembered that exactly the same thing had happened the night before. Then I remembered that this was the room haunted by Sam the hooker.

Shivering in spite of myself, I dressed and tiptoed away down the stairs.

A short history of Washington State

As in Oregon, except that the arrival in the twentieth century of Boeing, Microsoft, Amazon *et al.* has brought sprawling suburbs and constant traffic jams, giving Oregonians even more reason to feel smugly but quietly content.

An hour after leaving Portland, chilled to the bones in the increasingly northern air, we crossed another state border, arrived in the little town of Chehalis, and decided to have a hot breakfast before we went to the vintage motorcycle museum down the street.

As we were cupping our hands gratefully around cups of coffee, the door opened and an old-timer came in and introduced himself as Frank Mason, the museum's founder and sole proprietor.

'Saw the bikes and thought I'd come in and say hi,' he said, giving us both a bone-crushing handshake.

A sixty-five-year-old retired engineer, he'd started the museum in 1979 by accident when a friend who was getting divorced had offered him three pre-1915 motorbikes.

'I went to see John Alexander, an old friend who owns the local bank, as his dad had before him, and he gave me a good deal on a loan to buy them. Very handy having a bank owner as a buddy, I tell ya,' he said after we'd told him about the trip. 'I've concentrated on that era ever since, although good bikes are going for upwards of $100,000 now. But we still take them all for a spin every so often. Just a hundred miles or so, nothing like you fellas are doing, but it's about enough for the old dears. Hey, there's John walking past.'

John saw us, came in and gave us another knuckle-grinder of a greeting.

Since those early days, he'd built up his collection of banks to a dozen, but was now seventy, retired, and spent most of his time riding around on several vintage bikes, including Vincents, Triumphs, BSAs and Harleys.

He was telling us about them when Sarah, the waitress, came over with our corn chowder in a bowl made of bread.

'Enjoy, boys,' she said, holding out her hand to crush what was left of ours.

'God, she's gorgeous,' said Clifford, going off to take her photo for his book of beauties.

In spite of the irrevocable damage to our hands, it was all so homely that I wanted to rush across the street to the general store, tie on a manly apron and get a job behind the counter immediately.

'You know,' said John, 'I've been thinking of touring down to Mexico over the summer, but I hear you need to make darned sure all your documents are in order.'

'Tell me about it,' laughed Clifford, simultaneously examining his photo of Sarah and his hand for broken bones.

'But I'm going to Italy first. First time back there since I was in the navy in the Fifties. Didn't see too much culture then, for

I was just looking for bars and honeys. Guess my focus has changed a bit over the years.'

He laughed, although there was a sad edge to it: his wife had died of cancer the year before, and the loss was still in his eyes.

We finished our chowder, waved to Sarah but ran out the door before she could come over and finish off our paws with another handshake, and wandered down the street to spend a happy hour admiring Frank's old dears: mouth-wateringly beautiful ancient Harleys, Pierces and Indians with the chief's head on the front fender which lit up after dark, as well as dozens of makes I'd never even heard of – Henderson, Excelsior, Thomas, Yale, Reading Standard, Thor, Flanders, Emblem, Iver Johnson and Flying Merkel.

There was even one from Sears and Roebuck, the mail order company who sold everything from toothpicks to prefabricated houses which came with everything but the kitchen sink, hence the expression, and whose motto was: 'We stand behind everything we sell – except our manure spreader.'

On the wall, an old Indian advertisement said: 'The Motorcyclist often loses half the enjoyment of a pleasure trip when he goes alone. The beauty spots of summer land are made doubly enjoyable when he takes a congenial companion along.'

Down the back of the museum was a workshop in which Clifford and I both came over all emotional, for it was exactly like the sort which both our dear old dads had owned. Not that we would admit to our feelings, of course, for we were men of steel who rose at dawn, rode motorcycles all day and could survive for weeks without food, beer or a kind word.

Well, maybe not beer.

Talking of which, it was looking increasingly unlikely that Deadhorse would be our final destination after all, since recent investigation had revealed that:

a) It was not really part of the Pan-American Highway, which ended in Fairbanks, 500 miles south.

b) The road from Fairbanks to it was mostly gravel and potholes, navigable only by 4×4s and with no filling station for 240 miles at a time.

c) Because it was an industrial dormitory town for the nearby oil refinery, no beer was allowed.

Of the three, the last was the most compelling reason not to go there.

In any case, investigating the map of the road from Fairbanks to Deadhorse one night, I had happened to notice a hill just north of the Arctic Circle called Gobblers Knob. There was no apostrophe, it presumably having dropped off in the cold. Who could resist finishing the journey in a place with a name like that?

'You leaving the Triumph at the dealer in Anchorage?' said Frank, interrupting my thoughts. 'He's a good friend of mine, but my memory's so crap these days I've forgotten his name. Think it's Y something. Hang on a second and I'll call Roy, who knows him as well. Roy's eighty-six with terminal cancer, but tough as hell.' He hauled out his mobile phone and rang a number.

'Hello, Martha? Is the shop mechanic there? He's gone off riding for three days? Can you remember the name of the Triumph dealer in Anchorage? Don Rosene? That's it. I knew it began with a Y. Say hi to Roy when he gets back.'

Eighty-six with terminal cancer, and still riding motorbikes. There was more than one way to be a man of steel, I thought, as Frank and John demolished what was left of our hands and we rode off into the afternoon.

That night, we landed up in a lakeside lodge owned by Jon Hawkins, a thirty-two-year-old who had been working as a steel broker. Until he got kidnapped by the mafia while setting up a deal in Russia.

'I was beaten up, stuck in a room and told I wouldn't be going home alive,' he said as we sat out on his deck that evening watching the sun go down over the lake. 'After six weeks, my boss paid them $250,000 and I was released, but even on the flight home, I was thinking there had to be more to life than this, no matter how much money I was making. Not only that, but I was spending a lot of time in LA, and it was getting to me. It's got no heart and no soul, and after a while the people get the same. They'll bump into your shopping trolley, give you a mean look, call you an asshole and storm off.'

Then, by one of those pieces of serendipity that change lives, he found out that the lodge on Lake Quinault, half a mile from the house where he had grown up until his parents moved to California, was for sale. He took all he had out of the bank, borrowed some from them, and bought it.

Then, when his parents came up to see it, they fell in love with the place all over again, bought back that old childhood home, and now they were all working together, chopping logs, planting trees and hauling rocks to make the lodge a success. It was a heart-warming story, with a bittersweet edge: his girlfriend, fed up with playing poker and counting the trees all winter, had upped and left two months ago.

'Anyway, I prefer the company of animals,' he laughed, as Sara the retriever and Little Jack the schnauzer chased a racoon across the lawn, watched imperiously by the cat, who was above such things.

Next afternoon, we were riding along minding our own business when I spotted Den Chastain doing a spot of tricky dental work on a 10ft grizzly bear. Fortunately, it was made of wood, and he was using a chainsaw.

The son of a logger, Den started carving with chainsaws in 1968, and soon discovered such a talent for it that it was now a full-time job for him and his wife, Margaret.

'When I was a kid, the only thing I was good at was recess and art, and I'd always loved whittling, so I guess it came from all that,' he said. 'I sometimes wish I'd done an art class, but some folks say it would ruin me, and maybe I'm better going my own way. It'll never make me a fortune, but it's good working for yourself, and it's good working with Margaret. She's a people person, and I'm a chainsaw person. And we're not the only mad ones around here. Guy called Matthew Bertik, who makes cute sculptures from forks, moved all the way here from New York because he wanted to live in Forks up the road.'

Logging, of course, was primarily a male occupation, and a dangerous one, as was evidenced by the fact that Den was a couple of fingers short of a full set, and while the men were out wielding saws, women like Elizabeth Barton were at home doing interesting things with fluff.

Known to everyone in Forks as Missy, Elizabeth was the granddaughter of a legendary pioneer dubbed The Iron Man of the Hob, because at a time when you could only bring west what you could carry, he walked from Iowa with a cast-iron stove on his back. Her mother, a brilliant chemist and political campaigner, was just as remarkable.

When Elizabeth was forty-six, four decades ago, she went to art class and discovered a hidden talent for painting. Then, six years later, she started thinking about lint. You know, the stuff left over when you tumble-dry clothes. The result is the strangest collection of fine landscapes and portraits you will ever see, every single one of them made from old fluff.

Suitably amazed, we rode off, wondering about one of the great unanswered questions of life. Why, no matter what colour of shirt you wear, is the fluff in your tummy button always the same?

Since by now we were becoming addicted to lakeside lodges, we found ourselves that night in another one called Lake Crescent Lodge, whose collection of local beers I enjoyed so much that next morning I leaped out of bed, grabbed a bottle of shampoo and poured it all over my hair, only to discover that it was mouthwash.

Still, I was not the only one to make a cock-up around these parts: the government had built a railroad on the other side of the lake in the First World War to carry spruce south for making aeroplanes. They hammered home the last spike two weeks before the armistice.

With my hair freshly minted, we set off for Hurricane Ridge, a lofty viewpoint from which you could, according to the locals, see all the way from Los Angeles to Vancouver. As we rode along in the Sunday morning sunshine, waving gaily to weekend bikers, my thoughts turned to the end of the great adventure, which was now only 2,000 miles away. To the riders we were waving at, or indeed any normal person, this would have seemed like a huge undertaking, but after what we had been through, it felt like a skip and a hop.

It was going to be strange going back to work and sitting at a desk rather than in my little office, with its row of dials.

Strange to go to work without a crash helmet on, come to that.

And, most of all, strange to wake up every morning in the same place, strange not to look at the horizon, wonder what was beyond it, then get on a motorbike and go to find out.

'You know, Pancho,' I said to Clifford as we arrived at the top of the ridge, got off the bikes and crunched through snow which was thick on the ground, even in May, 'if it wasn't for Cate, I wouldn't really want to go home at all. And Kitten, of course.'

'I don't,' he said. 'I could quite happily just keep travelling for ever.'

'I know. Bruce Chatwin had a lot to answer for when he wrote that we're all essentially nomadic,' I said as two skiers swooshed past, noticed our motorbike gear, and gave us a very strange look indeed. I gave it back, since we had enough strange looks of our own to be going on with, and we went inside the wooden ski lodge for hot chocolate.

Afterwards, we rode back down through the snow and trees, leaving winter behind and returning to a spring of bluebell meadows, people walking around in T-shirts and, once, ten tiny ducklings following their mother across a river.

It was all very confusing, really: we had started in South American summer, gone through spring in North America and would finish in the perpetual winter of Alaska.

It was a bit like going back in time, and perhaps I would be a teenager again by the time we finished. Like I'd notice the difference.

In the meantime, the thrilling news, according to a roadside placard, was that Finlay Mickelson had just been elected Sequim Irrigation Festival Princess. Hurrah! That girl will go far, mark my words, I thought as we wheeled on through forests, meadows and lakes, with the odd eagle soaring overhead, followed by the even one.

By teatime we were in Fairhaven, an ancient village where we were spending the night at a matching inn. As we stopped at the village's only traffic light, a man on a Honda pulled up alongside wearing, to our surprise, a Joey Dunlop replica racing helmet.

'Nice helmet. I used to race against him,' said Clifford to him.

'You're kidding me. You rode with the man?'

'Sure did. And not just once.'

'Holy shit. Let me shake your hand,' said the man, reaching across and then, as the lights turned to green, disappearing into the distance at a rate which suggested that his emulation of his hero was not confined to headgear.

The next morning, as Clifford went off searching for an internet café, I was aimlessly wandering down the street when I looked up to see a sign saying American Museum of Radio and Electricity. Inside, I found Jonathan Winter, the museum founder, playing with his Tesla machine, named after the Croatian genius who invented alternating current, which meant that electrons could swing both ways for the first time, giving them a whole new choice of current affairs. A Tesla machine, for those of you who don't have one at home, is a bit like a Van de Graaf generator in a bad mood.

'Stick your hand up,' said Jonathan as forked lightning streaked from the machine all over the room. Rather stupidly, I did so, and was zapped in the palm by a 10,000-volt bolt. Fairly wakes you up, I can tell you.

Fortunately, the rest of the exhibits were a little more sedate, including a mechanical music box given to Jonathan's grandmother by the fire chief of San Francisco and which, using a ferruled zinc and tin disc, still produced the most beautiful sound in the world. It sounded like childhood, if I had to put a name to it.

There was, too, a reproduction of the wireless room on the *Titanic*, although a little less damp than the original, and the first mobile phone, the 1909 Collins Wireless Telephone. Sadly, when Collins was demonstrating it by pretending to speak to someone on the other side of the country, he was actually speaking to someone on the other side of the wall, and he was later jailed for fraud.

Nearby was the first home entertainment system, a 1927 Sparton Visionola, with a movie reel linked to a 78rpm phonograph, which still worked. As did the 1930s Zenith, a magnificent walnut radio on which you could tune in to recordings of broadcasts of the time, from *The War of the Worlds* to *The Lone Ranger*, and from Abbot and Costello to Tchaikovsky.

Strangely, it sounded exactly like the AM radio I'd discovered in a motel we had stayed in a few days before, on which I had found crackly signals, breathy with atmosphere, of discussions about politics, religion or books, live baseball games and cheesy advertisements.

There's one great thing about America: it does wonderful little museums, I thought as I wandered back down the street to find Clifford emerging from the internet café.

We loaded up the bikes, and set off for Canada, and the frozen north.

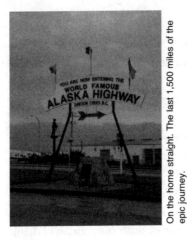

On the home straight. The last 1,500 miles of the epic journey.

19

A short history of British Columbia

1800–1858
Entire region ruled by Hudson's Bay Company and populated only by bears, natives and fur trappers.

1858
Gold discovered, attracting 25,000 would-be millionaires and increasing career opportunities by a third, except for bears.

1876
Railway makes it as far as Vancouver, transforming it from two huts in a swamp into laid back, hedonist hub of province which supplies quarter of all North America's timber, hydroelectric power, fish and minerals.

The Canadian border guards, as usual, grilled us for three hours, demanded impossible bribes, then beat us with rubber truncheons, attached electrodes to our dongles, locked us in a padded cell and forced us to watch Jerry Springer re-runs for three days.

284

Oh, all right, only joking: they waved us through with a cheery grin, wished us a pleasant stay in Canada, and actually sounded as if they meant it.

'Is it Fitzroy?' I said as Clifford put away his passport.

'Nope,' he said.

We set off in sunshine and showers, and before long were rolling into Vancouver, one of my favourite cities in the entire universe.

Even including Planet Zog on Wednesdays, when they have half-day closing so that everyone can go off, play volleyball on the beach, eat cheeseburgers and fries with mayonnaise, drink beer and talk absolute shite for hours on end, one of the greatest but most underrated pleasures known to humankind.

Anywhere, where was I?

Ah yes, in Vancouver.

It was to here that I had first come in 1991, at the end of a month spent travelling across Canada by train. It was here, too, that I had come after finishing Route 66 on a Harley, to meet Cate, then my girlfriend of only three months, to wander hand in hand through the streets then head for the Rockies in a Jeep called Arf.

We found a hotel and parked the bikes. Clifford went off to meet a cousin, and I went exploring.

As I walked through the same rain-dappled streets I had walked six years before with the woman who was now my wife, listening much as we had then to Van Morrison's 'Brown-eyed Girl' wafting out of dark cafés and buying tiny, mysterious delicacies from Chinese bakeries, it was hard not to fall in love all over again with Vancouver's indolent, satisfied soul.

Canadians already love it, of course. They emerge blinking from their endless, landlocked winters and come down to this Camelot by the waves to sniff the salt air and be astonished that flowers bloom in February.

And the rain! They love the glorious rain which washes down the dusty streets and drips from the trees which shelter every pavement. Canadians don't have rain. In the prairies and the east, they go straight from frostbite to sunstroke without the balmy, breezy days of spring. They even make a joke about it: that there are only two seasons in Canada, winter and Labor Day.

But in British Columbia they have so much rain that they export millions of gallons of it every year to California. And that still leaves plenty for the rest of the Canadian population to come here, unfurl their umbrellas and splash through the streets.

Or drive up the mountains which rim the city, to see even more water: salmon splashing their way up through the rapids of Capilano Canyon to mate.

Or terrify themselves by walking across the suspension bridge up there, a swaying curve of wood and rope hundreds of feet above the rushing river.

Or take the Sky Ride the 3,800ft to the top of Grouse Mountain, to stand in the clouds as they tear themselves to shreds on the rock and are reborn among the softness of trees.

And then ride the Seabus across the harbour to Gastown for an aquatic encore, as the steam clock in Gastown sounds off the quarter hours with a misty chorus high into the damp air above the Gastown streets. Time to sit and take a dry martini, it says, and look at the folks from the prairies slowly blossoming as they walk to restaurants in the rain, and remember where they came from, where it rained all the time.

Time to think that maybe if I had a million a year and an umbrella, I might love Vancouver even more. But wait, I do have an umbrella, I laughed, finishing my martini and going back to the hotel to fetch Clifford, since we had arranged to go and visit an old friend of his for dinner.

Ian McGuffie, now seventy-nine and living on the north shore of Vancouver with his wife, Elizabeth, had once worked as an apprentice mechanic in Clifford's dad's motorcycle shop. In 1953, he left Scotland on a boat to Halifax and got on a train to Edmonton. As it pulled into Toronto at dawn on the fourth day, an elderly man got on and sat down beside him.

'Where you headed, young fella?' he said to Ian.

'Edmonton.'

'What the hell are you going there for? There's nothing in Edmonton. Get off here instead,' said the other man.

Ian lifted his toolbox and suitcase down off the luggage rack, got off the train and was walking up Yonge Street looking for the YMCA when he passed the owner of a motorcycle shop opening up for the day.

'Do you need a good mechanic?' he said to him.

'Why, do you know one?' said the man.

'I am one.'

'Well, you'd better get started, then. You've a lot of work to get through before teatime.'

After a month, he'd saved enough for Elizabeth to come out and join him, and after two years, they had enough to buy an old Mercedes and set out for Vancouver. There, he walked into the garage of Trevor Deeley, then just starting on a multimillion-dollar career selling and promoting motorcycles, and asked for a job.

Deeley not only gave him the job, but a BSA Gold Star to race. For three years, he won every race in Canada on it, then returned to Europe as a works Norton rider. Sitting on his first brand-new Norton, he decided the tank wasn't comfortable, and took a hammer to it until it was. The season after, he got a Manx Norton.

'Pile of crap. Absolute garbage. Took it for a spin and the gearbox seized after five minutes. I pulled into the side of the road, someone offered me 200 quid for it, and I took it and went back to Canada,' he said.

I thought of how my dad had longed for a Manx Norton in his racing days, and laughed.

Now, after a successful career in aeronautical and motorcycle engineering, Ian hadn't been on a motorbike for years. Mind you, after dinner, he drove us back to the hotel at a rate which suggested that, even at seventy-nine, his mastery of speed remained undimmed.

The next morning, Clifford set off to buy a new chain for April, and I went out for breakfast, sitting by the window of a café in Gastown, nursing a mug of hot coffee and looking out at streets hissing with rain.

On the table in front of me, a newspaper lay open at the casting ads placed by the city's film companies. 'Wanted: 55–65yrs Quebecois man, broken, agitated, charming and strange, to play Laporte in *Some Letters to a Young Poet*,' said the ad at the top.

Outside, the rain stopped at last, and I finished my coffee and walked to Granville Island, where the beautiful people of Vancouver come down to the sea to play. Rumours that they are rich are unfounded, for they are very rich. In this little corner of God's green acre, even the Hell's Angels were freshly laundered as they rolled down to the island on a Saturday afternoon to wreak unlimited credit on grateful shopkeepers and café owners.

Squeezing their gleaming Harleys into the space between the yachts and the convertibles, they stomped politely into whichever bar was fashionable that week, drank themselves sober on low-alcohol lager, then rode back to the west of the city to park the bike back in the garage before it started to rain again.

On their way home, they would pass many small Chinese women driving German cars. These were the wives of the Hong Kong millionaires who poured into Vancouver as soon as the UK announced it was handing the colony back to China. As they did so, they pushed house prices so high that they forced the beautiful people of Vancouver ever closer to the mountains, over which the sun was already climbing to show that the day was passing on.

I walked on, and by three was in Stanley Park, the 1,000 acres where the ordinary people of Vancouver come to play on a Saturday afternoon. I was standing eating a very nice maple and pecan ice cream when I looked down to find a large racoon nibbling the toe of my boot.

'I wouldn't do that if I was you, chum,' I said. 'After where those have been the past few months, you'll get food poisoning.'

He looked up at me with a pair of moist, fey eyes, then pottered off.

In the zoo, the polar bear was asleep, the penguins were ambling back and forth like ancient butlers, and a Japanese girl was playing a violin beneath a tree.

In 1942, the substantial Japanese population of British Columbia, many with Canadian citizenship and some of whom had fought for the Allies in the First World War, was interned. Their possessions were sold to pay for the privilege, and in 1949 many of them were forced to emigrate to Japan.

But there was not even the ghost of a shadow of irony in her face, as she played 'There's No Place Like Home'. She looked up once, as a breeze from the ocean brought cherry blossoms fluttering down around her, but that was all.

On the grassy slopes below the zoo, several hundred people were watching the finals of the British Columbia rugby championships. On the balcony of the clubhouse, some of the wives had tired of the game and turned to watch a cricket match, munching silently on their hamburgers as they listened to the sweet click of willow and cork and watched the white figures running eagerly to and fro.

It was just like an English shire, except that the sun was shining. The wives looked anxiously at the sky from time to time, but the rain held off, and the day passed on. Before long it was seven in the evening, and the steam clock in the centre of Gastown announced the hour with a gurgling eulogy into the humid night.

In Hill's Indian Crafts Shop on Water Street, two American tourists were buying a Coast Salish totem pole for $15,000. Around the corner, the addicts were shooting up for the night, and the bums were huddled in front of the TV at the drop-in centre watching the hockey playoffs. 'No Drugs, No Knives, No Profanity, No Sleeping, No Fighting, No Panhandling' said the grimy notice above their heads.

Outside, two of the beautiful people stopped briefly at the lights in their new yellow Mazda convertible. The hood was down, and the Rolling Stones were on the CD player.

'You can't always get what you want, you get what you need,' sang Mick Jagger, millionaire, to the beautiful people of Vancouver. The lights changed, and they drove on. The bums hadn't raised their heads, and the rain came at last, until you could hardly see them behind the steamy windows of the drop-in centre.

Down the street, the beautiful people stopped, put up their hood and drove home in their Japanese convertible, passing on their way a Chinese millionaire's wife driving a German car and a Canadian policeman riding an American motorcycle through the hissing streets of this little corner of God's green acre that is forever British.

Within minutes of leaving Vancouver the next morning, we were into the wilderness, with fjords and islands on one side, eagles soaring above, and forest, waterfalls and lakes on the other.

All around, men were doing manly things: rebuilding roads rutted by winter, beavering away at dams damaged by spring torrents or just wrestling grizzlies with one hand tied behind their backs, stopping every two hours to chew some gravel.

Well, except in Whistler, where some dudes were, like, you know, boarding.

It was the strangest of days: so warm that even when we climbed thousands of feet and were riding past deep snow, we were in shirtsleeves. Mind you, every time we rode past a waterfall it was like being smacked in the face by a frozen kipper, and when we found the road blocked by an avalanche, we had to admit defeat and put our jackets back on while two industrious chaps with bulldozers cleared the way.

By nightfall, after riding through a scene as wild and rugged as Charles Bronson first thing in the morning with a hangover, we were in Lillooet. I recognised it the moment we rode down the main street, for I had been here before: when Cate and I had driven around the Rockies in Arf, we had driven up this same road.

We had gone up for glider flights in Pemberton Valley, gone skinny-dipping in snowbound Joffre Lake for, oh, a good two seconds before our lips turned blue, gone 'Wow' at every corner, and finally stopped at Lillooet for coffee and pie before branching off east to Kamloops. Who would have thought that six years later, I would be riding up this same street on a motorbike, having come all the way from Chile?

Funny old thing, life, as Abraham Lincoln said on his way to the theatre to see *Our American Cousin*.

In 1860, Lillooet was a gold rush boom town second in population only to San Francisco, and the seat of Judge Sir Matthew Baillie Begbie, who had a reputation for listening carefully, wisely and fairly to the mitigating arguments of criminals, then hanging them anyway. Today, it was a sleepy logging village with a hotel, a huge video shop, a liquor store and, naturally enough, a Greek restaurant.

On the way home from the latter, brimming with moussaka and ouzo, we passed the office of the *Lillooet News*, the window of which bore the admirably courageous promise: 'A chuckle once a week and a belly laugh once a month – or your money back!'

Next morning, after giving the very same paper a world exclusive interview, we rode out of town, passing on the way the wiry figure of George Vanderwolf, standing on the sidewalk scratching his chin. He'd been doing that now for four decades, since the autumn he found a huge jade seam up in the mountains. Unfortunately, when he went back in the spring, he'd forgotten where he left it, and has never found it again.

We had better luck at Williams Lake, where we were wandering down by the water at teatime when we spotted two kayaks lying on the lawn in front of a house. We knocked on the front door and asked the owner if we could rent them.

'No, but you can borrow them!' he laughed.

We paddled about the mirrored flat for an hour, disturbing loons and turtles, and I thought of seeing Cate again in what was now only a couple of weeks. I tingled all over, and it wasn't just the evening chill. I had never felt quite that way before, and I'll tell you how good it felt.

It felt better than the moment, later in the evening, when I discovered that the Overland Pub stocked Sleeman's Cream Ale, possibly the finest beer in Canada, hauled all the way from Ontario by a team of hand-picked racoons, one of which was the cousin of the one which had tried to eat my boot in Vancouver.

That's how good it felt.

It was a very emotional experience loading up Tony these mornings, checking the oil and tyres, and knowing that the days of these little rituals were now numbered, and that soon I would be saying goodbye to this most faithful of friends.

The best way of looking at it, I guess, was that at least I had given him the most exciting start possible to his life as a motorcycle. Unlike the mileage on most cars or bikes, which represented nothing more than work and back or Sunday jaunts, every single mile on Tony's mileometer had been an adventure and a challenge overcome.

Particularly the ones through the Atacama Desert, when I had ridden for day after nerve-wracking day through the endless sands with the engine warning light on, patting his tank occasionally in the way I imagined cowboys patted the flanks of their horses, and saying: 'Just one more mile, chum. Every mile is another mile north.'

Talking of faithful friends, Pancho had finally received word from home that he had to be back in work by the end of the month, which meant he would just about make it into Alaska before angling south towards Anchorage to fly home, whereas I would go on to Fairbanks, and Gobblers Knob if I could make it up the fearsome Dalton Highway.

In the same way that I had conceived the start of this journey alone, it seemed, after all, that I was destined to end it alone.

In the meantime, we set out from Williams Lake for

Barkerville, named after Billy Barker, a Cornishman who set out in 1858 to find gold in this solitary wilderness. In 1861, he arrived in a wooded valley surrounded by rugged mountains, and started digging. He got to 50ft, and had just given up when his mates told him he was a lily-livered woosicle, and should have another go. He picked up his spade, dug another two feet, and uncovered what was to be the biggest gold find ever in British Columbia, worth $3.5 billion.

Before long, every inch of the valley was being dug up by gold-crazed men, and today the boom town that grew up around them was still, remarkably, intact.

Wandering down its dirt street, lined by boardwalks and wooden buildings, and with the stagecoach coming and going, we could almost feel the tinderbox heat of emotions which must have resulted from such a group of wild, obsessive maniacs, both men and women, piled into such a small space, with half of them getting rich and the other half living on credit from the saloon, the grocery store and F.J. Barnard, the shipping agent who brought in everything from champagne and oysters to rubber boots, for which he charged an eye-watering $12, or $400 today.

Shipping agents obviously made a packet even in those days, I muttered to myself, thinking grimly of Judith as we climbed on the bikes and I led the way out of town, passing two bears and a wolf on the way. Fortunately, they were in fields at the side of the road.

Unlike the huge female moose who leaped out of the roadside trees right in front of me. It happened so fast that I didn't have time to swerve, just duck to the left as her head flashed by an inch from my helmet.

'You missed death by a millimetre, man. It wasn't even an inch,' said Clifford when we stopped for fuel half an hour later. 'If you'd hit that monster, both of you would have been killed. She braked so hard that she skidded onto her bum, then jumped up and leaped across to the other side of the road in a single bound, followed by a calf.'

He was right, though: we'd read enough horror stories of hundreds of people in Canada every year being killed or maimed for life, hitting moose in cars. On a bike, you had no chance.

'Well, that's another life gone. That's two I've used up this trip,' I said, going in to pay for the fuel and buy us a Magnum bar.

In Prince George, we pulled up outside our hotel to find Schubert wafting out from the foyer and several Indian drunks lounging outside against a sign proclaiming optimistically that the rejuvenation of downtown was well underway.

'We're all optimists here. We have to be,' said a man we met in a bar when we went out for a beer later to celebrate me being alive. 'Take trees, for example. You see all the brown pines in the forest around here? Pine beetle. No known cure. Disaster is around the corner, but in the meantime we're making a fortune from pulp, which is all the infested trees are good for. Anyway, you were lucky with the moose, but watch out for grizzlies when you head north. They eat a couple of tourists every year, and they're even meaner than usual this year for some reason. We tell tourists to take pepper spray and carry little bells when they go into the woods, but to be honest that's just so we can tell the difference between grizzly crap and black bear crap. The grizzly crap smells of pepper and has bells in it.'

Thanking him for the advice, we shook his hand and went to bed, then got up the next day and rode through a landscape which passed through pine forests, lakes and rugged mountains until finally we descended through rolling meadows which looked for all the world like Kent.

As darkness fell, we rode in a downpour into Dawson Creek, the start of the Alaska Highway, and the last 1,500 miles of our long journey.

A short history of the Alaska Highway

March 1942
Worried about Japanese invading Alaska, US Army picks 25,000 volunteers to build road from Dawson Creek in Yukon

1,520 miles to Fairbanks, Alaska. In spite of mountains, mud, mosquitoes, bogs, rivers, ice and dense forest, road is completed by October. First convoy of trucks to Fairbanks averages 18mph in worst winter on record.

1943
Road already needs rebuilt. Volunteers sigh and return, alleviating boredom by shooting several species of wildlife to verge of extinction.

1948
Road opened to civilian traffic, which breaks down in such quantities that road is closed again for a year.

For our first few miles up the Alaska Highway, we were joined by the local Christian bike club, who'd heard about our trip through the tourist board. Among them was a woman who taught kids in the back of beyond, and since 85 per cent of the people in the world's second biggest country live within 100 miles of the border with the US, that left an awful lot of back of beyond.

'We send books out to them during the summer, and sometimes get excuses back like "The huskies ate my homework",' she said over lunch of soup and chocolate cake. 'They tend to be the kids of fur trappers and the like, and they live way out. One girl is 600 miles from the end of the nearest road, and when she tried a spell at a real school, she hated it. She complained that there weren't any good trails to exercise her dog team, so she eventually harnessed them up and went home.'

'What age was she?'

'Nine.'

We shook hands with them and rode off, but only after they'd insisted on not only buying lunch, but giving us $50 towards our diminishing finances.

All afternoon we rode, increasingly chilled to the bone. Every hour or so, when we could no longer feel our hands or feet, we stopped at little cabins with hand-painted signs outside saying Marv and Cherry's or Bob and Jane's, to cup our hands around mugs of hot chocolate, then get back on and ride until we went numb again.

By nightfall, we were in Fort Nelson, home of Marl Brown, who, with his long white beard and hair that appeared to have recently been connected to a Tesla machine, may have looked like the wild man of the woods, but was actually a brilliant engineer who started the town's museum in 1987.

'Before that I came up the highway in 1957 and worked as an army mechanic, then ran a service station on the old Alaska Highway until they moved it, leaving me eight miles out in the bush with no customers,' he said. 'To get started on raising the money for the museum, I auctioned my beard for $10,000, and haven't shaved since.'

The result was a splendidly eclectic collection of frontier memorabilia such as paraffin lamps, sleighs, radios, canoes and rifles. In an adjoining shed were twenty-three cars, from a 1907 Brush to a 1965 pick-up, and including a 1924 Model T Ford Marl had owned for fifty-six years.

Next door to that was a trapper's cabin, authentic down to the bottle of Perry Davis painkiller on the windowsill. When that froze, it meant it was 60 below and too cold for even the most hardy to go out.

We knew how they felt, as we pushed north the next morning, past lakes and rivers still petrified by the icy grasp of winter. Our only companions in this wilderness of rock, forest and ice were the buffalo and bear, moose and wolves we saw variously grazing, lolloping or strolling unconcernedly across the road in front of us.

It was ironic, I thought, that I had once spent several days in Sweden with a guide looking for wolves and not seen a single one, and yet here they were wandering about willy-nilly.

The only humans we saw, meanwhile, were those in monstrous recreational vehicles with mock-heroic names like Adventurer, Commander, Wanderer and Old Farts from

Florida, and big truckers barrelling down the road with Dolly Parton on the stereo to keep them company. They all had one thing in common, though: they were sitting in nice warm, cosy vehicles.

Warmth! The concept seemed so utterly alien these days, as we sped along chilled to not only the bone but the marrow, that it was impossible for us now to imagine the baking deserts of Peru. Even the idea of riding in T-shirts, as we had only a few days before, seemed so ludicrous that I would have laughed out loud, if I could have stopped my teeth chattering for long enough.

At one stop, Pancho came out after our hot chocolate to find me hunting around in the panniers.

'What are you looking for?' he said.

'That heat we had in Ecuador. I stored some of it in here for days like this, but it's completely vanished.'

'Stolen by polar bears, almost certainly,' he said.

'Whose stupid idea was it to come to this part of the world in May anyway?' I said, wrapping my scarf around my neck as many times as it would go.

'Big fella with a moustache. I'd know him if I saw him again,' said Clifford, turning his hands over and admiring the particular shade of purple they had turned, then shoving them into his gloves. I did the same, although only after digging out of my pocket a pair of black silk glove liners I had taken to wearing over the past few days, even if they did mean having to explain to every petrol pump attendant that I wasn't really a cross-dressing transvestite.

Still, by way of compensation for the bitter cold, we had the fierce majesty of the mountains, the serene grace of a stand of silver birch in snow, the aquamarine shock of Muncho Lake between gaps in the ice and, best of all, the blessing of Liard River hot springs, where we sat up to our noses for half an hour until we could feel our extremities again.

That kept us going for the last haul of the day, and then, as we crossed the border into the Yukon, the sun appeared from behind the clouds, warming us by a few precious, glorious degrees.

A short history of the Yukon

Cold.

Gold.

Cold.

Late in the afternoon, we arrived in Watson Lake, home of the famous signpost forest.

Carl K. Lindley, a homesick soldier working on the Alaska Highway, started it all when he stuck up a signpost showing the direction and distance to his home town in the US in 1942. Today, there are 42,000 of them, which means that Watson Lake's a great place to come to if you can't find your way home.

'Anywhere good to eat in town?' I asked the gas station attendant as we were filling up with fuel.

'Nope,' he said.

Thankfully, he was wrong, for we found a pub with great pizza, that well-known Yukon delicacy, down the main street. The only street, now that I think of it. The staff were almost completely spherical, having obviously tested their products to destruction.

'Washed my hair this morning,' muttered the old-timer at the next table to the waitress at one stage. 'First time in six months.'

For his sake, I hoped he got it dry before winter set in.

We went to bed at nine, then rose in the ether-cold dawn and rode north-west from Whitehorse through the snowbound mountains, and along the vast expanse of Kluane Lake, frozen solid even in May. The landscape here was one reduced to monochrome, and haunted by such a spectral light that we must have looked like ghosts as we rode along the shore.

Like the spirits, perhaps, of all the adventurers who had

come this way before us: men looking for gold, or freedom, or themselves.

An icy wind drove off the lake as we came around the bluff, stripping what heat we had left in us. And then the road turned to muddy gravel, one of the unholy trinity of surfaces, along with corrugated tarmac and wet metal bridges, most hated by motorcyclists. Well, this particular one, at least. Oh well, I thought grimly as I rode on reciting Al Shepard's prayer, at least things can't get any worse. Just as it started to rain: freezing needles just this side of hail.

Thank God, then, for Burwash Landing, with a large wooden sign outside saying Rooms Grub Booze. What more could a man want, apart from the hot chocolate and pecan pie we found inside?

And besides, if we thought we had it hard, we were lily-livered woosicles compared with George Johnston, the first native to own a car around these parts. After a successful trapping season in 1928, George bought himself a Chevrolet in Whitehorse and had it shipped north. The reason he had to ship it was because there was no road, but that didn't deter a man like George: he simply built five miles of one so he could play with his new toy. He painted it white so he could use it for winter hunting, and when the Alaska Highway arrived in 1942, he painted it black every summer and used it as a taxi. In 1962, he finally traded it in for a new pick-up truck, and today it sits in the Teslin Museum.

By nightfall, or what would have been nightfall if night ever thought of falling here at this time of year, we were in Beaver Creek, population 145, the most westerly settlement in Canada and the site of the coldest ever temperature recorded in North America: $-61°C$.

As we were unloading the bikes outside Ida's Motel, a biker from San Diego pulled up on his way home from Alaska. He introduced himself simply as Mike, since, like most Americans, his surname had lapsed through lack of use.

In some Midwestern states, they were actually banned by

law under the 1974 We're Real Friendly Critters When We're Not Bombing The Shit Out Of Someone Bill.

'Set off up the Dalton Highway, but didn't make it as far as Gobblers Knob. Road was terrible. Mud and gravel so sharp it was like knives. I got as far as the Arctic Circle, then got a puncture and turned around,' he said, then rode on.

'A quid says you don't make it as far as Gobblers Knob,' said Clifford.

'Done,' I said, shaking his hand, then going to check my puncture repair kit.

That evening, our last together, we went out for a buffalo burger and a beer, and looked back on the most remarkable journey of our lives.

'Do you remember that time when … ?' Clifford would say, sparking off a chain of memories which would end, pause, then start again with me saying: 'Aye, but what about when … ?'

Already, the events we were talking about seemed like things we had done years ago, as much younger men.

We walked down the street, still talking, and found ourselves in the village hall, a huge circular log cabin with a fire in the middle, just in time for the start of the *Beaver Creek Rendezvous*, an old-fashioned but witty musical about the history of the Alaska Highway.

As we were leaving afterwards, we spotted on the wall a map of the world, went over to it, and stood looking in disbelief at the journey we had almost completed.

'Bloody hell. I can't believe we've actually come all that way. Wow,' I said.

'Wow is right,' said Clifford.

Final farewell. Clifford and Geoff, not to mention April and Tony, part company at Tok Junction, Alaska.

20

A short history of Alaska

15,000 BC
First native Americans arrive on land bridge from Asia.

1728
Danish explorer Vitus Bering discovers that land bridge is now a strait, which is named after him. Shortly after, Bering, in dire straits, dies of scurvy.

1741
Russians arrive, enslave natives, convert them to Russian Orthodoxy and force them to hunt sea otters to near-extinction for hats in Moscow, leaving only small family of otters hiding very quietly behind iceberg, intent on writing alternative history of state entitled *How the Otter Half Lives*.

1867
Russians flog Alaska to America for $7.2 million, or two cents an acre. Americans celebrate by slaughtering descendants of quiet otter family, then attack native souls with same vigour, dividing state into twelve denominations. Natives, who were still trying to get used to Russian Orthodoxy, take to drink.

1880–1902
Gold discoveries in Juneau, Klondike, Nome and Fairbanks
lead to huge influx of wild, lawless men. Most return home
broke, and rest stay behind to found salmon industry.

1968
Oil discovered, creating very rich corporations, and very
drunk natives.

Clifford woke at six, farted, cleared his nose, then had a noisy
cold shower.

All the little rituals which I would miss as much as he would
miss me greeting him every morning with a cheery: 'Get up,
Pancho, you lazy bastard; we have to be in Alaska by teatime.'

Except today, at last, it was true.

We crossed the border in a minute, or approximately two
hours and fifty-nine minutes less than the Central American
equivalent, and rode, at last, into Alaska. As we rode up the
road for one last time together, I looked in my rear view mirror,
gave a questioning V-sign, and got an answering thumbs-up
from Clifford, as we had done for the past three months, to say
that all was well in our little world as we hummed along
beneath the wind.

And then, all too soon, we were at the moment we had both
been dreading: the junction at Tok at which Clifford would
take the road south for Anchorage and home.

We got off the bikes outside an abandoned log cabin,
uncertain what to do or say.

'You take the best of care, Pancho,' I said at last.

'And you, Don,' he said, and we gave each other a manly
hug.

'By the way, what does the F stand for?'

'Frederick,' he said.

'That's a bit obvious, isn't it?' I laughed.

He laughed too, then got on the bike, gave me a manly
salute, and started the engine. To be honest, we were both close
to tears, not only at the thought that this was the last time we

would see each other on the great adventure, but at the fact that it was the last time Tony and April would be together as well. This must be what divorce feels like, I thought: sharing a whole lifetime of ups and downs with someone, then seeing them ride off down the road.

I stood there and watched Clifford Frederick Paterson disappear into the distance as the wind moaned through the windows of the log cabin behind me, and then, without warning, I felt tears trickling down my face.

'Buck up, old thing,' I said to myself – the expression Cate and I used mockingly to each other when we were feeling down – but that made it even worse. Eventually, realising I was doing a Ewan, I dried my eyes and distracted my attention with thoughts of something else.

A place called Chicken, to be precise. It was sixty-six miles north up a side road called the Top of the World Highway, which led back across the border to the shore of the Yukon River, on the other side of which lay Dawson City. The first settlers in the area had wanted to call it after the birds which inhabited the area, but after several attempts at spelling ptarmigan, they had given up and settled for Chicken.

Mind you, it wasn't the only place around these parts with a weird name: Tok was christened after the pet puppy of the all-black 97th US Engineers, who built this stretch of the Alaska Highway.

I had almost been to Chicken before. After driving from Whitehorse to Dawson City in the early summer of 1991, I had been idly studying the map when I had spotted Chicken, and decided immediately to go there for reasons which will be obvious to any right-thinking person. The problem was that the only way there was across the ice on the river, which was already getting thin. I had stood on the bank with Buffalo Taylor, the local fire chief, tourism chief and pretty much everything chief, as he looked at the ice wisely in that way you only get from years from looking at ice.

'Well, she's cracking up all right,' he said finally, stroking the luxuriant moustache which had given him his nickname for so long that everyone had forgotten his real name, including him. 'You might drive over, but you won't drive back.'

So I never had made it to Chicken, but today I was going to change all that.

I climbed on Tony and rode north, finding myself looking instinctively in the rear view mirror every few minutes for the familiar sight of Pancho, only to see nothing but the empty road. An hour or so later, I was greeted by a large wooden sign saying Welcome to Beautiful Downtown Chicken. The sign, in fact, was larger than the place it described, which consisted of a store, a gas station and a café.

I bought a sticker for Tony in the first, filled up at the second and had lunch in the third. Chicken and baked Alaska, naturally.

And then, in honour of the occasion, I wrote a Chicken poem, which went like this:

There is a town called Chicken
Where no one ever goes,
The population's twenty
And half of those are crows.

It wasn't quite as good as my Latvian Eurovision Song Contest entry, or indeed my Irish haiku –

Writing a poem
In seventeen syllables
Is very diffic

– but it would do.

By evening, I was in Delta Junction, which claims to be the end of the Alaska Highway on the basis that the road on to Fairbanks was already there when the highway was built. Mind you, Fairbanks claims the same title with as much fervour as both Chile and Peru claim to be the birthplace of *pisco*. The best answer was probably to have a celebratory *pisco* in both Delta Junction and Fairbanks. And I would probably need one tomorrow, as I passed through Fairbanks on my way north up the horrendous road to Yukon Crossing, base camp for the final assault on Gobblers Knob.

In the meantime, I had an early supper and went to bed in the unaccustomed solitude of a single room.

The next morning, I had just passed a sign saying 'North Pole 10 miles' when I met a woman from Wales walking the other way, pulling a small trailer. She turned out to be Rosie Swale, the legendary adventurer, just out for a dander around the world. She'd already walked across Europe and Russia, and was on her way home via Canada.

'Rosie, you're mad,' I said, giving her a hug.

'I know. It's great, isn't it? Careful with those ribs, dear. I broke a few when I fell on the ice in Siberia,' she said.

Setting off with renewed heart that I was not the only lunatic in the world, I passed a log cabin with a sign outside saying 'York Wentrup: Attorney'. It was as unlikely as walking down Fifth Avenue and seeing a notice saying 'Sven Olsen – Fur Trapper'. Wondering exactly what a lawyer did in the woods, I got off the bike and knocked on his door to find out, but there was no reply. York was obviously off settling a tricky moose paternity suit.

An hour later, I arrived at the North Pole; not because I'd taken a wrong turning, but because in 1963 the hamlet on this site was renamed in a cunning ploy to bring in business. Unlike most cunning ploys, it worked, attracting mugs like me to Santa Claus House – you can't miss it, it's the one with the 22ft Santa outside – to buy 'I Snogged Rudolph at the North Pole' stickers and read the thousands of letters on the wall from children addressed to Santa Claus, North Pole.

Among them was one from Dan Jones asking for a big halibut, and one from Sandra Massey requesting a rechargeable Remington shaver, which made me suspect that little Sandra really should lay off the steroids for a while.

Soon after, I reached Fairbanks and turned north, and within an hour and a half had reached the start of the Dalton Highway, which led 56 miles to Yukon River Camp, then 70 miles beyond that to the Arctic Circle and Gobblers Knob.

I stopped the engine, got off the bike and stood there looking at the rutted gravel and mud road climbing into the mountains. Even from where I stood, I could see the impossible climbs and even more impossible descents, with sheer drops on either side. I had heard stories of hardened truckers setting off up this road, abandoning their trucks after a few miles, and walking back.

The part of me that wanted to get back on the bike and ride south to safety wrestled with the part of me that refused to be beaten by anything as I stood there, feeling sick with fear. But then I remembered all the times that I had felt sick with fear on the trip, and had carried on. And I remembered that courage is not the absence of fear, but action in the presence of fear.

I got back on the bike, took a deep breath, started the engine, and gave Tony a pat on the tank. 'One mile at a time, chum,' I said. 'Every mile is another mile north.'

It started bad, and got worse, but for some reason not quite clear to me now with the sane hindsight of calm reflection, I kept going.

Alongside the road, for mile after endless mile, ran the Trans-Alaskan pipeline, snaking silver through the woods as it carried oil south from Prudhoe Bay at two miles an hour a lot more smoothly than I was proceeding in the opposite direction. Probably faster, too.

Then, just when I thought it couldn't get any worse, I came to a mile of roadworks in which they had got as far as laying the base layer of large rocks, then spraying it with water to keep down the dust for the occasional trucks and 4×4s which were the only other traffic.

If you can imagine riding a fully-laden motorbike over a mile of large, wet rocks, I admire your imagination, for I can't even after doing it. Still, it least it cured my fear of gravel to the extent that if I ever got home, I planned to haul out my Royal Enfield and take up speedway racing.

Late in the evening, utterly spent, I arrived at Yukon River Camp, basically a construction barracks with a few rooms on the side for the sort of lunatics who came this far for fun.

I was the only resident.

And besides, if I thought I'd had a bad day, it was nothing compared to that of Hank, if the conversation at the next table over supper was anything to go by.

'Say, is it true that Hank got jumped by a big old bear?' said the waitress as she poured another coffee for a man who was six and a half feet tall in any direction you cared to name and had a crew cut which went all the way down to the neck he didn't have.

'Sure as hell. He was just sitting there fishing when she jumped on him. He put six shots in her belly from his pump, but she still climbed on him and started chewing. Somehow he pulled out his .36 and shot her in the mouth, and that finished her for sure.'

'Holy shit. Is he OK?'

'Sure, just a few scratches like he'd rubbed up against a wall or sumthin'.'

'He shoulda climbed a tree, I reckon.'

'Ain't no point. Only difference you climb a tree is you know what kinda bear's chasin' you. A brown bear'll climb the tree and eat you, a grizzly'll knock down the tree and eat you.'

I sat there, thinking that it was more than a common language that divided Britain and the USA. Back home, a chap went fishing with a box of flies. Here, he took a pump-action shotgun and a revolver.

The man with no neck drained his coffee, stood up to go on night shift maintaining the pipeline, and noticed me.

'Say, you on that motorcycle out there, son?'

'Aye, that's me.'

'Where'd you come from on that?'

'Chile.'

He looked at me.

'Where's that at?'

'Oh, it's way south of here.'

He paused.

'South of Vancouver?'

'Yeah, it's south of Vancouver all right.'

'Hell, you've had quite a journey, son.'

Satisfied, he went out, and I finished my chicken, staggered down the corridor, fell into bed and was asleep before my head hit my thoughts coming the other way.

I woke at five, and set off again, through a landscape which slowly changed from stunted trees to the scene of a vast fire which had left several million frazzled trunks sticking up from the blackened earth, like matches after that childhood trick where you let one half burn, then hold it while the other half does.

Then even they disappeared, and the land became desolate, frozen tundra.

After several hours, I passed a sign informing me that I had crossed the Arctic Circle, and shortly after that, I crossed a frozen creek, climbed a long hill and found myself at a sign saying Gobblers Knob.

In truth, there was nothing there except a rubbish bin, the world's most outside toilet and a raven sitting on a rock looking at me in that arch way they have. I climbed a small rise, with the wind howling around my ears like the lost souls of wolves.

I stood there, and thought of all the milestones that had got me to this point.

Lying in bed reading the *Adventure Motorbiking Handbook*, then sitting down for two years to plan the trip, through days when I was so deep in despair that even getting out of bed was a superhuman struggle.

Meeting Clifford. Saying goodbye to Cate. Unpacking the bikes in Puerto Montt, feeling like boys on Christmas morning. Leaving Quellón to a one-hundred-granny farewell. The long days through the desert with the warning light on. The moment the engine had failed to start at the Chile–Peru border.

Sitting bleeding beside a wrecked bike in Colombia, sick at heart and sure the trip was over. And then the moment Diego started Tony's engine again, and we knew we could go on.

The endless wait in Cartagena, then the nightmare that was Colón, and the even greater nightmare that was the Mexican border. The glorious feeling of riding away from that, and the even more glorious feeling of crossing the border into the States. California, Alice's Restaurant, Vancouver, the moose, the bitter cold, and saying farewell to Pancho, the most faithful of travelling companions.

I looked out across the endless miles of solitude, feeling in my heart that I had, at last, reached the end of the longest and most difficult journey of my life.

And then I said goodbye to the raven, climbed on my motorcycle, which would not be mine for very much longer, and rode south for the first time in a long time.

It was the morning of my fiftieth birthday, and I was going home to the woman I loved.

Acknowledgements

Thanks to Clifford Frederick 'Pancho' Paterson, the most faithful of travelling companions, without whom the trip would have been completely impossible. As opposed to almost completely impossible.

And to Brian Davis, Naomi Waite and Richard McQuillan at main sponsors Nambarrie, who also sponsored the Delhi to Belfast on an Enfield jaunt with Paddy Minne, but thankfully failed to learn from their mistake the first time.

The Camphill Community and the Arts Council of Northern Ireland also provided funding for the trip.

At Triumph, Andrea Friggi in the UK marketing department said yes to lending me a Tiger 955i, although she'll probably never lend me one again after what I did to it. Also in the UK, Chris Willis in the technical department was endlessly patient with an idiot phoning him constantly from the Atacama Desert asking him why a motorbike wouldn't run on diesel. In the USA, Monika Boutwell gave support well above and beyond the call of duty, as did Mark and Alex at Rocket Motorcycles in San Diego, Charlie at British-Italian Motorcycles in Vancouver and Don and Michael at the Motorcycle Shop in Anchorage. Thanks also to Philip McCallen in Northern Ireland for giving us a crash course in maintenance. As it were.

Clifford's Aprilia was supplied by Michael at J. Paterson and Sons, who is no relation apart from being his brother, and prepared by mechanic Andy MacIntyre and KASE Engineering of Kilkeel.

Jane Wells and Joris Minne at JPR, and Andrea Hayes at Flybe, came up with flights from Belfast to London, and Larry Dillon at Varig gave us a bit off flights from there to Chile. On the way back, the endlessly helpful Debbie Marshall at Zoom and Lorna Inglis at Media House got us from Vancouver to London.

The bikes were shipped from the UK to Chile courtesy of All-Route and Ocean Express, whose man in Northern Ireland, Carson McMullan, is the Dalai Lama of global transportation.

My Roof helmet, which was tested to destruction in Colombia, was supplied by Ricky Drain at Provincewide in Ballymena. They're a Harley dealer, so whatever you do, don't tell Triumph.

Gordon Brown and Caroline Broderick at the Ulster Bank came up with the multimillion-pound guarantee for the carnet de passage documents, which were rustled up by Paul Gowen at the RAC. The fact that I would have had to sell the house if I'd lost either the documents or the bike didn't trouble me for a moment. Honestly.

Grant Hurst at Stratis provided the HP Ipaq wotsit for sending back daily bulletins from the road, thus saving us a fortune in pigeon feed. Mark Yetman in IT at work was infinitely patient in showing me how to work it.

We only managed to finish the trip thanks to the generosity of the tourist boards from California to the Yukon, who came up with free accommodation, and in many cases dinner, so thanks from the bottom of my wallet and Clifford's stomach to Leona Reed in California, Joanne Korfhage and Teresa O'Neill in Oregon, Julie Johnson and Carrie Wilkinson-Tuma in Washington State, Josie Heisig, Ian Giesbrecht and Sundance Topham in British Columbia, and Sheila Norris in the Yukon.

We used a combination of Rough Guides, Lonely Planet, Footprint, Cadogan and Bradt guides.

And finally, for those of you who have read *Eats, Shoots and Leaves* and feel deeply that there should be an apostrophe in Gobblers Knob, here it is.

,